The Home Buyer's Advisor

The Home Buyer's Advisor

A Handbook for First-Time Buyers and Second-Home Investors

ANDREW JAMES McLEAN

WILEY

John Wiley & Sons, Inc.

For general information on our other products and services please contact our Customer Care Department within the United States at (800) 762-2974, outside the United States at (317) 572-3993 or fax (317) 572-4002.

Wiley also publishes its books in a variety of electronic formats. Some content that appears in print may not be available in electronic books. For more information about Wiley products, visit our web site at www.wiley.com.

Library of Congress Cataloging-in-Publication Data:

McLean, Andrew James.
   The home buyer's advisor : a handbook for first-time buyers and second-home investors / Andrew James McLean.
      p. cm.
   Includes bibliographical references and index.
   ISBN 0-471-46641-7 (paper)
   1. Residential real estate—Purchasing—United States—Handbooks, manuals, etc.   2. House buying—United States—Handbooks, manuals, etc.   3. Second homes—Purchasing—United States—Handbooks, manuals, etc.   4. Mortgage loans—United States—Handbooks, manuals, etc.   5. Real estate investment—United States—Handbooks, manuals, etc.   I. Title: Handbook for first-time buyers and second-home investors.   II. Title.

HD259.M39 2004
643'.12'0973—dc22

                                                                         2003057065

Printed in the United States of America.

10 9 8 7 6 5 4 3 2 1

1. *Get your financial house in order before you buy.* Start by checking your credit, and fix it if it needs mending; make your saving and investment plans before you buy.

2. *Determine precisely how much house you can afford to buy before you start looking.* Realtors and mortgage lenders can only tell you the maximum that you're eligible to borrow.

3. *Don't buy if you can't stay put.* If you can't commit to remaining in one place for five years or more, then owning is probably not for you. The short-term costs of buying and selling are prohibitive, and maintaining the property as an absentee landlord is not recommended (too difficult to oversee, or you lose direct control when a property management company oversees it).

4. *Real estate is a better long-term investment than a short-term one.* Over the long haul, you'll make more money holding on to your realty investments, rather than "flipping" them (selling them quickly), because if you sell them, you'll have to find another property to invest the proceeds from the sale.

5. *The best time to consider the sale of your house is before you buy it.* When looking at prospective purchases, take into consideration the features and amenities of the home that other buyers would find desirable. In other words, pretend you are looking at the home's amenities through the eyes of other buyers, because if you don't, it will be difficult to find a buyer or get a good price when you sell it.

6. *It is wise* not *to begin serious house hunting until you are familiar with mortgages and preapproved for a loan by a mortgage lender.* This way you'll know precisely how much house you can afford, and that you are in fact financially capable of buying a home within established limits.

7. *You can easily save thousands of dollars by shopping for a mortgage that's just right for you.* If you intend to own the home for more than five years, a fixed-rate mortgage is usually more cost effective than an adjustable-rate mortgage. And notably, mortgage money is a commodity just like automobiles and gasoline, and commercial lenders have to compete to stay in business.

8. *Have the courage to be a nonconformist.* During the year, the best time to buy is toward the end of the year (between Thanksgiving and New Year's), when few others are interested in buying. Since real estate prices tend to be cyclical, the best time to buy is at the bottom of a cycle, when no one else thinks it's a good time to buy.

9. *What you don't know will hurt you when it comes to investing in real estate.* Become informed and knowledgeable about real estate. Furthermore, buying a

home is nothing less than a team effort. Choose your players wisely, and you can count on minimizing the likelihood of problems with your purchase.

10. *Take the time to choose the best possible full-time real estate agent that you can.*   An experienced, knowledgeable agent will be very helpful in locating and negotiating the best deal for you. Choosing an inept or mediocre agent can add needless expense and unnecessary delays to what should have been an efficient and hassle-free transaction.

11. *If the deal you're getting on the purchase of the house seems too good to be true, then it probably is.*   Investigate why the house is so underpriced (perhaps there are future plans to build a penitentiary or a bus depot across the street), otherwise you'll suffer the consequences later.

12. *Avoid buying a lemon.* Never try to skimp on the cost of a proper home inspection. Have the house thoroughly inspected *before* you buy it.

13. *Avoid overpaying.*   Knowledge of values and comparable sales in the neighborhood where you intend to purchase (along with the assistance of a good realtor) will be beneficial in negotiating a good deal.

14. *Be aware that buying a home is a very emotional experience for most people.*   The better prepared you are—knowing comparable values and prevailing mortgage interest rates, along with how much house you can afford—the easier it will be to control your emotions and procure a better deal.

15. *Remember that everything is negotiable.*   Shrewd buyers are fully informed of market conditions and neighborhood values. They also know when it's wise to make a lowball offer, and otherwise realize that there are situations when it's best to make the initial offer the best offer they can afford.

16. *Never enter into a bidding war.*   It's always better to buy from a motivated seller who will make concessions, instead of competing with other buyers who are trying to outbid each other. Remember the old saying, "there are always more fish in the sea," and likewise, there will always be more desirable homes on the market—you only need to spend the time to find them.

CONTENTS

PART V
THE SOURCES

PART VI
THE MIDDLE GAME

ACKNOWLEDGMENTS

Special thanks to my publisher's senior editor, Mike Hamilton, for his input and forwarding all that great topical information. And, to my lovely wife Jennifer, who helped prepare and edit the manuscript.

Congratulations for taking the time and effort to discover the *Home Buyer's Advisor*. Whether you're a first-time home buyer, or already own a home and are seeking other types of investment property, this all-in-one guide covers everything you need to know to invest successfully in today's real estate market—safely, confidently, and profitably, while taking full advantage of the new tax laws.

I've tried to cover all the angles—from buying a condo or a co-op, to acquiring a resale home or a new home in the suburbs—or you might choose a home in an adults-only community, or one secluded behind protective gates—or perhaps you'd choose a quiet home in the country? To that end, I've attempted to present all the options to make it easier for you to select the best house you can possibly buy.

Later on, the book shows you how to tap the wealth built up in your home—how it can be the foundation of future financial growth through investment in a second home—such as a profitable rental next door, or numerous other properties. The home you buy can even be a practical source of retirement income!

Everything from what to look for, how to get the best financing, what to do with the home once you've got it, how to fix it up, rent it, or sell it and pay less taxes is included. It's a practical how-to guide full of ideas, strategies, and sound business advice.

Of course, no one is born knowing how to buy a home without making costly mistakes at their own expense. But that's what this book is all about—Teaching you how to go beyond the school of hard knocks—the one that, unfortunately, gives you a crash course in making costly mistakes at your own expense—so you can be an informed investor in today's real estate market.

In creating this work, I have tried to provide you with a condensed yet thorough, informative as well as graphic, easy-to-read guide to a happy home-buying adventure. Both first-time home-buyers and real estate pros alike should find it very beneficial, while at the same time enlightening.

Along the way you'll discover an array of special *insider tips* from the pros in the know. Learn the ins and outs of "land banking" and lease/purchase options, the how-tos of buying foreclosures and buying at special auctions, and how to profit by buying Department of Housing and Urban Development (HUD) and Veterans Administration (VA) repossessions. Useful topics featured at the end of most chapters include answers to the most commonly asked questions about home buying and advice on how to avoid the most common mistakes home buyers make. Simply put, the methods demonstrated should clarify what others tend to complicate. There are even solutions for those who lack a sufficient down payment, or have a shaky or less-than-perfect credit rating. The book also includes special methods of saving for a down payment on a home.

Buying a home will likely be the largest purchase that you'll ever make. To make that experience not only very informed, but very profitable and hassle-free, the common mistakes most home buyers make are discussed, so that you can easily avoid falling prey to them and confidently do things right the first time. Furthermore, by learning the how-tos from the savvy pros in the know, you'll discover how to save thousands of dollars the first time you buy a home.

Unlike other books on real estate, this text goes beyond the how-tos of the initial home-buying experience. It provides you with special know-how about profitable investment techniques for purchasing your second home, or other types of income property you may invest in.

Throughout the book you'll be enlightened on many proven investment concepts gained not only from my own experience, but also from the sage expertise of other pros in the know. These real-world examples are illustrated with Landlord Tales, which tell it like it is and present the good along with the bad and ugly facts about real estate investment. Through these tried and tested examples you'll gain confidence with the necessary know-how of home buying.

All in all, the *Home Buyer's Advisor* is the practical guide I wish was on hand when I bought my first house 32 years ago. It offers useful information about all the facets of home buying. The book's design features also include special icons that highlight certain attractions and noteworthy tips.

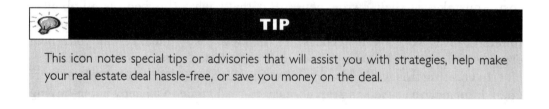

TIP

This icon notes special tips or advisories that will assist you with strategies, help make your real estate deal hassle-free, or save you money on the deal.

BEWARE

Countless pitfalls await the naive home buyer as well as the seasoned investor. This icon marks the pitfalls and shows you how to sidestep them.

NOTEWORTHY

This icon denotes important points that are sometimes repeated because they're noteworthy and should be highlighted so you don't forget them.

LANDLORD TALE

This icon marks a collection of real-world examples from my own personal experiences working and investing in real estate, as well as several tales from other savvy investors. You'll find a sampling of them throughout the book, and we hope you find them enlightening and beneficial to your own home-buying experience.

A Get-Rich-Slow Plan

This book is *not* designed to be a get-rich-quick scheme. Actually, if anything, it's a *get-rich-slow* long-term plan, because to get the most out of your realty investments—to make them the most profitable and hassle-free—it concentrates primarily on long-term holding strategies. Several quick buy-and-sell techniques are included for those of you who might prefer fast turnover profits, however.

So, whether you're investing in your first home, or you're a seasoned investor looking for new ideas and sound investment concepts, this all-in-one guide was written especially for you.

In addition, this book offers the following benefits:

- It can assist you in choosing the ideal home that's best for your lifestyle and needs.
- It shows you how to save thousands of dollars on your mortgage loan by taking advantage of the full range of today's real estate financing methods.

- It fully explains the key ingredients to profitable real estate opportunities.
- It goes beyond the precise how-tos of purchasing the first home; it also provides sound strategies for using your home as a solid foundation for future financial growth.
- It reveals proven management techniques to assist you in the profitable operation of your holdings, without hassles.
- It teaches you how to be tax wise and dollar smart with the latest tax implications of real estate ownership.

Above all else, this guide will help you achieve a satisfying and rewarding experience investing in that wonderful parcel of earth that belongs solely to you, and which has often been called "home, sweet home."

Good luck with your home purchase, or other real estate investments.

Author's note: To protect the privacy of individuals, in many of the Landlord Tales and other special instances discussed in the text I have changed the names and specific identifying facts. But all told, the experiences you'll read about are real. It is my intention that you benefit from the experience of others. In this way you can apply the lessons wisely, and enjoy your home-buying adventure.

PART I.

THE PRELIMINARIES

In this part, you'll discover all the reasons why real estate outperforms other forms of investment. We also discuss whether buying a home is right for you, and illustrate the great benefits of home ownership. Other topics include the important things to know before buying a home, along with several things you should avoid. And you'll learn why home prices do what they do.

CHAPTER 1

Why Buying a Home Is a Great Investment

Home is where the heart is, said Charles Osgood, host of the popular CBS television show *Sunday Morning*. That particular show, which aired April 27, 2003, had a segment about how Americans have retreated to their homes for safety since the attacks of September 11, 2001, and have made them their sanctuary from the rest of the world.

But the home has much more virtue than just sentimental value, or its value as a great refuge. Not only is the home a great investment, it also is a natural wealth builder and a superior tax shelter. Your home can even be the foundation for a pyramid of other profitable realty investments, yielding a lifetime of worry-free income.

Reasons Why Real Estate Outperforms Other Forms of Investment

A monumental event involving America's stock market took place in the spring of 2003—on March 24, the bear market turned three years old. During that time, the Dow Jones average had lost over 30 percent of its value (measured not in billions, but in trillions of dollars), and unfortunately the bear's birthday coincided with the onset of a new age of uncertainty. Americans faced a steady media drumbeat of war, terror, fear, and recession. The United States initiated its first preemptive war, against Iraq. Fear of terrorism stymied economic growth. Scandals put distrust in financial statements and Wall Street research. Seasoned investors now no longer view the stock market as a direct route to a comfortable retirement. The sound investment strategies that earned great returns in the 1990s don't work any more.

Meanwhile, what do you think happened to America's median home price—half sold for more, half for less—during that same three-year period of declining stock prices? It jumped 8.8 percent year-over-year in the October to December quarter of 2002. The increase broke a six-month trend of moderating home price increases. As Figure 1.1 shows, home price increases ranged from a low of 3 percent to a peak of 8.8 percent during that three-year period.

The 8.8 percent jump was the biggest such increase reported by the National Association of Realtors (NAR) since 1981. And the upward push on prices is widespread: 39 metropolitan areas registered double-digit price increases for the quarter, triple the number of metro areas with such growth in 1999. NAR chief economist David Lereah is quoted as saying, "The big jump reflects the explosive

FIGURE 1.1   Housing prices increases, showing a peak rise at an annual rate of 8.8 percent.

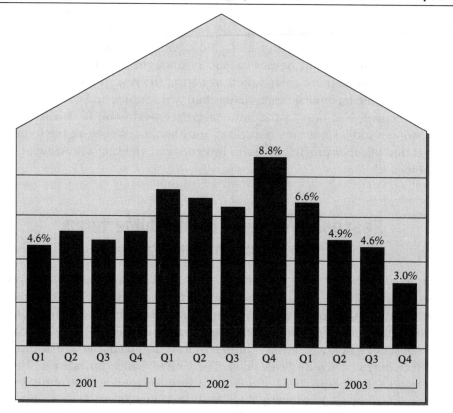

The median home price jumped 8.8 percent year-over-year in the October to December 2002 quarter. The increase broke a six-month trend of moderating home price increases. (*National Association of Realtors*)

mix of tight supplies of homes for sale and mortgage interest rates below 6 percent, the lowest in four decades."

Like many other housing economists, Lereah forecasts that the growth in home prices will decelerate to just 3 percent by the end of this year. His scenario: a strengthening U.S. economy leading the way to higher mortgage interest rates, and a modest cooling in what continues to be a red-hot housing market.

What's the end result after three years of declining stock prices in an economic recession? The average stock market investor took a beating in the portfolio. Conversely, over the same three-year span, the average home owner or real estate investor experienced steady appreciation with solid gains in value.

This comparison has served to emphasize the enduring benefits of owning a home. Most Americans prefer safe investments with historically good track records. Housing is one of those standards of enduring value, and adult Americans have most of their wealth invested in their homes. Two out of three adults living in the United States own their own home. Investment in a home gives the owner a hedge against inflation, an opportunity to shelter income from taxes, and, more important, a chance to accumulate wealth for the future.

"Okay," you may be saying, "you've convinced me that real estate has looked good in the past three years, but what does the future look like?"

Expect Increasing Rents and Appreciation

Although short-term economic recessions may temporarily cause a rise in vacancies and depress rents, rent levels and appreciation will go up over the long term, because future demand will increase faster than future supply. Here are four reasons why:

1. *Growth in America's population.* Moderate growth projections for the next 20 years reveal that the U.S. population will increase from its current figure of 284 million to a figure of 334 million—an increase of 50 million people. In just two decades, America will add more people than are currently living in the three states of Florida, Michigan, and Texas.

2. *Growth in the number of households.* Americans presently average 2.2 persons per household. But continuing with a declining trend, that figure is likely to fall to around 2.0, given the relative trend of families having fewer children, more singles living alone, and more baby boomers of the mid-1940s moving into retirement. Thus, America will need 25 million additional housing units just to adequately house a net gain of 50 million people.

3. *Growth in personal income.* People need money to rent apartments or to buy homes. Accordingly, people earn more money when the national economy is growing. But what does the future hold for growth in the U.S. economy—will

it be productive, and can it adequately supply the employment needed to generate this income? It's gratifying to know that the outlook for growth in the national economy is very promising. Expansion of markets for U.S. products due to globalization, continued corporate cost cutting, higher levels of competition among businesses, and technical innovation will bring more gains to incomes and economic productivity. In addition, a growing number of two-earner households increases overall household buying power.

4. *Growth in second-home ownership.*   Currently, approximately 8 million households own a second home. Taking into consideration the prevailing market conditions that tend to stimulate more real estate investment—low interest rates for mortgage loans and dispirited stock investors bailing out of the market to invest in real estate—forecasters expect this number to expand significantly over the next 20 years. They're predicting that by 2024, about 20 million households will own at least two homes.

As you can see, expanding population over the next two decades will generate record numbers of people needing adequate housing. This additional demand on the housing market will put a lot of upward pressure on the nation's overall housing supply, with corresponding increases in both rents and home prices. Yet, you might respond, "What about the law of supply and demand—that builders will expand their capacity to erect more new housing to satisfy the demand? Or, is it possible that they could go overboard and build too much, and glut the housing market?"

The answer is no to both questions. Here's why:

In the classic economic theory, supply increases to satisfy demand. Shortage of a product increases the demand for it, which inevitably makes its price rise. As the price continues to escalate, more suppliers see the profit potential and begin competing to produce the product, which eventually adds to the supply and curbs runaway prices. This theory is credible for long-distance telephone rates and airfares. However, throwing cold water on a red-hot housing market when home prices are going through the roof is not so easily done. Builders and developers are unable to construct enough homes and apartments to meet people's needs, because they're hampered by the following five factors:

1. *Insufficient habitable land.*   All in all, the United States is blessed with an abundance of land—unfortunately, the majority of it is situated where people don't want to live. Most of the desired habitable land is already built on, and that which is still unimproved costs plenty to own.

2. *High costs.*   Even with today's easy-qualifying low-interest mortgages, most people still can't afford to buy or rent new construction. The median price of a new home is now $178,000. The cost to construct new apartment

developments approaches $85,000 per unit. And in contrast to giant corporations like General Motors or Chrysler, home builders can't easily cut costs through economies of scale (that is, lower the production cost of each individual unit by producing a large number of units of the same type) or across-the-board layoffs.

3. *Inadequate infrastructure.* New housing and apartment developments usually require new or expanded infrastructure, such as roads, schools, and sewer and water systems, to service the new community. In situations in which developments lack sufficient infrastructure, governments assess developers thousands of dollars per unit in impact fees or as an alternative, often block new construction.

4. *Oppressive regulatory approval procedures.* Before construction can begin on any major land development, governments require dozens of lengthy and costly permits. Large-scale projects necessitate an investment of millions of dollars and several years of preparation before the first apartment or home is ever completed.

5. *Negative public interest.* Even if developers are able to get through the maze of bureaucratic red tape, they must still contend with environmentalists, unhappy neighbors, and public interest groups who all want to restrict development.

Considering all five of these restrictive factors, it would be very difficult for housing developers to respond both expeditiously and economically to sudden demand. Granted, from time to time, some local markets have to endure an oversupply of housing, which produces excessive vacancies and depresses home values. Yet, in the best of times and in most markets, builders are invariably trying to keep up with housing demands. Over the next two decades, home owners and real estate investors will surely benefit from the restricted supply of new housing.

On the whole, given the market fundamentals—the growing numbers of home buyers and renters with money competing for a constrained housing supply—rents and property values should increase to all-time highs.

Other Benefits of Real Estate Investment

Besides a promising future outlook with regard to value appreciation and increased rents, there are many other benefits of real estate and reasons it will outperform other investments. These include:

- You have personal control.
- You don't need much to get started.

- You get forced savings via the wealth-building benefit.
- You get tax benefits.
- It's easy to learn the how-tos of profitable real estate investing.

You Have Personal Control

Owning real estate means having a home of your own to live in, and a second home you can rent out, invest in, and profit from without losing control to so-called professional investment advisors. And most important, you'll have personal control over your investments in historically stable markets.

In simple terms, there is virtually no better investment available, none which gives you such total control, nor which historically appreciates over the long term and offers big tax breaks (mortgage interest plus property taxes) and up to $500,000 in tax-free gains to boot. Second-home investors or investors with other types of income property not only share the great benefits home owners have, they have the added advantage of reducing rental income through depreciation and expense allocation. (See more about these topics in Chapter 22.)

I want to emphasize the phrase *personal control*, because there is an important lesson here. Unlike acquiring stocks or bonds, with real estate you don't have to depend on third-party agents to handle or manipulate your hard-earned investment money. That's because *you* make the critical decisions as to what to buy or invest in. Granted, you may take the advice of knowledgeable Realtors or friends, but it is you who will ultimately live in the investment and care for it, or decide who rents it, and it is you who will thereby have command of its usage.

You Don't Need Much to Get Started

Most often, all you need to get started with buying a home is a few thousand dollars, and at times you don't even need that. This book shows you no-money-down techniques of acquiring real estate. With FHA financing you only need as little as 3 percent down. And if you're a qualified veteran, you can use a lot of *leverage* to finance a $203,000 home with virtually nothing down.

In the financial world, leverage is the use of a small amount of cash to control a much greater amount of assets. Zero leverage would be a full-cash purchase; a purchase 90 percent leveraged would combine a 10 percent down payment with 90 percent financing. Due to the impact of inflation and appreciation on real estate values, you can achieve the greatest yield on your invested dollars by getting as much leverage as possible when purchasing real estate.

As a simple example of leverage, consider buying a home using 95 percent leverage (a 5 percent down payment), as opposed to purchasing the same property with zero leverage. In this example, suppose you bought a house for $100,000 with a $5,000 down payment (5 percent), and a year later you realize a $5,000 increase in the value of the home. Therefore, the house is now worth $105,000. Because you put only $5,000 down on the house and it appreciated $5,000, you realized a 100 percent return on your investment ($5,000 return on $5,000 invested).

Now suppose you bought a similar house with $100,000 cash (zero leverage), and a year later that property also increased in value to $105,000. In this case, your investment is $100,000, the appreciation is still $5,000, but the return (yield) is only 5 percent on investment ($5,000 divided by $100,000).

Unlike buying stock, you can own $100,000 of real estate with as little as a $3,000 down payment. To purchase $100,000 of stock, you'll have to come up with at least $50,000 in cash (50 percent). And if the stock you purchased declines in value, you'll get a margin call requiring that additional cash be added to the account. If you do not meet the broker's margin requirements, the stock could be liquidated, and you'll be stuck with the loss. But there are no margin calls in real estate. Even if your home declines in value, your mortgage lender cannot require you to invest more cash into the home just to maintain a specified loan-to-value ratio.

Overall, not only can you invest in real estate with far less cash than would be needed to invest in an equivalent amount of stock, but financing real estate is not nearly as risky, and it is much less complicated than using leverage to buy stocks. Using leverage to invest in a volatile, unpredictable stock market is a risky game played mostly by brave speculators.

You Get Forced Savings via the Wealth-Building Benefit

Figure 1.2 shows what happens to a $10,000 down payment on a $110,000 home over 30 years based on three different rates of inflation. Based on a 4 percent rate of inflation, as the loan pays down over 30 years the home owner can expect an equity growth of $300,140. At 5 percent, he or she can expect a $10,000 down payment to increase to $491,350. And at 6 percent, a similar down payment would grow to $589,350 in equity.

Typically, when you own a home for many years, it becomes an important part of your financial *net worth*—that is, the difference between your assets (financial things of value such as stocks, bonds, mutual funds, CDs, savings accounts, retirement accounts, and so on) and your liabilities (debts). Over the decades a home will likely not only appreciate in value, you'll also be paying down the mortgage. The resulting *home equity*—the difference between the home's market value and the outstanding mortgage balance—can develop into a substantial amount of wealth that you can benefit from in several ways. If you're like most people who plan to retire someday, the home's equity can be a great source of retirement income. (See the section titled "How to Retire on the House" in Chapter 23.)

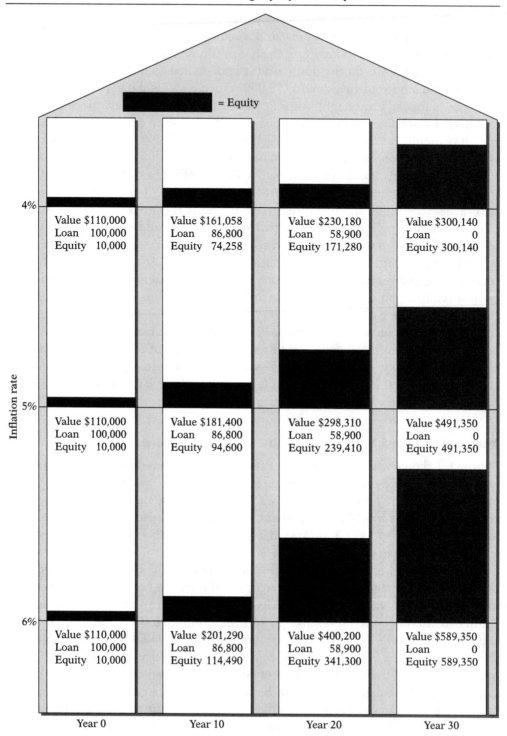

FIGURE 1.2 Growing equity over 30 years.

= Equity

Inflation rate

4%

Value $110,000
Loan   100,000
Equity 10,000

Value $161,058
Loan   86,800
Equity 74,258

Value $230,180
Loan   58,900
Equity 171,280

Value $300,140
Loan   0
Equity 300,140

5%

Value $110,000
Loan   100,000
Equity 10,000

Value $181,400
Loan   86,800
Equity 94,600

Value $298,310
Loan   58,900
Equity 239,410

Value $491,350
Loan   0
Equity 491,350

6%

Value $110,000
Loan   100,000
Equity 10,000

Value $201,290
Loan   86,800
Equity 114,490

Value $400,200
Loan   58,900
Equity 341,300

Value $589,350
Loan   0
Equity 589,350

Year 0   Year 10   Year 20   Year 30

10

You Get Tax Benefits

Chapter 22 reveals in more detail how the income tax law favors home owners and real estate investors. For now, here are two major points: First, in contrast to getting absolutely no tax relief as a renter, as a home owner the points, loan interest, and property taxes you pay are deductible against your federal, state, and local income taxes. Second, compared to the fully taxable dividends you receive from stocks, in most cases when you sell the home, a gain of up to $500,000 is exempt from taxes. In addition, income property owners are allowed to shelter some of their rental income from federal, state, and local income taxes.

Notably, too, if you sell a winning stock intending to move the proceeds into another stock or a managed fund, you'll be required to pay a good portion of your gain to the Internal Revenue Service (IRS). With an Individual Retirement Account (IRA), 401(k), or other tax-sheltered retirement plan, you may defer some of the taxes on the gains; yet many regulations and restrictions apply to these plans. However, you avoid these kinds of income taxes in real estate, which means you get to keep your entire accumulated wealth as long as you own properties. In addition, through home equity loans, refinancing, or installment sales, you can extract cash out of your realty holdings with little or no payment of income taxes.

It's Easy to Learn the How-tos of Profitable Real Estate Investing

Successful real estate investors and satisfied home buyers didn't get that way by recklessly throwing their money around, making ill-advised investments, such as overbuying in a declining neighborhood, or paying too much for the wrong type of financing. To the contrary, they made educated, informed decisions.

You're not going to need a real estate license or a college degree. You don't even need experience. What you do need is perseverance, commitment, and a willingness to learn and apply the lessons portrayed in the following chapters. That, along with a good knowledge of your local neighborhoods and property values, will take you a long way toward achieving your real estate investment goals.

Why Home Prices Rise and Fall

As a prospective home buyer, you may be concerned about the future direction of home prices. You, of course, wouldn't want to purchase a home just before prices plunge. But then, who in their right mind wouldn't enjoy buying a home just before prices dramatically increase? In order to understand what drives home prices, you must analyze what drives the supply of and demand for homes.

NOTEWORTHY

Through this discussion of what drives prices and real estate markets, please keep the following in mind: You're likely to own a home for many decades. Fretting about precisely timing your purchase is just not worth the trouble. Precise timing—that is, making your purchase when prices are at rock bottom, and selling when you think that home values have peaked—is very difficult to achieve. I know people who started waiting for lower home prices 10 or 20 years ago and are *still* waiting!

Predicting future real estate prices in a certain neighborhood, town, or region over the next one, two, or more years is not easy. In due time, the demand for and prices of homes in a region are driven primarily by the economic health and vitality of that region. When there's an increase in employment, especially with jobs that pay well, the result is more demand for housing.

Besides the economic health and vitality of an area, other factors are important to the lifeblood of a healthy real estate market.

Factors That Drive the Supply of and Demand for Homes

Because houses cost money to purchase and maintain—and you're not likely soon to inherit lots of money from a deceased rich uncle—you need a steady source of income in order to buy a home. Where does that income come from? A steady job.

The abundance and quality of jobs in a region directly affect the ability to pay for housing and the demand for housing in that area. In other words, when good-paying jobs are plentiful, the demand for housing increases, because more people have money to pay for housing. Conversely, when the number of jobs in an area is shrinking, demand for housing shrinks, and real estate prices decline. Regions that are ideal and where home values appreciate at a relatively high rate share the following characteristics:

- *Job diversity.* If a community does not have a diversified job base, if it is dependent on one or two employers for half its jobs, you should be wary of investing in a home there. Should both of those companies fail, the market for homes would most definitely fail with them. A similar scenario actually occurred in the 1980s, in New Orleans, when the bottom fell out of the petroleum market and oil prices fell dramatically. The petroleum industry experienced massive layoffs in the region when oil and natural gas production in the Gulf of Mexico was substantially curbed.

TIP

The U.S. Bureau of Labor Statistics compiles employment and unemployment data for U.S. metropolitan areas. Check out its web site at www.bls.gov, or visit your local library or chamber of commerce.

- *Job growth.* There's an old saying in the city of Detroit: "When General Motors catches a cold, Detroit comes down with pneumonia." The city of Detroit had millions of jobs, yet during the 1970s—primarily as the result of competition from new, low-cost, quality Japanese models in the auto industry—Detroit experienced declining real estate prices due to a deteriorating job base. Job growth is the lifeblood of a thriving real estate market. Check out the rate of unemployment in the area you're interested in and examine how the jobless rate has changed in recent years. A declining rate of unemployment is a good sign.

- *Job quality.* The quality of the jobs in a region affects the real estate values in that area. Compare northern California's high-tech Silicon Valley to an area that's producing mostly low-paying, low-skill jobs (such as jobs at fast-food restaurants). When most of the jobs in a region are derived from stagnant or shrinking employment bases (such as shoe and apparel manufacturers, small retailers, and farms), real estate values are not likely to appreciate in the coming years. To the contrary, regions with a preponderance of high-tech jobs in growth industries are more apt to experience rapid appreciation in real estate values.

Available Housing and Land

Whereas jobs produce the demand for housing, the quantity of available housing is the supply side of the supply-and-demand equation. Even though an area has a low employment growth rate, a housing shortage could induce faster appreciation in real estate values. On the other hand, if jobs are being created in a region, housing values may remain stagnant when there's an oversupply of available housing.

How can you determine whether an area has an abundance or a shortage of available housing? Examine the vacancy rates to determine how the existing supply of housing is being utilized. The average vacancy rate is 5 percent. Generally, a good indicator of future real estate appreciation is a vacancy rate under 5 percent. Low or declining vacancy rates mean there's more competition for the limited rental units still on the market. The added competition for fewer available units tends to drive up rental rates.

Conversely, high vacancy rates indicate an oversupply of rentals, which mean lower rents. As a general indicator, a high vacancy rate—above 7 percent—means cheaper rents and reduced real estate prices.

Besides examining vacancy rates, there's another way to determine how well the available housing supply is being utilized. Check out the trend in the number of building permits being issued in your area. Before a new house can be built, a building permit has to be issued. A considerable increase in the number of permits could indicate a potential oversupply of future housing. Scenarios such as this often occur in areas where real estate values have significantly increased. When prices are at a premium level, home builders scramble to erect new housing in order to capitalize on the higher prices.

To the contrary, depressed prices can stifle the development of new housing. That's because home builders would be reluctant to risk building in an area without a significant profit motive, although this trend of curtailed development should strengthen local real estate values over the long term.

The supply of habitable land also is a significant factor in the supply-and-demand equation. Without habitable land to build on, the supply of housing cannot be increased. Whenever a region is beset with a limited supply of land (as is the case in Japan, Hong Kong, Manhattan, and San Francisco), real estate has appreciated very well over the years, and today tends to be very expensive. Conversely, home prices usually remain stable or rise slowly in regions of vast tracts of undeveloped habitable land, such as Texas, the Midwest, and the Southwest.

Interest Rates

Interest rates on mortgage loans are also a significant factor that drives the supply of and demand for homes. Lower interest rates make housing more affordable and enable more people to own homes. Consider a $110,000 mortgage loan for 30 years at a fixed interest rate of 9.5 percent. The monthly mortgage payment is $925. At an interest rate of 6 percent, the same mortgage loan is significantly reduced to a monthly payment of $660, for a monthly savings of $265.

Clearly, when interest rates are low, more people can qualify for housing, which increases demand for housing. And although low interest rates make housing more affordable, low rates likewise make building more housing at less cost possible. A greater supply of housing tends to stifle increases in real estate values.

When interest rates are high, as they were in the early 1980s, home prices plummet because hardly anyone can afford to buy a home.

All that having been said, what can you conclude from this lesson on why home prices rise and fall? Be wary of buying a home in a region that's dependent on one or two employers, or in an area with a high vacancy rate. You can expect real estate values to appreciate at a higher rate in areas of diverse employment, and where vacancy rates are below 5 percent.

The Realities of Home Ownership

Without a landlord making decisions about the residence, home owners are generally in control and can do whatever they want with the property. Are you tired of that beat-up old carpet in the house? Get a new one without asking permission or waiting eight months for the landlord to have it installed. As a renter, you would likely need permission and be required to pay a deposit to have a pet. As a home owner, you have the last word on such decisions.

Renting versus Owning

Aside from the advantage of being in control, when you take into consideration the factors of appreciation and tax benefits, owning is substantially less expensive and more beneficial than renting over the long term.

Compare two similar families, each with two working adults and one child, a $45,000 combined gross income, and $10,000 to invest (see Table 1.1). One family invests the $10,000 in a down payment on a $110,000 home and takes out a $100,000 fixed-rate mortgage at 8.5 percent interest for 30 years. The other family continues to rent a home at $850 a month and invests $10,000 in a certificate of deposit (CD), which earns 6 percent interest compounded quarterly.

Under the assumptions that family incomes, rents, and the value of the purchased home increase 5 percent a year and inflation rises 4 percent, at the end of the first year the home owner pays $3,200 less in federal income taxes, and the value of the home will have increased by $5,500, compared to a $612 gain for the renter's CD.

At the end of five years, the home owner has paid $15,112 less in federal income taxes, and the home is now worth $140,391, for a gain of $30,391. Were the home owner to sell the home and buy another of greater value, the gain would be tax deferred. Conversely, the renter's CD would be worth $13,457 after five years, for a gain of $3,457, which would be taxable.

TABLE 1.1   Owning versus Renting—$10,000 Invested in a Home Down Payment versus a Bank CD

Occupant	Tax Deduction	Gain in Value	Equity Buildup	Tax on Gain
After One Year				
Home owner	$3,200	$5,500	$727	Deferred
Renter	0	612	0	$171
After Five Years				
Home owner	$15,112	$30,391	$4,007	Deferred
Renter	0	3,457	0	$968

Table 1.1 illustrates the tremendous gains attained through home ownership. Also note the additional gains in equity build-up, which benefits the home owner as the mortgage is paid down.

From the examples given in Table 1.1, the net gain to the home owner after five years, compared to that to the renter, is a difference of $47,021 in favor of home ownership.

The Negatives of Home Ownership

Now for the downside. Real estate is illiquid—it takes a long time to sell, and there are stiff selling costs. Some tenants are bums, and managing them can be a big headache. And the depreciation could turn out to be real, not just on paper—in which case your maintenance budget could fall far short of covering a new roof or pipes or other capital expenditures. You can earn a decent return on your investment, but just try to remember that all that glitters is not necessarily gold.

That having been said, in the following Landlord Tale I'll share with you a real-life example of why, at times when there's no stability in your career, it can be better to be a renter.

Is Real Estate Right for You?

Let's face it, buying a home for the first time can be an unnerving experience. All those pitfalls we can fall prey to—sellers who fib, faulty mechanical stuff, mold, the wrong type of mortgage, and cracked foundations—diminish what otherwise appears to be a good solid investment. It's a wonder anyone is happy with their newly purchased home.

But not to worry, because this book addresses all these negative issues and shows how to turn some of them into profitable opportunities. For instance Chapter 19 points out how to avoid a real estate lemon. The same chapter also offers specific guidelines on what to look for in a property in order to maximize its value.

 NOTEWORTHY

To some home owners, being illiquid is a plus, because it's a form of forced savings. In other words, if your equity in the house was converted into ready cash, you might be inclined to spend it frivolously. But since it's tied up, you don't have access to it. If you can look at it that way, being illiquid is an advantage.

LANDLORD TALE

In the spring of 1995 I accepted a supervisory position at the new land-based casino in New Orleans, Louisiana. Harrah's had won the bidding competition to build a casino there, and while it was being built, we (Harrah's management team) would train local people and operate a temporary casino facility at a city-owned auditorium.

After a few months, with everything apparently going well, I decided I liked working at Harrah's and living in New Orleans, and thought it was time to settle down and buy a home. In October I found a nice place, 2,000 square feet with three bedrooms and two baths in a nice area near City Park.

But I started to have bad feelings about the deal when I tried to get preapproval for a new mortgage. The lender was hesitant, and the hesitation was not about my credit-worthiness. The reason was that the lender didn't believe Harrah's would be a permanent employer in New Orleans.

Yet, I was not to be deterred. I applied for another mortgage with a different lender and had no trouble getting a 30-year loan. Then, just 30 days after I took possession of the home and started to settle in, the nightmare most of us thought would never happen, happened. Harrah's failed. It declared bankruptcy in November 1995 and closed its doors, and I was subsequently laid off.

A week afterward I accepted employment out of state. Not wanting to rent the house and be an absentee landlord, I decided to sell. Inevitably, mostly due to high unemployment in the city and a weak real estate market, the house took six months to sell, and I took a $10,000 loss liquidating it. In the end, though, considering I had invested in many homes and income properties over a period of 27 years, this New Orleans home would be the only loss I ever had to endure.

The lesson of this tale is, if you can't stay put for awhile, renting is better than buying.

Although owning a home can be profitable and fun, these things do not happen without a certain amount of work on your part. The chapters that follow present the appropriate guidelines that show the way to a profitable and hassle-free home buying experience. You, however, must implement these strategies. You must locate the right property to invest in, acquire the necessary mortgage loan, negotiate with the seller for its purchase, and make (or arrange) necessary repairs and improvements.

Only you can determine whether you're capable of completing these tasks. They are the drawbacks of owning improved real estate. Now consider all the advantages and great benefits of owning a home or additional income property. If you make the effort to implement the guidelines in the following chapters we'll show you how your home can even be a great source of retirement income.

When You Decide Real Estate Is Right for You

The chapters that follow present an array of guidelines and investment techniques for your consideration. Read all of them, then choose one technique that suits your particular desires and abilities. Choose your niche according to what you like to do, or what you do well. If you're a carpenter, then remodeling is likely your forte. The same for people who like to paint or wallpaper. A person who knows how to pour concrete would be ideal for building new foundations under older houses with faulty ones. If you are a patient person, a land-banking investment strategy could suit you. (See Chapter 19.) And if you have a green thumb, perhaps you can add value to your investments with special landscaping.

We think it's better to specialize in a certain investment technique. Much as an attorney specializes in a precise branch of law, you, too, can become an expert in your particular investment technique as you become more knowledgeable through specialization.

CHAPTER 2

Basic Guidelines for Successful Home Buying

Before tackling the specifics of choosing a house style, types of financing, and negotiating techniques, you must set some attainable goals and make a specific plan on how to achieve them. If you want to own a home or acquire a certain amount of wealth during your lifetime it's imperative that you start planning now. You need a plan with long-term as well as short-term goals. A well-thought-out plan revolves around estimating your future cash requirements and saving investment capital.

Establishing Your Investment Objectives

The self-made rich didn't get that way by being free spenders. And the folks who own big, beautiful homes free and clear of debt (and perhaps beautiful second homes and more) didn't accomplish such a feat by being frivolous spenders. They were smart buyers and savers. They scrimped, sacrificed, and initially lived frugal lives, while they watched their spending habits and saved their money to make smart investments.

If you haven't already saved enough for a down payment on a house, this chapter shows you how to survey your expenses and presents several ways you can save money, then allocate those savings toward a down payment.

Set Realistic Goals

For now, use a multiplier of three times gross income to determine how much house you can afford. For instance, if you and your spouse have a combined gross income of $40,000, the maximum price of the house you buy should not exceed $120,000 (3 × $40,000). (Chapter 4 goes into more detail about how much you can borrow to purchase a home.) This gives you a good idea of your home-buying capacity. Now, presuming that you don't have any savings to apply toward a down payment, you have to devise a plan for achieving this objective. To keep things simple, assume that you and your spouse desire a typical suburban three-bedroom two-bath house.

Now you've set a realistic goal. You have a reasonable idea of what you can afford, along with a general concept of what it is you're trying to purchase. Now all you have to do is devise a method to achieve the objective.

Survey Your Income and Expenses

To achieve your objective, you need to analyze your current income and expenses to determine where the investment capital (the down payment) will come from. If the bottom line reveals insufficient money left over for savings, don't panic.

Examine where and on what you are currently spending your money. After completing a survey of spending for the first time, many people are startled. They're suddenly made aware of their spending habits. For instance, they likely had no idea that eating out cost them in excess of $500 per month. Or that just the interest on their credit card debt was setting them back $200 per month. The combined cost of these two items alone adds up to a yearly expense of $8,400. If these people could trim these expenses just in half, they could save $4,200 annually. That in itself, is enough for a down payment in many real estate markets.

Your objective is to decide where to trim the fat from the monthly budget. But how much do you need to save? Ten percent of pretax income is an adequate goal for most people. How much you should be saving depends on your goals in life and how much real estate you eventually want to invest in. Should you, for instance, not have much presently saved, would need to save much more than 10 percent to attain your goal.

How Much Down Payment Do You Need?

Why are you still renting? Perhaps you lack what you feel is a sufficient down payment. Or maybe you think it's cheaper to continue to rent. Whatever the case, if you're like most renters, you probably overestimate the actual amount of cash required for a down payment.

You only need about $5,000 in cash to buy a $100,000 home. For a home priced at $60,000, you only need $3,000. And if you're a qualified veteran and earn enough money, you can purchase a home valued at $203,000 with no money down.

If you're unable to save money, you have two choices: Either cut your living expenses or earn more money and keep your living expenses constant.

Ways to Save for the Down Payment

The following are several proven methods of trimming the fat off your monthly expenses, and allocating the earned savings toward a down payment:

Reward yourself. Don't think *budget*—it sounds too much like work. Instead, think *reward*. Consider the wonderful reward you can earn for yourself by allocating your money toward a beautiful home of your own. If a new home is truly what you want, stop spending on nonessentials, and begin allocating the money saved toward a down payment.

Chop up those credit cards. Do you have several credit cards with high unpaid balances? Are you paying 18 percent or more interest on these unpaid balances, which never seem to get smaller? Then join the crowd—in 2003, consumer debt per borrower averaged more than $15,000.

How are you going to pay off what you owe on your credit cards? The first step (and yes, it's a mighty one) is, you must cut up your credit cards! Without them you won't be able to charge anymore, and you will have a better chance of paying off the balances. Put yourself on a strictly cash diet. Nothing curbs frivolous spending like paying hard cash.

When you finally have a zero balance on all your accounts, you have a major decision to make. If you feel you can limit your charge purchases and can pay off the balance at the end of each billing cycle without incurring any interest, you can have one credit card reissued. Be sure that when the credit card is reissued, the sponsor waives the annual fee.

If you already own your home and have a substantial amount of equity in it, consider taking out a low-interest home equity loan (which is usually tax deductible) and using it to pay off all those credit card debts (which are not tax deductible).

Reduce your rent. Rent is the biggest expense for most people who do not own their own home. You can reduce or eliminate rent payments, and allocate the savings toward a down payment. Could you switch to a lower-cost apartment? Could you share a rental, such as you and two friends sharing a three-bedroom house? Is there an empty bedroom that you could rent to someone? Could you move in with your parents or relatives and go rent-free for six months? (At $750 per month, that's a total savings of $4,500.) Bank this rent reduction, and you'll never pay rent again.

Trim your food bills in half. Like most people, you probably eat out a lot and enjoy doing it. Yet, this is a key area for savings—you may be able to trim the fat from your food budget by not eating out. Try taking a bag lunch to work. Prepare your food in large quantities, and freeze portions in single servings. Instead of shopping at some of the big-name supermarkets, shop at the new warehouse stores that have recently opened in most cities. You can save 20 to 50 percent at these food discounters, especially when you collect and use as many coupons as you can find.

Get rid of the extra car, or downsize the one you drive.   If you have an extra vehicle, and you can do without it, by all means sell it. (Not only do you get rid of the unneeded vehicle, you rid yourself of all the extra costs, including loan interest, maintenance, fuel, licensing, and insurance.) Especially get rid of the cash-draining car payments. If the old car is almost paid off, and you're thinking of buying a new one, don't! Drive the most dependable, least expensive car you can find. Car payments are the bane of far too many renters, and they will most certainly get in the way of most home-buying plans.

Cut down on your bad habits.   Have you ever thought about the amount of money it takes to maintain many of our bad habits—such as smoking and drinking alcoholic beverages at bars and restaurants? By eliminating them, you could reward yourself by probably saving half the down payment you need to buy a beautiful home. (Saving just $4 per day—the approximate cost of one pack of cigarettes or one alcoholic drink at a restaurant in some parts of the country—multiplied by 365 days is an annual savings of $1,460.)

Have a garage sale.   Is your spouse a packrat, who has saved everything that you ever bought since the beginning of time? Is it now cluttering up your garage or storage unit? Consider a fantastic money-making garage sale. Not only will you make money from the proceeds, you won't have to take the stuff you sell with you when you move, or continue to pay storage fees on it.

Insulate your water heater.   Your water heater is likely to lose energy through its outside casing if it's kept in an unheated space, such as an unfinished basement or garage. You can buy an easy-to-install insulating blanket that will cost about $14 to $20 depending on the size and the *R-value. R* means resistance to heat flow. The higher the R-value, the greater the insulation value.

   Also get coverings for the hot-water pipes leading away from your water-heater, since they're more likely to freeze without them. Such insulation for copper pipes costs between $2 and $10, depending on the material used.

Keep some drapes and flues closed.   Among other fast, inexpensive ways to insulate your home, the U.S. Department of Energy recommends closing chimney flues when you're not using the fireplace, and sealing any unused fireplaces in the house. (Since heat rises, it is better contained in the house with the flues closed.) Also, keep the drapes closed on north-facing windows, and let the sun shine in through the south-facing windows.

Control the thermostat. One of the most obvious ways to trim your heating bill is to cut the heat. Keeping your thermostat low when you're sleeping or away from home goes a long way toward saving money. Energy consultants estimate that if you turn the thermostat down 10 degrees for 8 hours a night, you can save 7 percent on your heating bill. If you do the same thing during the day, and you're away from home for 8 hours, that's another 7 percent.

Contact the energy source. Thanks to both deregulation and greater consciousness about energy conservation, your utility company may be eager to help you save money. Contact your local gas and electric company to see if it has any special deals for energy-efficient customers. Some may offer a free leak or draft audit for your house, Thorne says.

Put off the purchase of new furniture and appliances. Most renters spend entirely too much for new furniture and appliances. Worse, they charge it and are hooked into many years of payments at a high rate of interest. Much like new automobiles, most furniture and appliances depreciate in value faster than they deteriorate in condition. To overcome this, pay cash for quality second-hand bargains. You can purchase high-quality used furniture for less than the poor-quality particle-board furniture at low-priced furniture outlets. With regard to buying used appliances, buy only top-quality equipment, and then only if the appliance comes with a transferable extended warranty.

Most new cars, furniture, and appliances lose 30 to 40 percent of their value once they leave the retailer. Shrewd bargain hunters only pay for the usefulness of a product. Remember, whether you're purchasing cars, furniture, or appliances, let someone else incur the initial out-the-door depreciation.

The Wise Use of Credit

Not all borrowing is detrimental to one's financial well-being. In fact, long-term borrowing for practical investment or education purposes makes a lot of sense. These may include borrowing money for a real estate purchase, for a small business, or for education that can likely pay future dividends.

When you borrow to purchase a home or for investment purposes, the interest you pay is usually tax deductible. When buying a home, for example, the mortgage interest, points, and property taxes are generally tax deductible (see

Chapter 22). You should also know that due to inflation, the effective after-tax cost of borrowing money is just 4.6 percent for the average income earner when fixed-rate mortgages go for around 7 percent.

If you own a business, you can deduct the interest expense on loans you take out for business purposes. And when you borrow money against your securities (stocks and bonds) using margin accounts (borrowing from the broker), the interest is tax deductible against your investment income for the year.

You can even make wise use of short-term credit by using your credit cards to make your money work harder for you. Use your credit cards for the convenience that they offer, not for their credit feature. For example, by paying your bill in full and on time each month, you gain the free use of the money that you owed for the previous month's charges.

The lesson here is to be creative, but be careful. You may not like living with a group of other people (renters), but if it means you can someday reach financial freedom, then it's probably worth it!

LANDLORD TALE

In my senior year at Michigan State University, I already owned a three-bedroom house in Lansing, which I rented out to three students, and it showed a tidy little profit. I still had $1,500 left over from an inheritance, and I thought how nice it would be to own a second house, especially one I could live in. Soon I found a great prospect. It was situated on a beautiful half acre of land on the outskirts of the MSU campus, and it had six big bedrooms. The problem was, in order to assume the existing low-interest loan, I had to come up with an $8,500 down payment, which left me $7,000 short.

It was at about this time that I discovered the Federal Housing Administration (FHA), and all the great things it has to offer home owners and potential home owners. The FHA, under Title II, has an insured loan program to assist in financing the renovation of an owner-occupied home. Since I would be occupying this property and intended to remodel it, a Title II loan would be ideal. At the time I also had three credit cards at my disposal, with a combined line of credit that would cover the $7,000 required for the down payment.

To pay off the $7,000 debt, I took out a renovation loan (a second mortgage) for $7,000 amortized over five years. After all was said and done, I moved into this beauty and rented out the other five bedrooms to MSU students. After paying all the utilities, the taxes, and the installments on both home loans, I lived in this moneymaker rent-free, and earned $150 a month over and above all expenses.

NOTEWORTHY

Most mortgage lenders frown on borrowing the down payment required for a mortgage. (In the preceding situation, the seller carried back the first mortgage, and wasn't concerned about where my down payment came from.)

The Basic Dos and Don'ts of Successful Home Buying

The following advice is mostly preliminary and fundamental, to offer you a better overall perspective of the home buying process. These topics are covered in detail later in the book.

- *Initiate the home-buying process by shoring up your credit.* Since you most likely will need to get a mortgage to buy a house, make sure your credit history is as clean as possible. A few months before you start house hunting, get copies of your credit report. Make sure the facts are correct. Fix any problems you discover. Remember, if you're not creditworthy, you won't be able to get a good mortgage loan. And if your credit report is slightly tarnished, the lender will charge you accordingly, because of the higher risk. (See Appendix B for a list of credit agencies.)

- *Real estate is a better long-term investment than a short-term one.* Over the long haul, you'll make more money holding on to your realty investments, rather than "flipping" them (selling them quickly), because if you sell them you'll have to find another property to invest the proceeds from the sale.

- *Determine precisely how much house you can afford to buy before you start looking.* Realtors and mortgage lenders can only tell you the maximum that you're eligible to borrow. (For now, use three times your gross annual income as guide. You can calculate more precisely as you gain more information in Chapter 4.)

- *The best time to consider the sale of your house is before you buy it.* When looking at prospective purchases, take into consideration the features and amenities that other buyers would find desirable. In other words, pretend you are looking at the home's features through the eyes of other buyers, because if you don't, it will be difficult to find a buyer or get a good price when you sell.

- *Get professional help.*   Even though the Internet gives buyers unprecedented access to home listings, it's still a good idea to use an agent. Look for an exclusive buyer's agent, if possible, who will have your interests at heart and can help you with strategies during the bidding process. (See Chapter 8.)

- *Buy in a district with good schools.*   This advice applies even if you don't—and won't—have school-age children. When it comes time to sell, you'll learn that a strong school district is a top priority for many home buyers—thus helping to boost your property value.

- *When house hunting, bring your camera.*   Or at least bring a notebook to jot down reminders, because after you have looked at a half-dozen or so houses, the details will begin to blur in your mind. The best choice would be either an electronic camera that lets you take notes right on the image, or a Polaroid, so that you can scribble comments in the margins. You can also take notes on each listing, then later have the Realtor make copies of the listings that interest you.

- *Do your homework before bidding.*   Your opening bid should be based on the trend in sales prices of similar homes in the neighborhood. So before making it, consider sales of similar homes in the past three months. If homes have recently sold at 5 percent less than the asking price, you should make a bid that's about 8 to 10 percent lower than what the seller is asking.

- *Hire a home inspector.*   Sure, your lender will require a home appraisal anyway. That's the bank's way of determining whether the house is worth the price you've agreed to pay. Separately, you should hire your own home inspector—preferably an engineer with experience in doing home surveys in the area where you are buying. Your inspector's job will be to point out potential problems that could require costly repairs down the road. (See Chapter 8.)

All of the preceding items are the recommended dos of successful home buying. The following are the absolute don'ts of home buying that you have to be aware of and learn to avoid.

Don'ts to Be Aware of before Buying a Home

Did you ever buy a suit or a dress (or anything for that matter), take it home, and then decide you didn't like it? When the item in question doesn't cost much, it's no big loss. But when it comes to such a major purchase as buying a home, that kind of ill-advised shopping can not only lead to financial disaster, it can also get you stuck with a house that few others will want either. And unlike an item from a discount store, you'll be unable to exchange a home without absorbing a costly loss.

The goal of this book is to educate you to be a wise home buyer, so that you avoid overpaying for a house and/or buying one that you come to despise. There are many important things that you should know before buying a home. Along the way, you'll learn to avoid the many pitfalls others have fallen prey to.

You can do a lot of research, look around, review comparable properties, and shop for the best mortgage to help with your decision. This is encouraged, and later chapters give the details of how it's accomplished. However, in your unabashed enthusiasm for buying a house and making it your own, there are two important things you must do:

1. *Avoid overimproving the house to such a degree that could lead to financial ruin.* Remember that improvements cost money, not to mention the high cost of interest to finance them. Take note that when it comes time to sell, improvements such as an in-ground swimming pool will only appeal to buyers who want a pool on the property. Do not neglect other important financial goals, such as saving for retirement or the down payment on a second rental home, in order to make an endless number of impractical improvements to your home. Have an overall, long-term plan or theme for the future renovation of your home.

2. *Avoid making the home too strange.* Oddball colors and renovations will seriously limit the range of buyers it will appeal to when it's time to sell—and you'll reduce the price you're likely to get. Should you decide to make renovations, focus on those that are appealing and add value, such as ceramic tile, hardwood floors, updates to bathrooms and kitchens, an added patio for expanded living area, and so on. (See Chapter 18.)

These two don'ts are certainly costly mistakes you most definitely want to avoid in your home purchase. Yet there are other notable perils too, which I call "The Six Nevers of Home Buying."

The Six Nevers of Home Buying

These are common, costly mistakes that countless home buyers have fallen prey to in the past.

1. *Never ignore logistics.* Consider your commute to and from the workplace. A home should be enjoyed, not despised because travel to and from the workplace is a hassle of wasted time and gridlocked traffic. Don't forget to consider the distance to and from shopping, restaurants, and entertainment.

2. *Never buy if you can't stay put.* If you can't commit to remaining in one place for five years or more, then owning is probably not for you, at least not yet.

With slow appreciation and the costs of buying and selling a home, you may end up losing money if you sell any sooner. On the other hand, you might say to yourself, "If I had to relocate to another city, why couldn't I rent out the house instead of selling it?"

There are two primary reasons that renting out the house when you have to relocate out of town is not recommended. First, it will be too difficult to handle property management tasks, such as showing the property when it's vacant. And second, you'll be required to turn your rental over to someone else to manage, which means you'll lose direct control over your investment. (See Chapter 20.)

3. *Never worry too much about job security.*   Feeling insecure about your job is only natural. Most working people do, including superstar athletes, chief executives of multinational companies, and corporate lawyers. And making a substantial down payment, along with taking out a huge long-term mortgage, can make you think twice about career longevity. Remember that you'll always have the option of selling the home, if you should become unemployed for an extended length of time.

If losing your job is a real possibility, especially if you have to relocate out of town for a new job, consider postponing the purchase of a home until your career situation stabilizes. (Most mortgage lenders will not lend you money anyway, unless you can demonstrate a recent history of stable employment—see Chapter 3.) When you have to move out of town to find another job, especially when you've owned the home for only a short period, the cost of selling your home and buying another can be excessive. The cost to sell might include required renovations, sales commissions, and moving expenses, which altogether can run into tens of thousands of dollars.

4. *Never buy more than you can afford.*   You don't want to become a slave to your home. Many first-time home buyers allow their desires to overwhelm their budgets. Fred and Laurie had good jobs in the airline industry, and together earned about $140,000 annually. They lived high on the hog—they ate at the best restaurants, shopped for the finest clothes, took expensive vacations, and essentially overindulged themselves.

Eventually they bought a home. Of course, they bought an expensive one, and borrowed the maximum amount the loan officer told them they were allowed. After they moved in, Laurie got pregnant and soon quit her job to spend more time at home. About a year after their child was born, the airline industry experienced a major setback, and Fred was required to work fewer hours. The result was a 30 percent reduction in take-home pay, not to mention the added expense of raising a child. They soon found themselves struggling to pay their monthly bills. To make matters worse, they began accumulating significant credit card debt. Ultimately, they ended up filing for bankruptcy and losing the house.

You want to aim for a home you can really afford. The rule of thumb is that you can buy a house that costs about 2.5 to 3 times your annual salary. But you'll do better to use one of the Internet's many calculators to get a handle on your income, debts, expenses, and how those affect what you can afford.

5. *Never buy less than you can afford.*   Just as you can overbuy when it comes to selecting a home, you can also make the mistake of underbuying. If you underbuy and end up with a smaller home than you need, or one that lacks the amenities you require, soon after you move in you'll realize your mistake—it's not the house you wanted.

That's what Mark and Kim did when they bought their first home. They could have bought a large $150,000 home, but instead tried to live within their means—a smart thing to do, but they became overly cautious. They took out a mortgage for $60,000 when they could have borrowed twice that amount. They figured they would live in the smaller house for a few years, then sell it and buy a bigger, more desirable home. Unfortunately, they failed to consider the hassle of moving twice, or the costs involved with buying another house and selling the first one.

6. *Never put off buying because you're afraid that escalating prices will lock you out.*   Over the past 40 years, residential real estate values have increased, on average, about 1.5 times the annual rate of inflation. Real estate values are historically cyclical—they go up and down depending on related market conditions (such as prevailing interest rates, job market, inflation, and so on). Yet overall, including the intermittent downswings, real estate values have always been in a general upward trend. And at times overinflated housing markets—such as in the Sacramento area, where average home prices escalated 27 percent in 2002— make some renters feel locked out of the game. Indeed, patient buyers who can wait out a market that has increased dramatically in value are often rewarded with steadying or, at times, falling prices.

This all boils down to the fact that if you postpone buying a home for many years, knowing that real estate prices are generally headed up (along with inflation), you'll be getting less home for your money than if you bought today, because home prices increase faster than the rate of inflation.

Achieving Your Goals

What are your goals in life? A short-term goal might be the purchase of your first home. A great long-term goal for many is financial independence. Whatever your aspirations, you must keep in mind the old saying, "A journey of a thousand miles begins with a single step." If your short-term goal is to buy your first home, then you must take the first step toward acquiring that home. If you're just getting started in real estate, and you don't have any ready cash for a down payment, cutting your expenses and accumulating the savings for a down payment is a great first step. To do that you need to get rid of any and all consumer debt—such as credit card balances and auto loans. Ridding yourself of such debt is vital to saving investment capital.

Once you achieve your first short-term goal, such as buying a home for you and your family, you can begin devising a plan to accomplish a long-term goal. Your home can be the foundation for future investments. Before you know it, because of the appreciation you earn on the home, along with the tax benefits and equity earned through paying down the mortgage, you'll have enough to invest in a second rental property.

PART II

FINANCE 101—HOW TO GET THE MONEY YOU NEED

This part presents all the options in selecting the right mortgage that's best for you—one that can save you thousands of dollars in interest costs over the life of the loan. Depending on your circumstances, discover which repayment plan is best—a fixed-rate or an adjustable-rate loan—or perhaps you prefer a hybrid convertible loan. Whatever you choose, you don't have to be intimidated by all the financialese the lenders use, because the following chapters define the financial terminology. Special types of financing are covered, such as no-qualifying assumables, wraparounds, land contracts, and an array of seller financing you can acquire. This part also guides you through the paperwork maze of the loan application process.

CHAPTER 3

The Mortgage Alternatives

If you were Microsoft founder Bill Gates, you could skip Chapters 3 and 4, which reveal everything that you need to know about how to finance a home. Billionaires like Gates can easily avoid doing business with mortgage lenders, who ask a lot of credit questions and require employment verification when they lend money. Indeed, anyone who has plenty of cash on hand, can buy a home without a loan.

The rest of us need to borrow the majority of the money (and in some cases all of it) in order to purchase a suitable home. This chapter aims to save you some money and keep you informed about all the necessary how-tos of home finance.

The Cost Is in the Mortgage

The most expensive thing you'll likely ever buy is not your home—it's the cost of the *financing* required to purchase that home. If you borrow to buy your home, as most people do, the mortgage itself is the biggest cost item. Many home buyers fail to take into consideration the aggregate interest cost of the mortgage. You should pay special attention to it, and here's why: Suppose you buy a $120,000 home and borrow $110,000 at 9 percent for 30 years. That mortgage, if paid off over the entire 30 years, will cost you $208,629 in interest—which is almost twice the amount you borrowed, and almost double the price of the home. And that's not even counting the $110,000 in principal that you have to pay back. In other words, over a period of 30 years you would actually pay $318,629 for a $120,000 home!

If you learn how to take advantage of the full range of today's financing methods, and take the time to shop for a mortgage that is just right for your needs, you can save tens of thousands of dollars on a long-term mortgage. By following the guidelines set forth in this chapter, you can avoid the costliest mistake many home buyers make—paying too much for the wrong financing.

Financial Terminology: Learning the Basics

Starting with the basics, you should first become familiar with the more common financial instruments and terms used in the industry. When the time comes to apply for a mortgage, you won't have any trouble speaking financialese (mortgage talk) with knowledgeable mortgage lenders.

Mortgages and *deeds of trust* are financial instruments that create *liens* (claims or rights) against real property. These instruments state that, should the borrower default on the loan (fail to make payments when due), the lender has the legal right to sell the property in order to satisfy the loan in a foreclosure sale.

Mortgage loans are typically comprised of payments repaid over a specified term (a time period of repayment). The payment is comprised of *interest*, which is what the lender charges for the use of the money you borrowed, and *principal*, which is repayment of the original amount borrowed. Most mortgage loans are *amortized*, which means it is paid off in regular equal installments. As the loan is paid down, you build up equity in the home. *Equity* is the difference between what is owed on the home and its value. (If the home is worth $120,000, and you owe $100,000 on it, your equity is $20,000.)

A mortgage involves two parties: the *mortgagor* (the borrower and property owner), and the *mortgagee* (the lender). A mortgage is embodied in two documents: a *mortgage note*, which is evidence of the debt, and a *mortgage contract*, which is security for the debt. The note promises to repay the loan, while the contract promises to convey title of the property to the mortgagee in case of default.

Deeds of trust (or trust deeds) are similar to mortgage instruments, except that an additional third party is involved, which makes the foreclosure process simpler and less time consuming. Under a trust deed, the borrower (owner of the property) is called the *trustor.* The lender is referred to as the *beneficiary.* An intermediate third party, whose responsibility is to hold title to the property for the security of the lender, is referred to as the *trustee.* Under a trust deed, if the trustor defaults on the loan obligation, the subject property will be sold at public auction by the trustee through provisions in the *power of sale* clause contained in the trust deed, without court procedure.

Foreclosure is initiated by a *notice of default*, which is recorded by the trustee, with a copy sent to the trustor. If after three months the trustor does nothing to remedy the situation, a *notice of sale* is posted on the property, and advertisements of the sale are carried in local newspapers once a week for three weeks. If during this period the trustor fails to pay the beneficiary sufficient funds to halt the foreclosure, the trustee will conduct the sale. Proceeds from the foreclosure sale are first disbursed to the beneficiary, then to any other lien holders according to their priority.

Second trust deeds and mortgages (or thirds, fourths, etc.) are similar to firsts, except that they are second in priority to a first loan, with respect to security and the lender's ability to claim any proceeds from a foreclosure sale. (Note that the specifics of foreclosure proceedings vary from state to state.)

Foreclosure under a mortgage instrument, as opposed to a trust deed, takes notably longer (periods in excess of a year are common). For this reason, more than half the states utilize the trust deed as the preferred financial instrument over the mortgage. (Learn the details about how to buy foreclosed real estate in Chapter 12.)

Buying and Selling Mortgaged Property

In certain cases, a buyer can pay for property by assuming an existing mortgage. An *assumed mortgage* is one in which the buyer assumes (takes over) the legal obligation to make the loan payments, while the lender releases the previous borrower from the liability. Many mortgages contain a clause that prohibits assumption.

In contrast, buying property *subject* to the existing mortgage is a method by which the buyer takes over the loan obligation without the existing borrower being released from the liability, and without a formal arrangement with the lender.

An *assigned mortgage* is one that you already own, and then transfer to another person. A mortgage that you own is an asset or a negotiable instrument that has value. It is a note on which someone is paying you principal and interest, and your security is the mortgage against certain real property. Therefore, as your down payment, you can assign (transfer) a mortgage to the seller of the property you wish to acquire.

 LANDLORD TALE

During a span of about three years in the early 1980s, when mortgage rates were averaging 10 to 11 percent, I purchased four houses in Las Vegas, Nevada. Every one of them came with low-interest assumable financing, which meant I avoided much of the time and costs that would usually be required to originate new financing. In doing so, I eluded all the customary expenses inherent in originating a new loan, such as the proverbial credit report, the appraisal, the points, and the high rate of interest, which then was at least two points above the rate I was assuming. To assume these loans, all I had to do was pay a nominal $50 assumption fee, with no questions asked.

BEWARE

Be cautious when buying property subject to the existing mortgage, because certain mortgages prohibit such arrangements.

Be aware of due-on-sale or alienation clauses in loan documents. Without going into great detail, they essentially mean the same thing—that is, if the title is transferred to another party, the lender can call the total amount owed due and payable within 30 days, or has the right to ask for assumption fees and an increased rate of interest.

A Point about Points

There is a difference in the two kinds of *points* mortgage lenders utilize. *Service points* are essentially up-front interest. This charge is often called a *loan origination fee.* Lenders charge points as way of being paid in advance for the expense of processing and approving your loan.

One point is equal to 1 percent of the amount you're borrowing. You pay the points at the time you close on your home purchase.

Discount points are different from service points, in that they are used to equalize varying loan rates, and are most often paid by the seller in a real estate transaction. For instance, both the FHA and the VA set the maximum permissible interest rate that can be charged on their loans. Frequently this maximum rate is pegged below the interest rates charged by conventional lenders in the open market. Therefore, in order to provide an incentive to originate VA and FHA loans, lenders are permitted to equalize the differential between this pegged rate and the open market rate by charging discount points.

For instance, assume the following interest rates are in effect:

Market interest rate	8.0 percent
FHA fixed interest rate	7.5 percent
Difference in rates	0.5 percent

NOTEWORTHY

FHA loans originated before December 1, 1986, and VA loans originated before March 1, 1988, are completely assumable with no questions asked. Both types of government-backed loans originated after these dates, however, require that special qualifying exceptions be met before they can be assumed by the new buyer.

Studies have shown that over the average life of a mortgage loan, a 1 percent difference in interest rates equals 8 discount points. (A 1 percent difference equals 8/8 discount points.) Thus, a 0.5 percent differential in interest rates equals 4/8. Therefore, each eighth represents 1 discount point. Then, to originate the FHA loan in the preceding example, the lender would charge 4 points to make the FHA interest rate equivalent to the market interest rate.

Other Lender Fees

In addition to the up-front service points to originate a loan, mortgage lenders charge other kinds of fees you should be aware of.

- *Application or processing fee.* This is a fee some lenders charge the borrower to apply for a loan. Mortgage lenders want to be compensated for all applications, in case some don't materialize into actual loans. Often this fee is waived if the loan is approved and funded.

- *Loan commitment fee.* Expect to pay 1 point if you want to lock in a guaranteed rate at closing for an extended period (usually more than 30 days).

- *Credit report.* This is a cost every borrower pays to initiate a new loan, or to assume an existing qualifying loan. The lender requires a history of your creditworthiness, which reveals how you've dealt with prior loans.

- *Appraisal.* You may wonder why the lender would require an independent assessment of the value of the property. Because they have such a high stake in the mortgaged property, lenders want to be sure that you're not overpaying. Unfortunately, over the life of a long-term mortgage, some bad things can happen—neighborhood values could decline, or you could end up in financial trouble and be unable to pay on the mortgage, in which case you might walk away from the property and leave the lender owning it.

    Nowadays, depending on the size and complexity of the property, you can expect to pay about $300 for an appraisal on most modestly priced homes.

TIP

If you know that you have some minor scars on your credit report, address these problems before you apply for a mortgage loan. Otherwise, you'll surely be wasting your valuable time and money, applying for a loan that will likely be denied. Often, a minor blemish, such as a small unpaid telephone bill from the past, can easily be explained in an interview with the lender.

	TIP

After you've paid on the mortgage for a few years, and your equity in the home is at least 20 percent, you're entitled to cancel the PMI policy and pocket the savings. Note that you must initiate the cancellation. (Many home owners are not aware of this entitlement and needlessly continue to pay this premium over the life of the loan.)

- *Private mortgage insurance (PMI).* On conventional loans, borrowers with less than a 20 percent down payment are required to buy insurance that protects the lender against default. PMI costs about half a point of the loan amount, or about $30 per month, and is added to your monthly payment.

Types of Repayment Plans

Real estate loans can be classified in several different ways. One means of classification is according to the repayment plan. The basic repayment plans are the following:

- Interest-only (straight-term) loans
- Fixed-rate loans
- Adjustable-rate loans
- Convertible loans

Interest-Only Loans

Also known as a *straight-term loan,* an interest-only loan requires the payment of interest only during the term of the loan. At the end of the term, the entire sum of principal is due and payable in one final balloon payment. For example, the annual payment schedule for an interest-only loan for $12,000 at 10 percent interest for a term of five years is $100 per month ($12,000 × 0.10 ÷ 12 = $100). Then, at the end of five years, a balloon payment of $12,000 will be due and payable.

Before the Great Depression, the interest-only loan was the most common method of financing real estate. Many borrowers took out these loans for short terms, expecting to renew them term after term, thus deferring payment of the principal almost indefinitely.

But the world economy severely faltered during the Depression, and most lenders were unable to "roll over," or perpetuate, these interest-only loans. The results were devastating. Lenders began calling loans, requiring borrowers to pay back the entire principal amount, which the borrowers did not have. Lenders then started foreclosing on these loans throughout the country, which unfortunately was comparable to pouring gasoline on a burning fire, and only helped to deepen the Depression.

Almost everyone, especially those within the financial industry, became aware of the inherent dangers in this type of financing. A more practical form of loan soon materialized—the fully amortized fixed-rate loan.

Fixed-Rate Loans

A great alternative to the interest-only loan is the fully amortized loan that comes with a fixed rate of interest, featuring equal monthly payments of both principal and interest over the loan's term. Unlike the interest-only loan, the fixed-rate loan commonly has a longer term of 15 or 30 years, and is completely paid off at the end of its term. According to the National Association of Realtors, nowadays 86 percent of the loans mortgage lenders make are fixed-rate.

Fixed-Rate Loans at a Glance

- The initial interest rate is higher than that of the adjustable-rate loan, but it remains unchanged over the life of the loan.
- Monthly payments of principal and interest remain the same and fully amortize the loan at maturity.
- There is usually a "due-on-sale" clause, meaning that it is not assumable.
- If it's a conventional loan, it could have a prepayment penalty.

Initial payments on the fixed-rate loan consist mostly of interest. But as the loan matures, more of each payment is applied toward the principal, since interest on an amortized loan is calculated on the loan's outstanding principal balance. Thus, each payment reduces the principal balance owed, resulting in a smaller interest portion and a larger principal portion on the next payment. Figure 3.1 illustrates the paydown of a 30-year fixed-rate mortgage.

So, with a fixed-rate loan (as the name suggests), you have a rate that is fixed (unchanged) during the entire term of the loan. This means you don't have to deal with feelings of anxiety or uncertainty about future changes in your interest rate, which inevitably lead to changes in your monthly payment.

Yet, in the eyes of a mortgage lender, long-term fixed-rate loans can be risky, especially in times of rising interest rates. Traditionally, long-term

FIGURE 3.1   Paying down a 30-year mortgage loan at 7 percent interest.

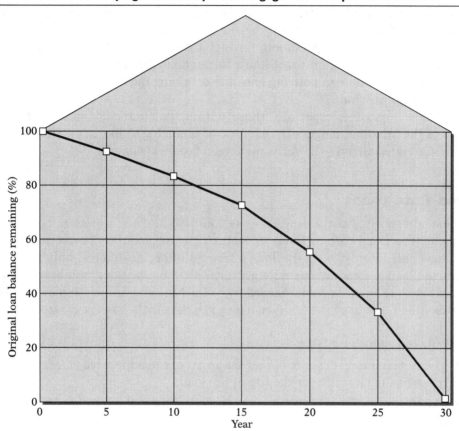

mortgage lenders loaned their money at reasonable interest rates (and rightly so, as their cost of acquiring that money seldom fluctuated). But along came the hyperinflationary times of the mid-1970s and the early 1980s, and the cost of money went up dramatically. Meanwhile, these lenders had billions of dollars loaned out at interest rates substantially below what it cost them to acquire the funds. Hence, the creation of the adjustable-rate loan.

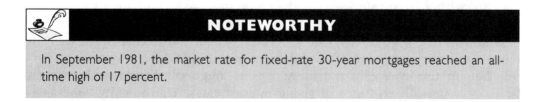

NOTEWORTHY

In September 1981, the market rate for fixed-rate 30-year mortgages reached an all-time high of 17 percent.

Adjustable-Rate Loans

Also known as adjustable-rate mortgages (ARMs), adjustable-rate loans were created for the purpose of protecting long-term mortgage lenders from radical changes in market interest rates. But before we go any further, let's take a brief look at some of the features of the ARM:

ARMs at a Glance

- The rate of interest fluctuates up or down depending on the index rate it's tied to.
- The initial rate of interest is more favorable than that on a fixed-rate loan: Increases over the term of loan are specifically limited.
- The borrower's monthly payment will rise or fall over the term, within specified limits.
- Because the initial rate is lower than that of a fixed-rate loan, the home buyer can qualify to borrow more.
- Most ARMs are assumable, with credit approval.

How ARMs Work. ARMs vary somewhat, but they are essentially similar in function. The initial rate (the so-called teaser rate), is allowed to fluctuate (along with your monthly payment) every one, three, or five years, over the entire term of the loan. The period from one rate change to the next is referred to as the *adjustment period*. Thus, an adjustable loan with an adjustment period of one year is called a one-year ARM.

Rate-Change Limits. Most ARMs are based on a formula that includes an *index* and a *margin* (amount of profit). When the index rate moves up or down, so does your interest rate, along with your monthly payments. There are limits, however, on how much your interest rate can change at any one time, and over the life of the adjustable loan. The interest rate change is usually limited to a maximum of 2 percent during each adjustment period, and an overall cap is placed on the interest increase.

Most lenders use indexes tied to some easily monitored rate, such as the U.S. Treasury securities rate. Then the lender applies a margin to the index used. The interest rate a lender quotes you on an ARM is equal to the index rate plus the lender's margin. Note that the amount of margin varies among mortgage lenders.

One lender may charge the Treasury index plus a margin of 2 percent, whereas another lender may use the same index plus a margin of 3 percent. The net result between the two lender's offerings is 1 point. Now let's look at the

difference 1 point makes on a hypothetical monthly payment of principal and interest on a $110,000 loan (Table 3.1).

In the example given in Table 3.1, the $75.31 difference in monthly pay-
ments represents the savings on a $110,000 mortgage loan for a 30-year term.
Over the life of the loan, the difference between lenders A and B is a substantial
$27,112!

Margins are an integral part of competitive pricing of mortgages, and reflect the lender's cost of doing business and resulting profit.

The margin used, the index preferred, and the choice of the adjustment period are the essential topics to discuss when shopping for an ARM. Besides comparing margins among lenders, you also have some options on how often your
rate will be adjusted. Keep in mind, however, that lenders will charge a higher
rate for longer adjustment periods.

Safeguard Features.   Many mortgage lenders offer certain caps, or specified limits on how much rates, or monthly payments, can increase in any adjustment period or over the term of the loan. Most ARMs have both payment caps and interest
rate caps.

Payment caps.   A payment cap sets a ceiling on how much your monthly
payments can increase in any one year.

Interest-rate caps.   Interest-rate caps limit the increases in the interest rate
itself. These caps come in two varieties:

1. Caps that limit the amount of increase in interest rate from one adjustment period to the next
2. Caps that limit the amount of increase in interest rate over the life of the
   loan

**TABLE 3.1   Effect of a 1-point Change in Margin on a
$110,000 Loan**

	Lender	
Factor	**A**	**B**
One-year Treasury index	5%	5%
Margin	+2	+3
Initiate rate borrower pays	7%	8%
Monthly payment	$731.83	$807.14
Difference between A and B = $75.31		

These caps act to insure the borrower, and like other forms of insurance, you have to pay to get them.

Though some adjustables are more volatile than others, they all float with the market level of interest rates. If the market rate fluctuates, so does your monthly payment. And therein lies the risk, because not only do you have to deal with such a major expense as a mortgage payment, with an ARM, you also have to face the fact that increases in your monthly payment may put a serious cramp in your budget.

Usually a borrower can originate an ARM at a lower interest rate than that of a fixed-rate loan, primarily because the lender is not at risk from fluctuating interest rates; instead, the borrower takes all the risk, because the rate can potentially be increased 6 points over the term of the loan.

Given all this, one might wonder why anyone would consider taking out an adjustable loan for an extended term of 15 or 30 years. The answer is that many first-time home buyers, and those trading up, tend to stretch their budgets and force themselves into accepting ARMs. They're actually lured by the ARM's initial lower interest rate, because such a mortgage enables the borrower to qualify to borrow more. Nonetheless, just because you can qualify for a bigger loan doesn't mean that you can afford to borrow that much, given your other financial needs and goals.

As you can see, compared to fixed-rate mortgages, ARMs represent a substantial risk to the borrower, especially in times of rising interest rates. If you don't plan or expect to remain in your home for a long time—say, up to five years—the ARM is usually the preferred loan type. The savings on interest charges for most ARMs usually come in the first two or three years, because an ARM starts at a lower teaser rate than a fixed-rate loan does.

On the other hand, if you expect to stay in your home and pay on the mortgage for a long time—more than five years—a fixed-rate loan would be more sensible, especially when you're not in position to endure the fluctuating monthly payments associated with an ARM.

If you do decide on an ARM, be prepared to ask potential lenders certain questions:

- How much margin is applied, and what index is used for determining mortgage interest rate?
- What will happen to the mortgage payments if interest rates rise, decline, or stay the same?
- How often will the monthly payments be adjusted?
- What type of caps are available for the borrower's protection?

Convertible Loans

Some ARMs are special, in that they have a convertible feature. The loan starts out as an adjustable loan, but it can be converted to a fixed-rate loan. It's special, because it's the hybrid of both the adjustables and the fixed rates. It gives you the best of both worlds—the lower initial rates of the ARM, and the option to lock in a fixed rate at some future time.

Convertible ARMs at a Glance

- The rate of interest fluctuates; however, the borrower can lock in a fixed rate when the time of convertibility is right.
- There is a slightly higher interest rate than that of the ARM, plus a conversion fee. (You pay for a valuable option.)
- When you convert to a fixed rate on your adjustment period anniversary date, the rate is usually 0.25 point higher than the going rate of your lender's fixed-rate mortgage.
- The convertible ARM is ideal for those who (1) like to take advantage of lower initial interest rates and fear the results of future rising interest rates, and (2) are likely to be selling the newly financed home within five years.

Unlike the nonconvertible ARM, the convertible ARM brings a certain predictability to mortgage needs. Most convertible loans allow the borrower to switch from an adjustable rate to a fixed rate on the anniversary dates of the loan closing, generally limited to a three- to five-year conversion period. The converted fixed rate will then remain unchanged until the loan matures. If the borrower never exercises the convertible option, the mortgage loan continues as a typical ARM with a cap on rate increases, limited to an overall 5-point increase over the life of the loan.

The cost of conversion varies with each lender, but generally it's in the range of $250 to $1,000. This can be a substantial savings compared to refinancing, which can often cost upwards of $3,000.

Convertible-loan rates are usually lower than those of fixed-rate loans, but slightly higher than those of similar nonconvertible ARMs. The cost of loan origination is about the same as for an ARM; regardless, be prepared to pay a premium to the lender (in addition to the conversion fee) for the right of convertibility.

Potential home buyers can also benefit by selecting from a wide array of available loan types. The following section discusses various government-backed loan programs that allow you to buy a home with virtually no down payment. It also shows which types of loans are fully assumable, and how under certain circumstances, the seller can also be the lender. To this end, the section presents the how-tos of these special types of financing, including wraparounds, land contracts, and purchase-money mortgages. Also included are sources of financing for home buyers with less than perfect credit, or even a poor credit rating.

The Loan Choices

Real estate loans are divided into two categories: loans insured or guaranteed by the federal government (and in some cases the state government), and loans that are not. The most common government-backed loans are those sponsored by the Veteran's Administration (VA) and the Federal Housing Administration (FHA). Home loans made without government sponsorship are termed *conventional loans.*

Conventional Loans

Compared to the guaranteed VA loan and the insured FHA loan, conventional financing usually has more stringent qualification standards, fewer benefits, and higher costs. These include the following:

- There are higher down payment requirements (at least 5 to 20 percent).
- There is the added cost of private mortgage insurance (PMI), which is about half a point, and is required when the down payment is less than 20 percent.
- The loan is usually not assumable.

FHA-Insured Loans

The FHA assists home buyers who might not be able to meet the higher down payment requirements and qualifying standards used for conventional loans. FHA works through local mortgage lending institutions to provide federal mortgage insurance for the purchase, rehabilitation, or improvement of affordable housing.

The borrower is eligible for approximately 97 percent financing, and is permitted to finance the up-front mortgage insurance premium into the mortgage. The borrower will also be responsible for paying an annual premium. Eligible properties are one- to four-unit structures.

The following are features of the FHA insured loan:

- You can borrow with as little as a 3 percent down payment.
- It is easier to qualify for than a conventional loan.
- There is no prepayment penalty.
- The loan is assumable, with qualifications.

TIP

Similar to the cancellation of PMI on a conventional loan, after you've paid on the FHA-insured loan for a few years and your equity in the home is at least 20 percent, you're entitled to cancel the mortgage insurance policy and pocket the savings. Note that you must initiate the cancellation. (Many home owners are not aware of this entitlement, and needlessly continue paying this premium over the life of the loan.)

VA-Guaranteed Loans

A VA loan is made by a lender, such as a mortgage company, savings and loan, or bank. VA's guaranty on the loan protects the lender against loss if the payments aren't made, and is intended to encourage lenders to offer veterans loans with more favorable terms.

Qualified veterans can use the VA loan to buy a home, build a home, improve a home, or refinance an existing home. Ease of qualification and no requirement of a down payment are the hallmarks of this great benefit, offered to those people who have served in the U.S. military. All you need is your form DD-214 (proof of discharge). Send it to the VA, and you get back a Certificate of Eligibility. Take your certificate to a lender that makes VA loans and get preapproved. The local VA office can provide more details.

The following are the features of the VA loan:

- You can borrow up to $203,000 with no down payment.
- There is no prepayment penalty.
- No private mortgage insurance is required.
- There is a limit on closing costs to the borrower.
- The loan is assumable, with qualifications.

30-Year or 15-Year Mortgage?

Besides choosing a particular loan type that's best for you, you have to decide which term you favor, 30 years or 15 years. Table 3.2 compares the two.

On a $110,000 loan at 9 percent, the monthly mortgage payments are as follows:

    15-year $1,115.69
    30-year   804.62

TABLE 3.2 Comparison of Accumulated Equity and Interest Paid on 30- and 15-Year Fixed-Rate Loans

Contract interest rate = 9 percent; loan amount = $110,000.

Time	15-Year Accumulation		30-Year Accumulation	
	Interest Paid	Equity Earned	Interest Paid	Equity Earned
After 5 years	$45,051	$ 21,890	$ 43,767	$ 4,510
After 15 years	90,824	110,000	122,061	22,770
After 30 years	—	—	179,663	110,000

A difference of $311.07. As Table 3.2 shows, the 15-year fixed-rate loan is ideal for those who can afford the higher monthly payments. Compared to the 30-year loan, the 15-year saves over $89,000 in interest payments, and lenders usually charge a half-point lower rate of interest than for a 30-year loan. Notably, though, the 30-year loan gives you a higher tax deduction for the interest paid.

Of course, the shorter-term loan costs you $311.07 more each month, but don't forget—you'll enjoy the satisfaction of owning your home, free and clear, in half the time it takes with a 30-year mortgage.

So, if you're looking for faster equity buildup and ways to save on interest charges, the 15-year fixed-rate mortgage could be the most sensible loan for you.

Loan Prequalification versus Preapproval

Imagine going to the supermarket and the following scenario occurs: You grab a shopping cart and spend an hour or so going up and down the aisles loading up the cart. When you finally get to the checkout counter, you unload the shopping cart, putting the items onto the counter where they're price-scanned, bagged, and placed back in your cart.

Then comes the moment of truth—the bill comes to $119. So you reach in your wallet and—oops!—realize that you don't have enough cash. You then hastily take out your credit card, and you start to get nervous when you notice that the three people in line behind you are getting really impatient. Meanwhile, you scan the credit card nervously, waiting for authorization approval—and if you have guessed what happens next, go to the head of the class. If you guessed that the credit charge of $119 will be disapproved, you're right! What a humiliating moment! Not to mention the embarrassment of having to walk out of the store empty-handed, while a clerk has to place all your groceries back on the shelves.

This scenario can serve as a good lesson when it comes to buying a home. Having your mortgage application denied after signing a contract to buy a property may cause you to lose the house, after having spent hundreds of dollars on a house inspection and loan application fees. Even worse, it's a real emotional drain, after you have spent countless hours and a great deal of energy trying to secure a desirable home. Many house sellers may need to sell quickly, and for this reason will be unwilling to wait for you to be approved by another lender. Other buyers, too, may have offers pending on the property, which the sellers could now accept. Which means you'll likely have to find another property.

How can you avoid this experience? Get preapproval for a mortgage by a specific lender before you sign a contract to buy real estate.

But don't confuse loan *preapproval* with loan *prequalification*. There's a distinct difference between the two procedures. Prequalification can be as informal as a phone call to the lender. The lender will merely give an opinion of the maximum loan amount that you can borrow, based solely on the input you provide. The lender doesn't verify anything, and is not required to make the loan when you're ready to buy.

Conversely, preapproval is a precise process based on documented verification regarding your employment, your income, the cash you have available for the down payment, your liabilities, and your creditworthiness. That's why it's recommended, especially if you have any reason to believe that you'll have difficulty acquiring the loan you need. Getting preapproval is a sign to house sellers that you're a serious buyer. A lender's preapproval letter could be beneficial in a multiple-offer situation, in which more than one prospective buyer bids on a property at the same time. Given the same price and terms, the sellers would most definitely give the edge to a home buyer who has been preapproved for a loan.

Prequalification usually doesn't cost anything. Some lenders will charge for loan preapproval, due to the extra work involved; others may offer free preapprovals to gain borrower loyalty. Those lenders may not have the best loan terms. Choose a lender based on the best loan terms, not because you're getting a free preapproval.

Special Types of Financing

Aside from the standard forms of financing, you also have a choice of special types of home financing. In certain cases, you can also let the seller be the banker.

Seller Financing

In seller financing, the seller of the house you are buying assists with the financing. Sellers do this by allowing you, the buyer, to owe them money instead of paying the full price of the house in cash at the closing.

In a traditional home-sale transaction, the buyer would normally use savings to pay for about 20 percent of the purchase price. The remaining 80 percent would be obtained from a lender, such as a savings and loan or a bank. Thus, the seller would receive all the cash for the sale of the house at the closing—part from the buyer and the remainder from the lender.

Seller financing can be arranged in two different ways: with a purchase-money mortgage or a land contract.

Purchase-Money Mortgage. The first, and most common, method of seller financing is when the seller of real estate carries back a mortgage from the buyer. This type of seller financing is also called a *purchase-money mortgage*. It's the equivalent of the seller making a loan to the buyer, yet the seller will not receive that money at the closing. In other words, the seller (the mortgagee) takes back the buyer's paper (the mortgage), instead of accepting cash from the buyer (the mortgagor).

Land Contract. The second method of seller financing conveys the property to the buyer on the installment method, also known as a *contract of sale*. Unlike a mortgage, in which the buyer receives title to the property at closing, in an installment land contract the buyer does not receive title to the property until all the required payments are made. Since the buyer does not have legal title to the property until it is fully paid for, this method is generally practical only when the seller provides all of the financing, because it would be difficult for the buyer to obtain additional financing from another lender. In other words, it would be difficult for another lender to use the property as collateral (place a lien against it) when the buyer does not have legal title to the property.

The two primary reasons an owner of real estate would offer seller financing are that it makes the property more salable, and it's a great secured investment, allowing the seller to earn interest income over the term of the mortgage.

Loan Assumption

Instead of originating new financing, often you can simply take over someone else's existing mortgage, and earn a huge amount of savings doing it. Instead of paying for an appraisal, a credit report, and loan origination fees, when you assume a nonqualifying loan, all you pay is a low-cost assumption fee.

Loan assumption is a transaction in which the buyer assumes (takes over) the legal obligation to make the loan payments, while the lender releases the previous borrower from the liability. Many mortgages contain a clause that prohibits assumption, such as a due-on-sale or alienation clause. Either one of these written stipulations in the mortgage contract make the loan due and payable within 30 days if the encumbered property is sold, or the mortgage is assumed.

Loan assumption can be either with or without qualification. VA and FHA loans originated prior to 1987 can be assumed without qualification. All that's required is payment of a simple assumption fee, with no questions asked of the borrower. VA and FHA loans originated after 1987 can still be assumed; however, qualification of the borrower (the assumptor) is required.

Adjustable-rate mortgages can usually be assumed, too, although qualification of the borrower is usually required. Conventional fixed-rate mortgages are usually not assumable.

Wraparound Mortgage

The wraparound mortgage, or "wrap," also referred to as an *all-inclusive trust deed* (AITD), is a unique and innovative method of financing real estate. But in order to legally use a wrap, all existing underlying loans must be assumable, without due-on-sale clauses.

The wrap is used when a seller of real property wants to maintain the existing low-interest financing, so the seller "wraps" the existing loans with a new wraparound loan at a higher interest rate. The seller continues making payments on the existing low-interest loans, while the buyer makes payments to the seller on the new wraparound loan. The seller then earns a profit on the spread in interest rates. Figure 3.2 gives an example of how it works.

In the example given in Figure 3.2, the seller creates and carries a new loan (the wrap) at 11.5 percent. Payment on the existing 9 percent loan is $850 per month. Payment on the new wraparound loan is $1,050; therefore, the seller earns $200 per month profit on the spread in interest rates.

By creating a wrap, you're in essence acting like an institutional lender. You're paying on borrowed money at one rate, but lending it out at a higher rate, and making a profit on the spread in rates.

FIGURE 3.2   Example of a wraparound mortgage.

Seller's original purchase price	$96,000	Buyer's purchase price	$115,000
Seller's original down payment	10,000	Buyer's down payment	5,000
Balance on existing 9% assumable loan	$86,000	Balance financed on a wrap at 11.5%	$110,000
Seller continues to pay on existing 9% loan at $850 per month.		Buyer pays seller $1,050 per month on new wraparound.	

Home-Equity Loans

A home equity loan, also referred to as a *take-out second loan,* is originated against your equity in the property. For instance, say you have $50,000 equity in your home. You could take out a second mortgage against that equity to make home improvements, pay off credit card balances, pay for a college eduction, or buy additional income property. The loan amount can range up to 80 percent of the equity in the property.

In October 2002, Wells Fargo introduced a new loan that combines a first mortgage with a home-equity line of credit. Notably, the credit line automatically increases as the borrower pays down the mortgage, and the home's value appreciates.

When interest rates are low, tapping home equity makes sense for many home owners. Nonetheless, you should keep in mind that if interest rates rise, your monthly payment will increase. That's because adjustable-rate home-equity loans are typically tied to the prime lending rate, which rises when the Federal Reserve Board raises rates. So, it can be very risky to borrow large amounts of money for long periods of time through a home-equity line, especially if the loan is a adjustable-rate mortgage.

A line of credit is a good bet (especially when rates are low) for borrowers who intend to make good use of the proceeds. This may include financing home

---

TIP

Home equity loans can be good, but they are not for everyone.

- They make the most sense for people who expect to repay the loan quickly.

- Those with long-term needs should use fixed-rate loans. In other words, adjustable-rate loans are better for short-term needs (three years or less).

- With adjustable-rate loans, pay attention to the interest-rate risk. Typically, your rate will rise if the Fed raises interest rates.

- Getting your home-equity line and mortgage from the same lender will often save you money. Since you're already a good customer, they are likely to cut you a break on the rate or fees. However, it often pays to shop around before you sign on the dotted line. Rates on home-equity lines can vary by as much as 2 points, not to mention that fees and terms can also vary greatly. If you are offered a low teaser rate, be sure to find out how long the initial rate lasts, and what the final rate will be after the teaser expires.

- Unlike auto loans and credit card loans, home-equity loans are tax deductible.

improvements that will be paid for in stages, or planning to repay the loan within two or three years. And, according to Wells Fargo [(800) 667-5831], borrowers can take out a home-equity loan entirely by e-mail.

Advisory: Home-equity borrowers need to pay close attention to fees. Some lenders charge small application fees on a line of credit and an annual fee, typically $50 to $75, to keep the line of credit open. Borrowers who don't draw down their lines may face a "nonusage" fee, typically $50. Those who pay off the line within the first three years may be charged with an early termination fee of $250 to $600.

Refinancing versus a Home-Equity Loan

A home equity loan could be better than refinancing, especially if the existing first loan has a below-market rate of interest. The decision to refinance or take out a second loan should be dependent on the rate of interest you're paying on the existing first mortgage. If the rate is equivalent to or lower than market rates, it's usually better not to refinance (retaining the existing low-interest mortgage), and instead take out a second loan.

Rule of thumb: Refinance your existing mortgage when the market rate for new mortgages is at least 2 points below the rate on your existing mortgage.

Sources for Home Buyers with Poor Credit

Should you have difficulty finding a lender because of your credit history, there are other less conventional methods for securing a mortgage. The qualifications are quite often less stringent with these options:

- *Non-qualifying assumable loans.* You can take over someone else's mortgage with no questions asked. But it has to be a nonqualifying mortgage, such as a VA or FHA loan that was originated prior to 1987.

- *Mortgage brokers.* Since mortgage brokers are independent agents who often represent mortgage lenders nationwide, they are likely to know of lenders who arrange mortgages for buyers with less-than-perfect credit histories.

- *Lease/purchase option.* You can find a seller who is willing to lease you the property and give you an option to buy it. For instance, you could negotiate a contract wherein you rent the property for $750 a month for three years. But in addition to rent, you pay an additional $250 a month toward the purchase price. At the end of three years, you would have applied $9,000 toward the purchase price. An ideal property for a lease/purchase option is one that the seller owns free and clear. There's no need for outside financing, because the owner can handle the financing with a purchase-money mortgage.

■ *Cosigned loans.*   Someone else can cosign on your mortgage, thereby giving you a better chance of being approved. However, this method makes the cosigner responsible for repayment of the loan should you fail to make the payments.

As you can see, there's a wide array of mortgage alternatives to choose from. Chapter 4 tells you all about getting the financing you need, including helpful hints on completing the loan application process. But first, here are answers to some important questions you might have about the mortgage alternatives.

Important Answers about Mortgage Alternatives

Question: What are the benefits of an adjustable-rate mortgage (ARM)?

Answer: Compared to a long-term fixed-rate loan, the ARM can be more cost effective if you plan to sell your home in five years or less. (The initial rate of interest is less than that of a fixed-rate loan.) Also, ARMs have lower income requirements, which means you can borrow more money. Most ARMs have the added benefit of being assumable (with credit approval).

Question: Should I take out a mortgage now or wait until interest rates go lower? Also, which is better—the fixed-rate or adjustable-rate mortgage?

Answer: In reply to the first question, there's no telling exactly when rates will go up or down. As a rule, however, interest rates are either in a rising or falling trend; seldom are they stable. Once the initial direction changes, they will usually continue in that direction for a while until a new trend develops. Therefore, if interest rates were rising, you could take an educated gamble that you would pay more for a loan if you waited. Conversely, if rates were falling, you could likely get a cheaper rate if you waited.

As to which is better—a fixed-rate mortgage or an ARM—it essentially depends on how long you intend to keep the mortgage. Both types of loans have inherent advantages and disadvantages.

As a rule, if you plan to own the property for three years or less, the ARM will be more economical. If you own the property for more than three years, the fixed-rate mortgage will cost you less. This is primarily due to the lower initial rate on the ARM, which in time will gradually reach and surpass the rate of the fixed-rate mortgage.

Bear in mind that ARMs shift the risk of increasing interest rates from the lender to the borrower. In return, the borrower gets certain caps that protect against drastic rate increases. More important, the ARM is assumable, whereas most fixed-rate mortgages are not. This assumability is advantageous, because this added flexibility makes your property more salable.

Question: Most mortgage lenders seem to be very competitive. Are all their rates the same? If not, how much can I save by shopping around?

Answer: Studies show that a home owner can save tens of thousands of dollars over the term of a typical mortgage by being an informed borrower. Rates can vary substantially among lenders, and the educated borrower can save plenty of money by making the correct decision.

In fact, a borrower could save $27,112 over a 30-year term on a $110,000 mortgage, simply by paying 1 percent less in rate of interest. Comparing an 8 percent to a 7 percent loan, the difference in monthly payment for P&I on a $110,000 loan for 30 years is $75.31. Multiplied by 360 months, that's a savings of $27,112.

CHAPTER 4

Getting Financing

How Much Can You Borrow?

As a quick gauge to determine how much you can borrow for a home loan, traditional mortgage lenders often use the gross income multiplier. A conservative lender uses 2.5 times your annual gross income, while a more aggressive lender might go as high as 3 times. So, if you earn $40,000 in gross annual income, you could afford to borrow $100,000 using the 2.5 multiplier, and you could borrow up to $120,000 using the 3 multiplier. Yet these quick formulas don't take into consideration the borrower's other monthly debt obligations, and mortgage lenders want to be sure that your home loan is no greater than you can reasonably afford.

To arrive at a more precise *affordable* home loan, this book follows the guidelines of most lenders. These allow a total debt-to-income ratio of no more than 36 percent. Total debt payments include all monthly payments toward any kind of consumer debt, such as car loans and credit cards, plus the mortgage payment, including taxes and insurance. The guidelines assume a housing payment-to-income ratio of 28 percent for the conservative estimate (the limit you'd expect from a conventional lender), and 29 percent for the aggressive one (the limit allowed on an FHA insured loan). Table 4.1 lists the 29 percent ratio for different annual and monthly income levels.

As you work the numbers to determine how much you can afford, bear in mind that mortgage lenders only look at your current financial situation. They're not aware that you may be planning to finance the new furniture for the home you buy, or that you may need to finance a new car in six months. You should make allowances for these big anticipated expenditures and decide how much of your future income you can realistically commit to housing, so you don't put a strain on your budget.

TABLE 4.1   Mortgage Qualification Guidelines

Annual Gross Income	Monthly Gross Income	29% of Gross Income
$15,000	$1,250	$ 363
20,000	1,667	483
25,000	2,083	604
30,000	2,500	725
35,000	2,917	846
40,000	3,333	967
45,000	3,750	1,088
50,000	4,167	1,208

Source: U.S. Department of Housing and Urban Development.

Maximize Leverage with
Owner-Occupied Financing

One great way to maximize your leverage and keep your financing cost to a minimum is to utilize owner-occupied financing. If you intend to live in the property you're buying for at least one year, you can qualify for owner-occupied financing. The terms are better than for non-owner-occupied financing (investor financing) because mortgage lenders typically consider investor financing to be more risky, since the owners of the property won't be living there. Thus, they charge investors more in interest and require larger down payments.

Numerous high loan-to-value (LTV) owner-occupied loan programs that offer 95 or even 100 percent financing are available for the purchase of single-family homes, condos, townhomes, and two- to four-unit buildings. (See following section.) However, if you or your property fails to qualify for owner-occupied financing (i.e., the desired loan qualifies as investor financing), most mortgage lenders will limit a loan to a maximum LTV ratio of 70 to 80 percent.

Besides giving you greater leverage, owner-occupied financing is easier to qualify for when buying a home to live in. The interest rates lenders charge for owner-occupied loans are usually 1 to 2 points lower than the rates charged for investor financing.

Here's a useful strategy: Once you have used owner-occupied financing, and you have stayed in the home for the required occupancy period, acquire another investment home (or two- to four-unit apartment building) using favorable owner-occupied financing, and move into it. Then find a good tenant for the home you vacated. Then repeat the process accordingly.

After you obtain owner-occupied financing, that loan can stay with the property even after you move on to another home. Since any additional properties you buy and move into still qualify for favorable owner-occupied financing, you can quickly accumulate several rental properties along with your own home—all without making sizable down payments.

Alternative Financing for Cash-Short Buyers

Although space doesn't permit a complete discussion of all the high-LTV possibilities, here are several of the more popular alternatives:

- *VA-guaranteed loans.* Eligible veterans can originate new mortgage loans with absolutely no money down. Ease of qualification and limits on borrower costs are some of the great benefits for persons who have served in the U.S. military.

- *VA qualifying assumptions.* These are existing loans that can be assumed by nonveterans. Find a property that was purchased with VA financing—especially one with built-in equity that was bought within the past five years—and you could acquire it with little or nothing down.

- *FHA 203(b).* This bread-and-butter FHA fixed-rate plan is used by more borrowers than any other finance plan. It only requires a down payment of 3 percent, but you don't need to use your own cash. You can use borrowed funds or gift money. And the qualifying standards rarely exclude anyone who can show steady income and the ability to pay their bills.

- *FHA ARM (251).* This program is similar to the FHA 203(b), except that it has an adjustable-rate mortgage (ARM), which allows you to qualify for a larger loan, because the initial rate of interest is lower than that of the fixed rate in the 203(b) plan. Another benefit with this program is that annual interest-rate increases are limited to 1 percent, and the lifetime cap is set at 5 percent.

- *FHA/VA 203(v).* This FHA program is offered only to eligible veterans. It has the same qualifying standards as the 203(b) plan, except that the required down payment is less.

- *FHA 203(k).* This program enables you to combine the home's purchase price and renovation costs all in one loan. This plan is great for home buyers who want to fix up, rehab, or otherwise create value in their home. It has the same down payment and qualification standards as the 203(b) program, although it offers several zero-down situations for first-time buyers.

- *FHA nonqualifying assumptions.* Millions of these fully assumable FHA loans were funded before 1987. Though many of them have been repaid or refinanced, those remaining can easily be assumed with no credit qualification on the part of the assumptor. The nonqualifying assumption is great for credit-impaired buyers, because they don't have to go through any loan approval process—instead, they simply pay a small assumption fee, with no questions asked. Another plus is that no down payment is required, which means you could keep your investment to a minimum, and negotiate favorable seller financing for the balance owed.

- *FHA qualifying assumptions.* FHA loans funded after January 1, 1987, are assumable, but require credit qualification on the part of the assumptor. These loans have all the benefits of the FHA nonqualifying loan, except that the assumptor is required to go though the loan approval process.

- *HUD repossessions.* When people fail to make payments on their FHA-insured loans, the U.S. Department of Housing and Urban Development (HUD), the parent of the FHA, eventually becomes the owner of these houses through foreclosure. Depending on market conditions, you can purchase these HUD repossessions with as little as $400 to $1,000 down, using any of the FHA loan programs for financing. (See Chapter 13 for more details about purchasing HUD property.)

- *New home builders.* Many new home builders offer great incentives to entice home buyers, which may include low down payments, no closing costs, or below-market interest rates on the financing. Read builders' advertisements in your local newspaper, or visit them on site at new developments in your area.

- *Lease/purchase option.* You might find a classified ad in your local newspaper from an owner who will lease the house and give you the option to buy it. In a lease/purchase option agreement, a cash-short lessee/buyer could arrange to pay a monthly option fee, in addition to rent, that could be applied toward the purchase price. For example, while you're leasing the

TABLE 4.2 30-Year Fixed Monthly Payment (P&I) at Selected Interest Rates

Amount	Interest Rate (%)										
	5.0	5.5	6.0	6.5	7.0	7.5	8.0	8.5	9.0	10.0	11.0
$ 50,000	$268	$284	$300	$316	$333	$350	$367	$384	$402	$439	$476
60,000	322	341	360	379	399	420	440	461	483	527	571
70,000	376	397	420	442	466	489	514	538	563	614	667
80,000	429	454	480	506	532	559	587	615	644	702	762
90,000	483	511	540	569	599	629	660	692	724	790	857
100,000	537	568	600	632	665	699	734	769	805	878	952

TABLE 4.3 15-Year Fixed Monthly Payment (P&I) at Selected Interest Rates

Amount	\multicolumn{11}{c}{Interest Rate (%)}

Amount	5.0	5.5	6.0	6.5	7.0	7.5	8.0	8.5	9.0	10.0	11.0
$ 50,000	$395	$409	$422	$436	$449	$464	$478	$492	$ 507	$ 537	$ 568
60,000	474	490	506	523	539	556	573	591	609	645	682
70,000	554	572	591	610	629	649	669	689	710	752	796
80,000	632	654	675	697	719	742	765	788	811	860	909
90,000	712	735	759	784	809	834	860	886	913	967	1,023
100,000	791	817	844	871	899	927	956	985	1,014	1,075	1,137

house over a term of, say, two years, you could apply an extra $150 per month option toward the purchase price. After 24 months you would have applied $3,600, which could serve as the down payment—a form of forced savings that's equitable to both the buyer/lessee and the seller/lessor. (For more details on the lease/purchase option technique, see Chapter 19.)

For more topical information about home buying made easy, go to the following web sites: www.HUD.gov or www.VAhomeswash.com.

Tables 4.2 and 4.3 illustrate monthly payments (principal and interest) at selected interest rates required to amortize (pay off) 30-year and 15-year fixed-rate mortgages. To compute your loan payment, simply go across the top of the table and select the appropriate interest rate. The entry where the loan amount and the interest rate intersect is the computed monthly payment (rounded to the nearest dollar) for principal and interest (P&I) that you will pay to amortize the loan. Note that if your loan amount is not illustrated, you can add smaller amounts to calculate the payment you need. For example, for $110,000, add the payments for a $60,000 loan and a $50,000 loan.

Table 4.4 illustrates the monthly P&I cost per $1,000 borrowed for both 30-year and 15-year fixed-rate loans at different interest rates. To calculate your monthly payment for amounts not found in the preceding two tables, follow this example: For a $5,000 loan at 11 percent for 30 years, first look for the column for

TABLE 4.4 Monthly Fixed Payment (P&I) Cost per $1,000 at Selected Interest Rates

Term	\multicolumn{11}{c}{Interest Rate (%)}

Term	5.0	5.5	6.0	6.5	7.0	7.5	8.0	8.5	9.0	10.0	11.0
30-years	$5.37	$5.68	$6.00	$6.32	$6.65	$6.99	$7.34	$7.69	$ 8.05	$ 8.78	$ 9.53
15-years	7.91	8.17	8.44	8.71	8.99	9.27	9.56	9.85	10.14	10.75	11.37

11 percent. Then select the 30-year row. Where the two intersect is a factor of $9.53. Multiply $9.53 by 5 (the number of thousands in your $5,000 loan amount), which results in a $47.65 monthly loan payment on $5,000 borrowed.

Shopping for a Mortgage Loan

You can save thousands of dollars over the life of a long-term mortgage by carefully shopping for a loan that suits your particular needs. But some might say, "Ahh, what's the big deal? I'm only paying an extra one-half of one percent in rate of interest." Some people don't know that over the entire term of a typical 30-year loan, paying an extra half a percent in interest charges can add up to some very serious money.

The All-Important Interest Rate

Consider two different rates of interest on a loan of $110,000 with a term of 30 years.

Principal and interest payment at 8.0 percent $807.14
Principal and interest payment at 7.5 percent $769.14

A difference of $38 per month. If you take that difference and multiply by 360 (12 months × 30 years), the result is a staggering $13,680 in savings over the life of the loan.

Yet just because one lender's offering is half a percent below another's, that doesn't mean you should blindly choose the lower rate. You must also become familiar with points and other fees that mortgage lenders charge.

Choose Carefully between Points and Rate

There is a direct inverse relationship between the service points you pay up front and the interest rate you pay on a fixed-rate loan. Often you have the option of paying additional points up front; in return, you get a reduced interest rate over the term of the loan. If you plan to stay in the purchased home for a long time— say, three years or more—it's usually a better deal to take the points. The lower interest rate will save you more in the long run.

Conversely, if you need to pay fewer points at the closing (due to cash constraints), you can pay a higher rate of interest. The shorter the term of the loan, the more sensible it would be to pay less up front and more later on.

Take a look at an example of the points—interest rate trade-off. Suppose that you want to borrow $120,000. One lender quotes you 7.5 percent on a 30-year fixed-rate loan, and wants a 1-point origination fee. Another lender quotes

8.0 percent with no points. Which offer is better? The answer depends entirely on how long you intend to pay on the loan.

The 8.0 percent loan costs $880.52 per month.

The 7.5 percent loan costs $839.06 per month, plus 1 point at $1,200.

You can save $41.46 a month with the 7.5 percent loan, but you have to pay $1,200 in points to get it.

To determine which loan is more cost effective, divide the cost of the points by the monthly savings ($1,200 ÷ $41.46 = 28.9). The result is the number of months (in this case 28.9) it will take to recover the $1,200 cost of the points. Therefore, if you expect to pay on the loan for less than about 29 months, choose the no-points loan. Conversely, if you expect to pay on the loan for more than 29 months, selecting the 7.5 percent loan plus 1 point will save you money.

The Annual Percentage Rate (APR)

The annual percentage rate (APR) is the actual cost of credit to the consumer in percentage terms. Regulations in the Truth in Lending Act require that borrowers are to be informed of the cost of credit, to allow a comparison of costs based on a uniform rate—the APR.

Prior to the enactment of the Truth in Lending Act, a lender could have offered a consumer loan of $1,000, advertising a rate of 6 percent interest for a term of 1 year. The lender could have also charged the borrower a $60 application fee, then deducted it from the $1,000 and given the borrower the remaining balance of $940. In doing so, the actual effective interest rate on $940, paying back $1,000, is actually 6.38 percent, not 6 percent. This type of deceptive advertising is the reason why truth in lending came into existence.

When you're making a comparison of overall credit costs between lenders, use the uniform rate that puts all the competitors on a level playing field— the APR.

Where to Start

The most common loan originators are savings and loans, banks, credit unions, and mortgage bankers. If you're already a customer of a savings and loan or credit union, start there. Established customers often can get preferred rates and terms.

Questions Asked of You

The mortgage lender you select is primarily interested in three things: Are you capable of paying back the loan? If applicable, do you have the required down payment? And can you afford the monthly payments?

Besides these primary queries, the lender will also require you to answer other pertinent questions. Be prepared to answer the following questions on the loan application:

- Are there any outstanding judgments against you?
- Have you ever been foreclosed on, or given a deed in lieu of foreclosure?
- Have you ever been bankrupt?
- Are you borrowing any part of the down payment?
- Are you obligated to pay alimony or child support?
- Are you a comaker or endorser on a note?

Questions You Should Ask

A home is probably the costliest thing you will ever finance, and you'll be contracting for terms that you will have to live with over a substantial period of time, until the obligation is repaid. Thus, it's very important that you become fully informed about exactly what you're committing yourself to. Use the mortgage cost comparison worksheet in Figure 4.1 as a guide to compare mortgage loans and lenders.

Working with a Mortgage Broker

Mortgage brokers are independent agents who represent mortgage lenders. Part of their service is to explain the wide array of loan choices, assist borrowers in selecting a loan, and guide them through the ordeal of the loan application process. Brokers also can be helpful in getting the best loan deal, because they can shop among the many lenders they represent. Furthermore, if your credit history is questionable, and you're finding it difficult to qualify for a mortgage, a good mortgage broker can direct you to special lenders that may be willing to give you a loan.

Mortgage brokers are essentially in the business of "selling" loans, and they earn a commission for their services, which is paid by the lender. The commission is usually in the range of 0.5 to 2 points of the loan proceeds, depending on the size of the loan. Keep in mind that the fee the broker earns from the lender is not set in stone, and often is very negotiable, especially on larger loans. Typically, the commission earned on a $100,000 loan is 1 point, $1,000. But the same commission rate on a $200,000 loan amounts to $2,000, double the earnings for the same amount of work by the broker. Don't be afraid to inquire how much the broker's cut is. Even though the lender pays the commission, you'll end up paying

FIGURE 4.1   Mortgage cost comparison worksheet.

Fixed-Rate Mortgages

	A	B	C
Lender name			
Lender phone			
Down payment			
Term			
Application fee			
Loan origination fee			
Appraisal fee			
Credit report fee			
Points			
Interest rate			
APR			
Assumable?			
Prepayment penalty?			

Adjustable-Rate Mortgages

Initial rate			
APR			
Index used			
Current Rate			
Margin			
Adjustment period			
Limit			
Payment cap			
Convertible?			
When?			
Cost to convert?			

the bill. Since it's your money, try to negotiate for a better deal, especially if you're applying for a sizable loan.

Borrowers who are best suited to using a mortgage broker are those who dread shopping around or who might be turned down by most lenders.

Online Lending Services

Realtor-arranged mortgages are allowed in more than 30 states. Real estate agents bypass mortgage brokers by linking their customers directly with lenders. In most cases, they use specialized lending services, such as online lending services like GoLoan and LoanWorks.

The Loan Application Process

Applying for a mortgage loan can seem like a never-ending paper chase—documents, verifications, account numbers, signing papers—at times it might appear to be a lot of work. Yet knowing what will be required of you is half the battle, because it will help you to get organized in preparation for the loan application.

Applying for a Loan

It's a good idea to get two copies of the loan application, take them home, and fill out the first one in pencil. Then, when it's complete, transfer all your data neatly in pen to the final copy. This will be the copy you submit to the lender, neat and free of alterations and messy dabs of correction fluid.

Information You Will Need to Provide

On the loan application your lender will ask pertinent questions about many things, including your employment, income, debts, account numbers, bank balances, marital status, and number of dependents. Be sure to fill out the application completely, with no spaces left blank. Here's a sampling of what you can expect on the typical loan application:

- *Addresses.*   List your current home address, and your prior addresses for the past two years. List your present employer's address so the lender can verify your employment.

- *List of assets.*   Name all your assets, such as stocks, bonds, cash in banks, retirement accounts, and CDs, along with all the appropriate account numbers and addresses. Remember that the lender is looking for where the down payment will be coming from. (Notably, leaders don't want you to borrow it.) If you're planning to sell certain assets, such as jewelry or a car, to help acquire the down payment, you should do it now, so that your bank balance is sufficient to cover the required down payment.

- *List of liabilities.*   Name all your liabilities, including credit card balances, outstanding loans, and previously paid off loans, along with all the appropriate account numbers and addresses.

- *Proof of employment.* If you're self-employed, you'll need copies of federal income tax returns for the past two years. If not, you'll need recent pay stubs to verify your income.

- *Extra income.* If you have regular sources of extra income, be sure to include them on your application. Past W-2 forms, pay stubs, or past tax returns will help substantiate this income.

- *Divorce papers, if applicable, along with child support agreements.* If you receive child support, you can use it as supplemental income to help acquire the mortgage you desire. If you are obligated to pay alimony or child support you'll need to report the amount.

- *Bankruptcy, judgments, and foreclosures.* If you experienced any of these in the past ten years, or were given a deed in lieu of foreclosure, you're required to report that information to the lender. (The lender is likely to learn of it anyway in the credit report.)

- *Social Security number.* List your number and that of any endorser or co-maker on the loan.

- *VA documentation.* If you're applying for a VA-guaranteed loan, you'll need to supply the lender with a certificate of elgibility. If you haven't already got one, it takes about a month to receive it from the VA after mailing in your proof of discharge, form DD-214.

How to Overcome Common Mortgage Problems

Got a glitch in your credit history? Lack a sufficient down payment? Don't despair if obstacles such as these stand in the way of owning the home of your dreams. You'll just have to be a bit more patient than usual, but I've never met anyone who had the determination to buy a home who couldn't overcome credit or other obstacles.

Dealing with a Poor Credit History

The best advice for dealing with mortgage lenders if you've had past credit problems is to be up front, be honest, and have a good explanation of what happened. Elapsed time and the development of good, on-time bill-paying habits do a lot, especially in a lender's eyes, to overcome past deficiencies in paying your bills.

Here's some advice on how to handle blemishes that might appear on your credit report:

- *Be up front.*   If you're aware that your credit report includes any imperfections, have a good explanation of why the blemishes are there. For instance, perhaps you were laid off unexpectedly, and temporarily became delinquent in your payments until you found another job.

- *Look for a more flexible lender.*   Some lenders aren't as strict about certain credit problems and may be more sympathetic toward past deficiencies. As you shop for a mortgage lender, make inquiries about whether previous credit flaws will pose any problem. Also, consider calling on a mortgage broker, who may have access to more flexible lenders.

- *Let the seller be the banker.*   You would be surprised at how many property sellers are willing to carry a mortgage; some won't even check your credit. And those who do a credit check are likely to be more flexible than commercial mortgage lenders in overlooking past deficiencies, especially if your recent history reveals good bill-paying habits.

- *Correct any errors.*   Creditors, and the credit reporting agencies they supply information to, often make mistakes. Regardless, unlike the American system of justice, you're guilty until you can convince the reporting agency otherwise. Initiate your case by identifying the faulty data on your credit report. Frequently, accounts you never had will show up under your name. If that's the case, notify the credit bureau that the erroneous information belongs to someone else.

  However, if the information belongs on your account, but the creditor made an error, you'll have to contact the creditor and instruct the creditor to make amends with the credit bureau. You often need lots of patience and persistence to get these sort of things corrected. By law, the credit bureau must respond to your inquiry within 30 days. If you don't get any satisfaction from customer service, try speaking with a supervisor until you get results. If this strategy doesn't get satisfaction, contact your local Better Business Bureau and file a written complaint. You can also have a statement of contention issued on your credit report, so potential creditors can see your side of the case. Just keep in mind that your objective is to have all derogatory information erased from your credit report.

- *Be patient, pay your bills, and save more.*   Sometimes, especially if your credit history and savings aren't what they should be, it may be better to continue renting. Meanwhile, you can save more money and spend a year or two developing a good credit record by paying all your bills on time. Before you know it, you'll have plenty of savings, with plenty of lenders soliciting you for business

- *Have a cosigner.*   As mentioned before, a relative or close friend can cosign on a loan, which is another way of overcoming one's credit problems.

Bankruptcy

Bankruptcy is more serious than credit deficiencies. However, don't let such a blot on your record keep you from originating a new loan. There are no legal time limits on how soon you can secure a conventional mortgage after a bankruptcy, yet some lenders will deny you a loan no matter how long ago the bankruptcy occurred. With VA-guaranteed loans, a bankruptcy is required to be discharged for at least two years; on FHA-insured loans, the wait is only one year.

Insufficient Income

The mortgage lenders may reject your application if they think you're buying more house than you can actually afford. If this is the case, you shouldn't feel rejected, because the lenders may be doing you a big favor. They could be keeping you from overextending yourself by buying a home that would tie up all your income and prevent you from saving money and attaining other long-term financial goals.

If you have your sights set on a particular home, and know that you can afford it, the following are some alternatives for getting your loan approved:

- *Use patience.*   When your income is low (perhaps because you've only been on the job a short time), it might be better to put off your loan request for a year or two, until you can earn more income.
- *Increase the down payment.*   When you make a down payment of 25 percent or more (some lenders only require 20 percent), many mortgage lenders will approve you for a no-income verification loan. Be aware that such loans require a higher interest rate, so be prepared to pay a premium for this type of mortgage.
- *Have a cosigner.*   If your parents or other family members are in good shape financially, you could ask them to cosign on a loan. Bear in mind though, that should you default on the loan, the cosigner is responsible for paying it back. The end result is that you not only tarnish your own credit history, but you taint the cosigners as well.

Excess Debt

If you are overburdened with too much consumer debt, you're just another average American—the average working adult is encumbered with a whopping $15,000 in consumer debt, and just the interest on that debt exceeds $2,000 annually.

If you've got too much debt, a mortgage lender will actually be doing you a favor by declining to lend you any more money. Over the long term, too much debt can seriously undermine your ability to save money and make real estate investments.

Should you have ready cash available, use it to pay off as much of the debt as you can. If you lack sufficient cash to retire some of that debt and make a down payment on a home, you have the following alternatives:

- *Trim your budget.*   The best alternative to financial soundness is to survey your spending, and identify where you can slash expenses. (See Chapter 2.)
- *Downsize.*   Purchase a less expensive home than you could otherwise qualify for. In other words, don't overburden yourself with a house that you realistically can't afford because of the excessive debt.
- *Get family assistance.*   Have a member of your family assist you in borrowing, either as a cosigner on the mortgage loan, or by lending you money to pay off the consumer debt.

Speeding Loan Approval

When you bring in the completed application, here are some things you can do to help speed approval of the loan:

- Bring your checkbook if you're applying for a conventional loan. Some lenders will charge you about $350 up front to begin the process. This will cover the cost of the appraisal and credit report.
- The lender will want you to sign the employment verification form that will be sent to your employer. You can speed up the process by informing the responsible person at your company that the inquiry is coming, and making sure that it's mailed to the right person.

Avoiding the Most Common Mistakes Home Buyers Make

Mistake: Taking out an adjustable-rate mortgage instead of a fixed-rate mortgage for a term of 3 years or more.

LESSON: Over the long term, a fixed-rate mortgage will most often be more cost effective for the home buyer. However, if the home buyer intends to own the house for 3 years or less, then the adjustable-rate mortgage is usually a better bargain.

PART III

CHOOSING THE
IDEAL HOUSE

Now that you've had a chance to look at the important preliminaries, and have determined how much house you can afford, it's time to get to the fun part: selecting a house that's ideal for you—one that suits your particular wants and needs. This part goes beyond choosing a particular house style. The intent is for you to think about and examine your present lifestyle, and consider potential changes in the future. The next few chapters cover all the angles—from buying a condo or a co-op, to acquiring a resale home or a new home in the suburbs. Perhaps you might choose a home in an adults-only community, one secluded behind protective gates, or a quiet home in the country. This part makes your selection easier by presenting all the options.

Which House Is Right for You?

Before choosing the ideal house that's suitable for your particular wants and needs, you should choose a location.

Choosing a Location

Much has been said over the years about the importance of location as the prime consideration when purchasing real estate. So much so that if you ask a Realtor what the three most important things one should look for when buying a home are, the classic reply is "Location, location, location." That axiom is mostly true. People will pay a premium to live in better neighborhoods. Conversely, deteriorating neighborhoods destroy property values. Even the magnificent Hearst castle would be difficult to sell if it were adjacent to truck terminals and a bus depot.

Yet buying a home in a good location, while important, shouldn't be your only home-shopping standard. Value—the quality of worth you get for your money—is significant, too.

This chapter shows you how to get maximum value for your investment.

Features of Good Neighborhoods

What is a good neighborhood? It depends on your particular wants and needs. If you're married with a couple of preteens, being near excellent schools is important.

However, if you're ready to retire, a quiet neighborhood with lots of outdoor activities might appeal to you, while living across the street from a junior high school would not. Neither of these neighborhoods would likely suit you if you're single or living with someone and don't intend to have children. Your choice of neighborhoods might include a singles' condo complex situated downtown, where you can enjoy the action day or night.

Regardless of personal preferences, all good neighborhoods have the following features:

- *Sound economics.*   Is the area declining? Are there a lot of "For Sale" signs in the area, which might be related to recent corporate layoffs or company shutdowns? If so, this is an indication of unsound economics.

  Be sure you're investing in a real estate market with sound underlying economics, which essentially means a local economy that's not declining in population, employment, and property values. For instance, consider Houston, Texas, during the late 1980s. At that time, Houston experienced what economists call a "rolling recession." A glut of petroleum supplies on the world market caused oil prices to fall drastically. This caused oil companies to cut back on employment, and many related businesses failed. Many banks also failed, partially owing to defaults on real estate loans. The result was an oversupply of new housing and foreclosures. Eventually, the value of housing in Houston dropped substantially.

- *Low crime rate.*   Nobody wants to live in a crime-ridden area. If you want the facts on an area, don't listen to hearsay. Communities compile crime statistics, and you can get them by calling the local police department or visiting its web site, or by checking the neighborhood reference library.

- *Quality schools.*   Schools are important, even if you don't have school-age children, because when it comes time to sell, most prospective buyers with kids will be deeply concerned about the quality of the school system. The only time this doesn't matter is when you're buying into an adults-only resort or a retirement community. To learn more about the schools in your prospective neighborhood, don't just get one person's opinion of their quality—visit the school first-hand, and speak directly with parents and teachers.

- *Amenities.*   These are special features, such as tree-lined boulevards, wide streets with cul-de-sacs, lush green parks, mountain views, and proximity to schools and shopping, that make a neighborhood attractive and desirable. Other, more exclusive neighborhoods may have all of these features, plus an ocean view, tennis courts, and a location near transportation and restaurants. However, not all home buyers can afford to buy in a neighborhood with all these wonderful traits. Nevertheless, the more of these features a neighborhood has, the more desirable it is to own a home there.

- *Pride of ownership.* Pride of ownership shows in a neighborhood full of well-maintained homes with manicured landscapes. Conversely, a lack of pride in ownership can easily be spotted, as well: You can see it in poorly kept houses, abandoned cars out on the street, junk-filled yards, and iron bars over windows and doors to keep out thieves. Unfortunately, this deterioration is related to crime and vandalism, and the decline of the neighborhood is a blight that seems to spread from one house to another. Avoid declining neighborhoods where dispirited owners no longer take pride in their property.

What to Avoid in a Location

Instead of knowing what to look *for* in a location, sometimes it's better to be aware of what to *avoid* in a location. Be careful of buying in a neighborhood that has certain nuisances that may detract from property values. Before purchasing residential property, ask the following questions:

- Is it located next to commercial buildings, such as a warehouse or factory?
- Is it adjacent to a cemetery or an undertaker?
- Is it next to a school playground, where noisy children may interfere with the quiet enjoyment of the premises?
- Is it near an airport, or under the flight path of incoming or departing aircraft?
- Is the property subject to floods?
- Does an unusual volume of traffic pass nearby?

These characteristics detract from the value of residential property. Check out the surrounding neighborhood carefully before committing yourself to a long-term realty investment.

Be cautious when investing in smaller urban areas that depend primarily on one type of industry. This is because the surrounding area will likely become depressed if that particular employer experiences bad economic times or has to shut down. Major metropolitan areas, such as Los Angeles and Boston, have diverse economies and will continue to thrive even if one major industry fails.

City or Suburbs?

In most parts of the country, you're apt to have a choice among homes in the city, the suburbs, or the country. Before you choose, you need to take several things into consideration.

For instance, if you hold a city job or work for any regional government entity, be sure to check whether you're required by law to reside within certain metropolitan borders.

Travel Time

Several considerations have to be made for commuting. If you'll be taking public transportation, do the scheduled departures and arrivals fit with your work itinerary? Which method of public transit will you take—bus or train? Also consider the commuting costs. How much is the monthly commuting fare? Will you have to buy a second car? If so, will you have to pay for parking?

Have you ever thought about *reverse commuting*? It's the opposite of living in the suburbs and working in the city. Instead, you live in the city, and on the way to work you avoid all the traffic on your pleasant journey, watching all the incoming commuters fight gridlocked traffic. Then you again elude all the heavy traffic out to the suburbs, on the way home.

You also have to consider how far the kids will have to travel to school. Can they still ride their bikes, or will they have to wait for a school bus? Or what about special activities at the new school—how much chauffeuring will be involved?

If anyone in your family is nearing retirement or has a chronic illness, consider a home in a neighborhood with quick access to health care services or a hospital's emergency room. Senior adults also have to think about transportation alternatives in case of an accident or illness. If you're unable to drive, is there a bus to the grocery market or the shopping mall?

A Home in the Country

A country home can be great, especially if you need lots of space to store your belongings—such as a boat or a recreational vehicle, which usually can't be stored on-site in the city or the suburbs. If you like plenty of peace and quiet, and you have interests such as growing a vegetable garden, hiking, or fishing, then indeed the country life might suit you just fine. And what about the commute to and from work, or travel time required to go shopping and eating out? Try to foresee what country life would actually be like before you buy.

Consider Your Present and Future Lifestyle

In order to choose the ideal house, you need to examine your present lifestyle and think about potential changes in the future. Finding the ideal home will require objectivity.

Should your lifestyle change in a way that alters your housing needs in the near future, you may not want to sell your home. Or it might be difficult to sell quickly and find another house suitable for your modified needs. And the alternative of renovating the house to fit your new requirements could be costly and inconvenient. The best alternative is to look ahead now, to ensure that the home you buy will be suitable—as much as you can envision without a crystal ball—to your present as well as your potential future needs.

Here are some considerations to think about:

- Will you have grown children visiting? If so, will they require their own rooms?

- Will your parents and your spouse's continue to live on their own? Is it feasible that an older parent or in-law might eventually move in with you? Should you buy a home with just an extra bedroom, or maybe a separate independent area, including a bedroom, bath, and living area?

- If you're single and want a good-sized house, will you want—or financially require—a rent-paying tenant to help offset expenses? If so, will you share your living area? If not, consider how the rented area can be independent, with its own kitchen and entry.

- If you have teenagers or preteens, they could be off to college or to work before you know it. Should you look for a large home now, and then downsize after they move out? Or if you opt for a larger home, will you want (or need) all that unused space when the time comes?

- Should you move to a resort area, especially one that's warm in the winter, you can expect plenty of houseguests (who are usually snowbirds from the north trying to escape harsh winter weather). The considerations here depend on what level of comfort you wish to afford them. You could furnish a complete guest bedroom. Or, instead of maintaining a room that won't be used all the time, will you have the guests sleep on a convertible sofa in the home office or family room?

- Are you approaching retirement, and planning that the house you buy now will be your retirement residence? If so, you should consider a single-level home, such as a ranch or patio home built all on one floor. This would be more appropriate to your future lifestyle, in the event that you or your spouse should eventually find it difficult to climb stairs.

As you can see, your present lifestyle is not the only consideration when you're trying to find the ideal home. If you want to avoid moving frequently from house to house just to accommodate your changing needs and desires, it will be necessary to foresee future needs.

LANDLORD TALE

Once upon a time, in 1976, we bought a beautiful custom-built chalet situated on a half-acre of wooded land that overlooked southern California's picturesque Lake Arrowhead. Nestled among the San Bernardino mountains, this three-story beauty was designed with a large family in mind, including extra space for extended overnight stays by flocks of visiting grandchildren. The main level, with a huge living area (about 1,600 square feet), had a panoramic view of the lake, and also featured a kitchen, a master bedroom, and a full bathroom. For the visiting grandkids, four separate beds were built into the knotty-pine walls, hidden behind doors that opened into the living area. Above the living area was a sizable loft, with lots of single and double beds, and a sturdy wood stairway ascended to it.

From the kitchen's oversized broom closet, you could climb down a wrought-iron spiral staircase to a private guest area situated on the property's lowest level. This guest area, about 600 square feet of living area, also had an outside entry, along with a bedroom, bath, and small kitchen area.

All in all, we figured 16 people could comfortably live in this three-level A-frame.

LESSON: This lovely resort home would, no doubt, be great for a lot of young people with big families. However, taking into consideration the three different levels, and the effort required to climb up and down the stairs to reach them (not to mention descending the cramped spiral staircase in the broom closet), this three-story beauty would hardly be appropriate for mature adults or an elderly retired couple.

Three Principles to Maximize Your Investment

It really doesn't matter what style of house you buy, whether it's California ranch, Victorian, Cape Cod, or southern colonial. You can maximize the investment yield on any property by following three fundamental principles in the selection of the home you purchase. As you read the following guidelines, bear in mind that they're not etched in stone—exceptions do occur.

Principle of Progression: Reason to Buy One of the Lesser-Priced Homes on the Block

This principle is based on the fact that in a particular neighborhood, the lower-priced homes tend to seek the value of the higher-priced homes. In other words, if you buy a modestly priced home in a higher-priced neighborhood, the more expensive homes in the neighborhood will eventually raise yours to a higher value. To that end, avoid the highest-priced house, or the one that has been over-improved for the neighborhood.

For instance, suppose you're house hunting in a neighborhood you like, and you find a particular jewel. It's priced at $125,000 and is definitely the least expensive home in the neighborhood. The other homes are selling for $160,000 to $200,000—and now that you know this, you can't wait to make an offer.

But wait, you've got some investigating to do. You must find out why this house is so underpriced. If it has certain kinds of curable defects, which can be overcome, you may want to buy it. However, if it has incurable defects, find another property to invest in.

Curable Defects

Curable defects are flaws in a property that can easily be overcome without too great an expense. Suppose, for example, that the previous owners had poor taste—they painted both the exterior and interior walls a hideous dark color, and to make matters worse, they covered the walls in the kitchen and bathroom with dreadful-looking wallpaper. This is merely a cosmetic defect, which could be overcome with a little elbow grease and a tasteful paint job.

Or perhaps this jewel you found is the only two-bedroom one-bath home in the area, but both bedrooms are huge, allowing you to convert the two bedrooms into three, with an additional guest bath added on. If you can do the renovation for no more than $12,000, you have a total cost of $137,000 ($125,000 purchase price + $12,000). Now you have created value, because you own a three-bedroom two-bath house in a $160,000 to $200,000 neighborhood.

You can add value to your investment by finding properties with curable defects that can be remedied inexpensively. Other relatively inexpensive remedies include painting, modernizing a kitchen with ceramic tile floors and countertops, upgrading fixtures in a bathroom, and rewiring the electrical system with a higher-ampere system to accommodate modern appliances.

Incurable Defects

If a house has major deficiencies, it's not worth buying at any price. Would you want a house next to a junkyard or a bus depot? Or what about a downright ugly home? Just because the seller made a fortune in the doughnut business, doesn't mean you (or anyone else) would want to live in a house designed in the shape of a giant chocolate éclair. There's no cure for a poorly located house. These are major deficiencies, incurable defects, that cannot be overcome at an economically feasible price. It wouldn't even be feasible to pay $150,000 for the doughnut house, tear it down, and build a new home on the site (unless that's what comparable vacant sites sell for). If you did that, and spent another $125,000 building a new house, you'd likely have the precarious honor of owning the priciest house in the neighborhood.

There is more information about fixer-uppers later in this chapter, and additional information about fixing up fixer-uppers in Chapter 18.

Gain Value by Fixing Up Lower-Priced Homes

Thanks to the principle of progression, the least expensive homes on the block are also the least risky ones to renovate. Suppose, for example, that you paid $125,000 for a home that needs renovation, right in the middle of a neighborhood of $200,000 homes. In this example, your maximum renovation budget should not exceed $75,000 in order to elevate your home's value to that of the other houses.

Principle of Regression: Reason Not to Buy the Costliest Home on the Block

This principle is the economic opposite of the principle of progression—the lesser-valued homes in the neighborhood bring down the values of the higher-valued homes. Or, put another way, if you buy the most expensive home on the block, the lower-valued homes around you bring down your home's value.

In order to attain maximum value for your investment, the wisest choice is to purchase one of the less expensive homes in a desirable neighborhood.

Principle of Conformity: Reason Nonconformity Is Costly

Conformity is good. Look for a house whose style fits in with the others in the neighborhood. A southwestern adobe-style with a tile roof (an architectural style that's common throughout New Mexico), is hardly appropriate in the hills of Pennsylvania. A house that significantly stands out in a neighborhood might be great for you, but others may not share your taste for alternative design, and it could make the house difficult to sell when the time comes.

What Exactly Is a Home?

Home is a very elusive concept. Up until now, this book has generally used *home* to mean anywhere you presently live. That definition could characterize everything from a row house in Queens to a sprawling ranch on 160 acres in West Texas as a home. Now, however, it's time to get more definitive. The following material describes the different types of housing you're likely to purchase. Essentially, these include detached residences and attached residences, such as condominiums and cooperative apartments. The rest of the chapter explores the pros and cons of each type of home in order to help you make a wise buying decision.

Detached Residences

Simply put, attached homes, such as condominiums and cooperative apartments, are those that are connected to the adjacent properties. Conversely, a three-bedroom ranch-style home that is not attached to any surrounding buildings is a detached single-family residence.

   The essential difference is that when you buy a detached home, everything within the invisible property lines that border your property belongs solely to you. When you purchase an attached home, such as a condo, you solely own your unit, but you share the ownership of all the land and all the other parts of the complex with the other condo owners. The shared ownership part is called the *common area,* and thus all the condo owners own a share of the swimming pool, tennis courts, exercise facilities, lobby, hallways, and so on.

Attached Residences

If you like the idea of having access to lots of amenities, such as tennis courts, a pool, a spa, and someone to mow the lawn, then communal living might be for you. Keep in mind, though, that you have to pay for these goodies (usually $80 to $200 per month), and you have to put up with the constraints of communal living to get the economic and lifestyle benefits.

Condominiums.   What is a condominium (condo)? A condo can be any type of building, from a Victorian flat in San Francisco to a highrise apartment in Manhattan. What actually makes a condo a condo is the way its ownership is

 NOTEWORTHY

Detached single-family residences are most desired. American home owners have always had a deep-seated love affair with detached homes. Compared to attached homes, such as condominiums and cooperative apartments, detached homes have historically held their value better in weak markets and appreciated more in strong booming markets.

structured. You have a deed to your individual unit, but you and the other owners share ownership of the land on which the condominium complex is situated,
including the high-rise building that contains your individual units. Therefore,
each and every condo owner owns a portion of the foundation, the garage, and
the roof—as well as a piece of the lobby, the tennis courts, the swimming pool,
and so on. These parts of the overall complex outside of the individual living
units are referred to as *common areas*, because you own them in common with
all the other condo owners.

Home Owners Association.   When you purchase a condo, you automatically
become a member of the project's home-owner's association. You don't have to
attend the association's meetings, but you do have to pay monthly association
dues. These dues can range from $80 to $200 per month and up, and they cover
the common area operating and maintenance expenses. These could include the
lawn and garden landscaping service, pool maintenance, staff salaries, garbage
collection, and fire insurance on common area buildings. A portion of the dues
are held in a reserve fund, to cover future repairs and replacement, such as
painting the exterior of the building and replacing the roof occasionally.

Condo Advantages.   Given that detached homes appear to be a better investment, why do some people prefer condos?

- *Condos have amenities that you couldn't otherwise afford.*   Could you imagine owning a detached home with amenities such as tennis courts, a swimming pool, and a fancy health spa? Most home owners could never afford
  expensive facilities like these. But in a large condo complex, the cost of all
  these goodies is shared among all the owners.

- *Condos raise your purchasing power.*   If you make comparisons in the same
  neighborhood, on the basis of square feet of living area, a condo will sell for
  20 to 30 percent less than a comparable detached home. That's because
  sharing the cost of the land, roof, and foundation with many owners is a lot
  less expensive that owing them yourself.

- *Condos are maintenance free.*   As people grow older, they often prefer having someone else shovel the snow or cut the grass. By owning a condo, you
  don't have to deal with the maintenance. Even better, many high-rise units
  have the services of a doorperson, who'll not only screen visitors, but will
  forward your mail when you're away on vacation, too.

- *Condos cost less to maintain.*   Consider the overall cost, for example, to
  maintain your landscaping and swimming pool and paint the exterior of the
  building. The owner of a detached home is solely responsible for these

items. However, if you were one of 100 owners of a Manhattan high-rise condo, you would share these maintenance expenses with the other 99 owners, and the cost per owner would be significantly less.

Condo Disadvantages.   Although the condo lifestyle does offer some advantages over living in a detached home, it's not for everyone. Here are some of the drawbacks to the condo lifestyle:

- *Condos lack privacy.*   As with apartment living, shared walls mean hearing your neighbors more easily. Noise is one of the biggest problems in condos, and it is one problem frequently overlooked by prospective condo owners. Should you have an interest in a particular unit, visit the unit at various times of the day and listen for noise. Talk to owners within the complex to learn whether they're annoyed by noise.
- *Condos are not as good an investment as detached homes.*   Compared to detached homes, condominiums historically do not hold their value in weak markets, and they appreciate less in strong booming markets.
- *Condos are financially complex.*   Nothing is worse than being hit with a financial surprise. For example, you buy a condo, and you're told the monthly maintenance fee is $115. But two months after you move in, you're told that the budget is too low, and that you'll need to pay an extra $40 per month to make up the deficit.

    Once you have purchased the unit, it's too late to do anything about it. But as a prospective buyer, you can avoid this situation by checking on the current operating budget. Be sure that it covers all building maintenance costs, including utilities, staff salaries, insurance, garbage collection, pool maintenance, and other normal operating expenses. Also be sure that the budget has an adequate reserve to provide for predictable major expenses. Usually, 5 percent of the property's gross operating budget is adequate.

TIP

As a rule, the most desirable condo units are those that share the fewest common walls with neighbors. This is why corner units are more desired, and sell for a premium. Unless there's a roof deck, penthouse units are also more desirable, because you won't have people walking on your ceiling. The most desirable unit with the best privacy—and which, of course, sells for a premium—is a penthouse corner unit.

LANDLORD TALE

In 1981, we bought a great condo in Las Vegas, Nevada. Being an avid tennis player, I was attracted to the tennis courts. And not 20 yards away was a large swimming pool with a whirlpool and sauna bath. The home owner's association maintained the landscaping and the exterior of the building, including the roof, which, notably, was replaced after we had owned our unit for six years. But a few years after we moved in, most of the home owners decided they wanted more privacy. So they hired a contractor to build security gates at both entrances to the complex. Owners could enter the complex by swiping a security card, and visitors to the complex had to be buzzed in from the owner's unit. To pay for all this, our maintenance fees increased $50 a month.

Well, not only did all this security become a big nuisance, it also became very expensive. People who couldn't get the gates to open, for whatever reason, kept breaking them down, and we constantly had to replace them. Naturally, our maintenance fees continued to rise month after month.

Cooperative Apartments

Condos and cooperative apartments (co-ops) are the most common types of attached housing. And like condos, what makes a co-op a co-op is its legal standing. You'll be happy to know that most of the advantages and drawbacks of owning a condo also hold true for co-ops. There are three key differences between condos and co-ops: how title is held, property management, and financing the purchase.

How Title Is Held.   When you buy a co-op, instead of getting a deed to your unit as with a condo, you get a stock certificate, which proves that you own a certain number of shares of stock in the co-op corporation, and a proprietary lease, which gives you the right to reside in the apartment you purchased. Although the corporation owns the building and holds title in its name, you're simultaneously a coowner of the building and a tenant in the building.

Cooperative shares are usually issued according to the size of the unit and what floor it's on. So, a penthouse apartment on the top floor is issued more shares than a similarly sized unit on the ground floor. The coowners with more shares have greater influence in the corporation, because each share represents one vote. However, a coowner's proportionate share of the corporation's total maintenance expenses is also predicated on the number of shares held.

Property Management.   Stock cooperatives are corporations run by a board of directors. Since a co-op unit is in a building owned by a corporation, it's governed by a board of directors elected by the coowners. And not unlike how a home-owners association oversees a condominium complex, the board of directors manages the co-op's daily operations and finances.

Financing Your Purchase. Acquiring a mortgage to purchase a co-op can be difficult, because many mortgage lenders consider shares of stock in a cooperative corporation as too risky for collateral. Most likely, you'll end up paying a high rate of interest, due to lender concerns regarding the greater risks co-ops pose and to the lack of lender competition. To make matters worse, the potential buyer must be approved by the board of directors. And accordingly, when the unit is sold, the buyer has to be given the green light by the board.

Maintenance Responsibility

Generally speaking, with a condo or co-op, you are responsible for the things inside the unit, and the association or board of directors is responsible for the things outside. Condo and co-op owners pay a monthly maintenance fee to cover the expense of maintaining the common area.

See Table 5.1 on page 84 to find out who's responsible for what in a condo or co-op.

Patio Homes

Another style of communal living is the patio home. These are usually single-story homes with a patio or deck in the rear. Notably, patio home owners purchase their own individual units, including the land under them and the front and back yards. Owners are responsible for their own outdoor maintenance. However, the home-owners association maintains the entrance to the community, along with publishing a newsletter, sponsoring some social activities, and so on.

Town Homes

These are usually two-story attached units that feature upstairs bedrooms. They can operate like a condo, with owners belonging to a home-owners association

 BEWARE

Buying and selling a co-op isn't always easy. Bear in mind that getting in and out of co-op ownership is a lot more difficult than buying or selling a condo. Usually co-op owners need approval from either the board of directors or a majority of owners before they can sell or otherwise transfer their stock or proprietary lease.

TABLE 5.1   Who's Responsible for What in a Condo or Co-op

	Responsibility	
Maintenance Task	Condo-Owners Association or Co-op Corporation	Unit Owner
Remove graffitti from outside walls	•	
Repair cracked or heaved concrete at one owner's patio	•	
Maintain cleanliness of hallways	•	
Mow grass, shovel snow, rake leaves	•	
Repaint or wallpaper the interior		•
Pay for the cost of periodic roof replacement	•	
Paint the exterior	•	
Repair water damage in an owner's kitchen when the dishwasher malfunctions		•
Sweep a patio reserved for the use of a particular unit		•
Landscape in front of one unit	Could be either	
Repair fire damage inside one's unit garage		•
Repair storm damage (broken window and rain on floor) on an owner's unit	Probably both, to varying degrees	
Replace landscaping at the entrance gate	•	
Repair storm damage to a wall or landscaping	•	
Landscape in an interior surrounded entirely by one unit		•
Pump out a flooded basement	Depends on whether the basement is common area	

and sharing the cost of maintaining the common areas. The significance of a town home is that the residents can own the ground under their units.

Advisory for Buying in a Community Living Complex

If you enjoy maintenance-free living and like the idea of sharing the expense of all the amenities communal living offers, then this lifestyle might be for you. However, before you sign on the dotted line, there are certain precautions you should be aware of.

- *Be wary of overbuilding.* Condominiums are popular, especially along Florida's Atlantic and Gulf coasts. Sometimes they can become too popular, as they did in Fort Lauderdale in the early 1980s. After one high-rise condominium went up, 10 others followed. Before long, the market was so saturated, there was a glut of units on the market, and the condo owners who had been first to buy lost much of their investment. It resulted in a terrible disaster—entire buildings remained vacant, while condo associations ended up going bankrupt.

You have to be very careful not to buy in a saturated area, where it could be difficult to sell later on.

■ *Be sure the complex is financially sound.*   Before you buy a particular unit, be sure to check into the entity's operating budget. Once you have purchased the unit, it's too late to do anything about it. Be sure that the budget covers all building maintenance costs. Also be sure that the budget has an adequate reserve to provide for predictable major expenses. Usually, 5 percent of the property's gross operating budget is adequate. If you don't make this necessary check, you could end up making up the deficit after taking possession of the unit.

■ *Check out the complex.*   Visit the unit at various times of the day and listen for noise. Talk to owners within the complex. They will usually be happy to chat about the good points of the community, and about any problems. And while you're there, try to get a feel for the place, and imagine what it would be like to call it home.

Gated Communities

Would you like a little more security in your neighborhood? Gated communities are the latest trend in keeping nonresidents from passing through. This concept means that it's safer for the kids to play outdoors. It also means you won't have solicitors ringing your doorbell. And it offers a little more security to your home and neighborhood.

Conversely, that security can be a nuisance, too. Keep in mind that every time you enter the complex, often two or three times a day, you'll need to swipe a security card or show identification. And don't forget that your monthly maintenance cost will be higher to cover the security gate, especially to pay the salaries for its staff, who may be there as much as 24 hours a day.

The Wisest Choice

Both condos and co-ops could be an appropriate home choice, especially considering the maintenance-free lifestyle and the many amenities that they often offer. The condo, however, excels as the wiser choice between the two.

The reason that it comes out ahead is that it's pure and simple real estate, not shares in a corporation like a cooperative. This also makes a condo less complicated legally, which means it will be easier both to finance and to sell when the time comes.

Nevertheless, the best investment of them all—one that holds its value better in slow markets, and appreciates more in booming markets, is very simple to sell and is always in demand—is the detached single-family residence.

CHAPTER 6

The Resale House

A resale house is any dwelling that has been previously lived in by another owner.

The Pros and Cons of a Resale House

A resale home is usually more affordable than a brand-new home, and quite often is better located. Besides these advantages, there are other benefits on the side of the resale home:

- Resale houses are usually situated in mature neighborhoods, with older trees and landscaping. You won't see that barren, stark appearance of a new development.
- In a resale house, the previous owners have already added many important things. You shouldn't have to buy window blinds or drapes, a garage door opener, or ceiling fans, or plant lawns and build fences.
- Certain vintage houses are sturdily constructed, with nice design features, and they are built with materials that would be prohibitively expensive today, or just are not available anymore.

There are, of course, disadvantages to all the charm you get with an older home. Such houses are usually more expensive to maintain. Who wants an ancient heating or cooling system? The electrical system might need to be upgraded.

> ### TIP
>
> If you're interested in a particular resale home, ask the seller for copies of the utility bills (electric, gas, and water) for the past 12 months, so you can determine the expense to operate the house. Should the utility bills seem overly expensive, check with your property inspector about the cost of making the home more energy efficient.

What about the expense to replace rotting window sills? And upgrading a 1950s kitchen into the twenty-first century, could be very expensive.

Features to Look for in Resales

Choosing the right neighborhood will have a substantial effect on what your home is worth. That's because the homes that surround the home you buy will either enhance or detract from its value. For instance, you don't want to buy on a street that's declining in value, or that has become off limits to sensible home buyers. Conversely, if you buy the most modest home in a thriving, high-priced neighborhood, you could expect the more expensive homes to enhance the value of yours. In other words, the higher-priced homes will increase the value of yours to a higher price than it would command in a lesser neighborhood.

You also want to be mindful of logistics—the travel time to and from work and shopping. Buying in a location where excessive travel is required is not only expensive and time consuming, it could eventually cause you to despise the home.

Look for Enclaves of Revitalization

A real estate renaissance is happening in cities, both large and small, across the United States, as older, well-located neighborhoods that were abandoned for suburban sprawl are being rediscovered and converted into enclaves of revitalization.

For years, Chicago's lakeside community of Rogers Park was shunned by home buyers and investors. Even though it has charming architecture and a great location—nestled along Lake Michigan, it's only a short commute to downtown— too much crime and insufficient shopping, restaurants, and other services kept potential home buyers away. But things began to change in the late 1990s.

Today, several of Rogers Park's old diamonds in the rough have been polished up and look like gleaming gems. They've been renovated, grocery stores and new restaurants are moving in, and the city is spearheading a $60-million development at one of the neighborhood's "el" train stops. Property values, as one would expect, are rising fast. Jim McFarlane, a real estate agent, says they've gone up 18 percent in the past year.

"We are literally a block from the lake," says Dina Frieri, who purchased a two-bedroom condo in one of the community's renovated vintage buildings in December 2002. The 36-year-old Saks Fifth Avenue manager paid about half the price of a similar apartment in her old neighborhood. "We think within five years we're going to double our investment."

It wasn't long ago that New York's Harlem was a crime-ridden slum. Not anymore. According to Klara Madlin, a real estate agent there, prices have doubled over the past three years. Across the nation in Columbia City, Seattle's southeastern neighborhood, prices have followed a similar trend. "I paid $99,000 for a craftsman-style bungalow in 1994, and sold it for $230,000 two years ago," says Darryl Smith, a Seattle real estate agent.

Young people aren't the only ones spiriting the renaissance. "A lot of empty nesters are moving into downtown Denver because they can walk around and go to shops or restaurants," says Bill Bronchick, an author and attorney who specializes in real estate investing. "Downtown Denver used to have rows and rows of boarded-up houses selling for $10,000, but now those houses are selling for $150,000 on the low end, and lofts are going for $1 million."

Robert Irwin, author of *How to Find Hidden Real Estate Bargains* says, "Even in small cities, people have incentive to move back to old neighborhoods, because they are often cheaper, they are closer to everything, and in many cases the architecture is better."

The following are four guidelines to live by, if you're considering moving into an "undiscovered" neighborhood:

1. *Get in early, but don't be first.*   Buying real estate in what you hope will be a revitalized neighborhood is one way to stretch your housing dollars and maximize your investment value. But if you want to be successful, your timing has to be right, and you must know the neighborhood inside and out, and plan to be in for the long haul.

To yield the most profit, of course, you need to get into a neighborhood early, but you don't want to be first. There's always the danger that other investors won't follow, that home values won't increase, and that you'll get robbed in the meantime.

"I always look to see if other properties have turned around, because if you're the first in, you may really get hammered," says Irwin. Other experts, along with Irwin, say it's important to see other real estate investors, including the city and business owners, committed to long-term revitalization of the neighborhood.

Still, if you're hunting for an unpolished gem in the rough, don't hesitate until it's too late. "Usually, if you read about it in the local paper as the next hot neighborhood, the best deals are already gone," says Bronchick, adding that Starbucks coffee shops are a telltale sign that a neighborhood has turned.

2. *Don't be afraid to get your hands dirty.*   Charming architecture is another feature to look for, says Dale Mattison, a real estate broker in Chevy Chase, Maryland. "The first neighborhoods to turn around are those where the housing stock is interesting," he says, adding that Victorians, Federal style, and other kinds of prewar buildings are particularly desirable.

Bear in mind that revitalizing such properties takes a lot of effort, whether you do the renovation yourself or hire someone to do it for you. The work can also be very expensive, depending on how old and in need of renovation the building is.

Often, as an added incentive, federal or local governments offer special deals on low-interest mortgages, or even grants for remodeling in communities that have been targeted for urban renewal.

3. *Check out the neighborhood.*   Before you invest the money and effort into restoring a Victorian in tomorrow's enclave of revitalization, be sure to do some research on the neighborhood itself. Dine in local restaurants, do a little grocery shopping, and even try out the el train for your daily commute.

Furthermore, some of the more important checking you do requires a little more probing. "You need to go to the city council, and see if there are any new businesses on the way, get crime statistics from the police department, and look into the school system," Irwin says, adding that schools are often the single biggest factor in price appreciation for a neighborhood. "In other words, find out what the future holds for this area."

4. *Invest for the long term.*   Renovating a property with the sole purpose of quickly selling it could backfire. You'll have a better chance at maximum profitability if you retain the property over the long haul. "A lot of people have gotten hurt in real estate because they're too short-sighted. They get in too late, and want to sell right away," says Bronchick.

There's greater danger in marginal communities, since they are often the first to see a decline in home prices when the economy fizzles out. "What happens in a recession is that people want to feel safe, they don't want to try anything new," says Robert Kucharski, a Realtor in Dallas.

Kucharski goes on to say that, the real estate market in Dallas today reflects what he believes is the worst housing recession since the oil bust of the 1980s. As such, he's adjusted his expectations for property he owns on the outskirts of Kessler Park, a trendy Dallas neighborhood. "I fix up homes and hold on to them, but now I'm seeing that I may be holding on to these properties longer than I had originally planned."

Other Resale Features

Other features to look for in a resale home are architectural style, construction materials, kitchen layout, number of bedrooms and bathrooms, and so on. Some of these features enhance the appearance and enjoyment of the home, while others are negative and detract from the function and potential beauty of a home. To invest wisely, you need to know what to look for, along with knowing what to avoid in a prospective home investment.

Just keep in mind that what appeals to one person's taste can repel another. Selecting features that add value and convenience to a home is an art, not a science, so it is difficult to give you a precise list of good and bad features. Home buyers are not all alike, and every situation is different. However, the following pages offer a general view of what home owners and home buyers consider the most (and least) desirable features.

House Style

Good style is a home that's in harmony with the neighborhood. For instance, a clapboard Cape Cod is appropriate in the New England states, but it would hardly be stylish among tile-roof Spanish-style ranch homes in Santa Barbara. Likewise, a southwestern adobe-style home would be difficult to resell if it's situated in a neighborhood of two-story Victorians.

A home that conforms to the neighborhood has a positive impact on the investment potential, whereas a style that does not conform, that is in disharmony with the neighborhood, negatively affects investment potential. So, if value and salability are important to you, avoid investing in a home that's unusual or out of the ordinary.

Construction Materials

Homes with a brick veneer are desirable in most parts of the United States and you'll save time and money on maintenance. Brick and vinyl-sided homes are popular too, and virtually maintenance free. Wood siding has to be painted periodically unless it's been treated and it is less desirable in the south, where termites are abundant. Aluminum siding over wood frame may or may not add to resale value, but it will definitely save on maintenance.

Stucco is an attractive material, widely used throughout the southwestern and western states. However, in the more northern latitudes, stucco homes are less desirable, due to their unjointed surfaces, which tend to crack in colder temperatures. Granite and stone veneers, however, have expansion joints, which can accommodate changes in temperature. These façades are usually charming and attractive too, which is a real plus on the resale side.

Garages

Most desirable is an attached two-car garage, especially one located on the side of the house. One that's extra big, 8 or 10 feet wider than the width needed for two cars, is better yet. The extra space comes in handy for storage of the lawn mower, bicycles, and other equipment.

Garages located under the house are not as functional, and very inconvenient. Take into consideration the inconvenience of climbing a flight of stairs every time you go from the car to the house, and of unloading groceries and carting them up the stairs. These are the primary reasons most home owners prefer having the garage on the same level as the house.

Attached garages are more popular in the north, because there's no need to shovel snow off the walkway to get to the car. A carport may give the car some protection against the elements, but it's not nearly as functional or desirable as an attached two-car garage.

Porches, Patios, Decks, and Pools

An extra screened-in room, or any place to eat or sit outdoors, is both functional and desired among prospective home buyers.

An in-ground swimming pool, on the other hand, is very expensive to maintain. You have to be concerned about the safety issue, too, when it comes to small children. And when it comes time to sell, the home with a pool will only interest people who are precisely looking for a home with a swimming pool.

Kitchens

Student realtors are often taught that it's the woman of the household who makes the decision about buying a particular home: The man only decides

NOTEWORTHY

Be wary of a home where the garage has been converted to living space. At first glance, it might appear that such a conversion could be lucrative. Perhaps you could rent out the space as a studio apartment for $350 or $400 a month. That's the good news. The bad news is that you don't have a garage, which could seriously impair the salability of the house. Most potential home buyers require at least a two-car garage.

whether he can afford the payments. If this is so, it is the features and convenience of the kitchen, more than anything else, that often determines whether the woman desires a particular home. With this in mind, nowadays many home buyers prefer eat-in kitchens, with a double sink under a window. They also prefer lots of counter space, especially if there is a convenient center island. Plenty of cabinet space, along with a handy broom closet, are also among the items most desired in a kitchen.

Bathrooms

Long gone are the days of the one-bathroom house. Today's home buyers want at least two full baths, or at a bare minimum one bath and a powder room. Bathrooms with outside windows are preferred over interior baths with only a vent fan.

Home buyers also prefer shower stalls to combination shower and tub arrangements, but still want one bathtub in the house. Bathroom vanities with a double sink are considered a plus, too, along with full-wall mirrors behind them.

Closets

A walk-in closet in the master bedroom is one of the most desired features for many home buyers. But overall, a well-designed home should have plenty of closet space. Here are some additional closet features to look for:

- A front-hall closet where you can hang jackets, coats, and guest coats
- One or two linen closets in a hallway for blankets and towels
- A broom closet near the kitchen

Bedrooms

Most home buyers require a minimum of three bedrooms in a home, and the larger the rooms the better. Unfortunately, homes are seldom built with more than one large bedroom. If one or two of the bedrooms are small, you should at least have adequate wall space for furniture placement and convenient access to a bathroom.

Attic bedrooms with sloping ceilings and dormer windows, such as those commonly found in a Cape Cod, are not a big home buyer favorite. Yet, they're a little more desirable than basement bedrooms, which are always damp and cold.

Living Rooms

When it comes to the living room, the more space the better, especially in a house without a family room. Nowadays most people desire only a family room (or a *great room*, as it's often called) rather than a separate formal living room.

Family Rooms

The family room is more important than the living room. And not unlike the living room, the more space you have, the better. Many home buyers in the south and west like combining eating areas with the kitchen, making it a great room. Most home buyers find basement family rooms undesirable and out of style. However, a grade-level family room with a fireplace is a most desired feature.

Dining Rooms

A formal dining room is useful, especially when guests are invited for dinner. But many folks believe an eat-in kitchen is just fine. If the house has a formal dining room, it should have direct access to both the kitchen and the living room.

Attics

The most useful and convenient storage attics are accessible by stairs. Less appealing to home buyers, and inconvenient to home owners, are attics that are accessible through a ceiling trap door.

Basements

Primarily found in the north, basements are convenient for storage, and a good place for a workshop. They should be well lighted and dry, and have direct access to the outdoors.

When you're snooping around the basement, investigate what type of heating system is in the house. Gas heating is preferred among most home buyers, because of its low maintenance requirements. Oil or coal heat is very dirty and requires periodic fuel deliveries. Electric heat, though low maintenance, is the most expensive type of heating. And be wary of heat pumps in the northern latitudes, which usually are an inadequate heating system in that part of the country.

Laundry Rooms

Washer and dryer hookups are more convenient when they're not located in the basement, which requires the owner to carry laundry up and down flights of stairs. The most preferred location is near the kitchen, especially if the room can accommodate an ironing board.

Choosing a Floor Plan

When you find an interesting resale home, it's always a good idea to make a rough floor plan to take home and study. Noting the locations of doorways, walls, and windows will help jog your memory after you leave the home, and it will be useful for answering questions that you may have overlooked the first time you walked through the house.

Few home buyers really try on a home for size when they first inspect it. They may casually look around from room to room, which is fine for the first stage of house hunting. But when you're seriously considering buying a particular house, you need more than just a mental image. You need to draw up a rough floor plan, take it home, and imagine living in it.

The following are important features you should look for when choosing a floor plan:

- You'll want to avoid floor plans in which bedrooms are situated in such a way that require you walk through one bedroom to get to another. The kitchen is the only room that's considered acceptable as a walk-through room.

- Where are the bedrooms located? Many home buyers prefer some distance between the master bedroom and the other bedrooms. This "split" bedroom layout allows more privacy by keeping a good distance between the master bedroom and the other bedrooms.

- Most home buyers prefer a home with short, well-lit hallways. Avoid a layout with long, dark hallways.

- How do you navigate from the kitchen to the backyard? Not only do you need to think about monitoring the children playing in the yard, also imagine going back and forth from the refrigerator to the patio chairs.

- Is the layout convenient for bringing groceries and other goods into the home? As mentioned earlier, it can be a real chore carrying groceries up a flight of stairs and into the kitchen.

During your walking tours, ask yourself these questions: "Would I enjoy living here?" "Could I sell this property when I want to, without incurring a loss?" and "Will this house appeal to many other buyers when I decide to sell?"

CHAPTER 7

Other Home Choices

If you're the type of person who doesn't like buying someone else's problems, or another person's style, then purchasing a new home could be ideal for you.

New Homes

Many new homes have some very appealing features:

Advantages of a New House

- New homes come with warranties on such things as the heating and air conditioning system, the plumbing, the electrical system, and the roof.
- New homes have the latest systems, with modern kitchens and the latest in built-in appliances, such as built-in microwave, stove, and garbage disposal.
- Choosing a new home built by a reputable builder can give you the peace of mind of knowing that your home doesn't contain lead-based paints, asbestos, or other hazardous and toxic materials.
- A new home will cost less to operate and maintain than a resale home. Operating expenses are minimized because of energy-efficient appliances and heating and cooling systems. And with a quality new home, maintenance expenses are virtually nil, because everything is new—the paint, roof, appliances, carpet—all you need to do is change the light bulbs.

- New homes often come with financial incentives to stimulate a purchase. Developers frequently offer to pay all the closing costs if the buyer closes on the home within a specified time.

Unfortunately, new homes also have some disadvantages:

Disadvantages of a New House

- *You don't get all the extra features that come with a resale house.* Often you have to install a lot of extra things, such as sod for the back yard, window treatments, ceiling fans, and an automatic garage door opener.

- *Prices are less negotiable.* New-home builders maintain price integrity, both to protect the value of their unsold inventory of homes and to uphold appraisals for loan purposes. Instead of reducing their asking prices, builders bargain with you by offering free upgrades, such as a better grade of carpet, or ceramic tile floors instead of linoleum.

- *New homes are usually more expensive than resales.* That's because the cost of land, labor, and materials are much higher today than they were years ago, when resale homes were built.

- *You get a less desirable site that lacks mature landscaping.* Because habitable land is scarce, today's home developers must build on whatever land is available. In other words, the earlier developments got the better sites. Years from now, though, today's less desirable site will be considered a prime area.

Negotiating on a New Home

Developers usually don't like to lower the sales prices of their homes. However, there are other items they will frequently be more flexible on. You can usually bargain for better financing and on any extras, such as a built-in fireplace and hardwood floors. Another area where there's room for bargaining is on the

TIP

Some home builders entice buyers by pricing houses very close to their actual cost. They make all their profit in overcharging for the upgrades and extras. After you've done some comparison shopping and discovered that these things are overpriced, go ahead and buy the house at the bargain price, but buy all the extras from low-cost suppliers, not the builder.

LANDLORD TALE

Dave and Sherri bought a new home in a new development in Gulfport, Mississippi. After taking possession and moving in, they had to buy and install the following items: window treatments (blinds and drapes), ceiling fans, electric garage door opener, shelving for the garage, clothing hooks, extra towel racks, peep hole for the front door, fencing and sod for the backyard, shrubs, trees, and fireplace logs.

They also saved $2,500 in closing costs by responding to the ad sent to them by the developer (if they bought within 60 days, saving on points and all related closing costs).

LESSON: Although they saved a substantial amount in closing costs, most of those items they were required to buy for their new home would have been included with most resale homes.

upgrades, such as a better grade of carpeting, or ceramic tile floors and countertops instead of linoleum and laminate.

Having a Home Built for You

Perhaps you like the idea of building your own home from scratch and having a say in each aspect of its design. Choosing a lot and building a home on it is a whole different experience from buying a resale home.

Shopping for a Site

When you go looking for available land to build a home on, you have to keep in mind that some sites may be impossible to build on. The land may not be accessible to utilities. It could have poor drainage or lie in a flood plain. It might be difficult to access, because it's so far off the beaten track. Or it might not be residentially zoned. Whatever the reason, the following are important points to consider when shopping for a home site:

- Avoid buying a site near a major highway. Check with your area's planning department, and investigate master plans and environmental agency reports in the area you're considering. This way you avoid building a home on a road that the state highway department will eventually widen into your front yard.

- Do some research down at city hall. Find out if the site you're interested in can be used as a home site. Also find out what type of building permit is required. Make inquiries about water and sewer hookups, and find out if your site is large enough to build the kind of home you want, according to local zoning laws.

- Check into what will be built around you. Again, check out the master plans to see what kind of zoning surrounds your site. It would be a good idea to be informed if a new high school or manufacturing facility were planned nearby, or across the street from your site.

- Be wary of a high water table, or unstable ground that's not capable of supporting a house. You have to be especially wary of a site that's located over a landfill, where flooding often occurs as the water table rises. This information is available at your city or town's engineering office.

- Check with your state environmental agency to find out about its plans for land-trusts and areas slated for a moratorium on development.

- Avoid buying a site that is too steep for constructing a home.

- Check into whether your site is serviced by public sewer and water. If not, you'll need to have a well dug and have a septic system installed.

- The topsoil has to be checked. If rock is too close to the topsoil, it will add to the cost of pouring the foundation, or it may not be feasible to build one.

- Be sure that you can obtain clear title to the site. You can pay a title search company to do this, or you can purchase title insurance, which will protect you from any future claims on the property. You can also do a title search yourself at city hall in the hall of records.

- Be sure that you have access to your site. It's illegal to sell landlocked sites in most states.

- Consider the shape of your site. Frontage on an improved thoroughfare is important: The more you have, the more valuable the site. Also, the higher the cost to develop the site, the cheaper your purchase price should be.

You also have to take resale value into consideration. A remote country site out in the boondocks might appeal to you, but later, when it's time to sell, will potential buyers find your remote site appealing?

How you'll pay for your site is another consideration. Most unimproved lots sell strictly for cash. Often the seller will carry a short-term mortgage, though.

You may have to check with mortgage brokers to help you find a conventional lender that will fund a loan if you intend to build soon.

Financing Your New Custom Home

Getting a mortgage loan for a custom home is a little different from arranging financing for a resale or a new-development home. Ideally, you need a mortgage lender that will fund a construction loan that automatically converts to a traditional mortgage after the home is constructed. That type of loan is called a *combo mortgage,* wherein both the construction financing and the permanent mortgage are combined in one loan package. Also, the value of the land that the home will be built on can usually be allocated toward the down payment.

The following are other items to consider:

- When considering the design of your home, think about its appeal to future buyers. In other words, don't make the home too unique or peculiar. Oddball homes designed by their so-called architect owners can stay on the market for years, waiting for an oddball buyer to come along. Examples of such homes include a one-bedroom house, a house with only one bath, a house built underground, or any other type of design that doesn't conform to the homes built in your area.

- It doesn't matter how carefully you plan or budget, the construction of your custom home will, in most cases, take longer and cost considerably more than you estimated.

- It would be wise to consult with a real estate attorney who is experienced in the matters of building a custom designed home.

Buying a House before It's Built

Although you'll likely have to endure a little inconvenience, buying a home before it's constructed has several advantages. New housing developments usually offer preconstruction prices during the first phase of the project's development. At this stage, the lot is being developed in preparation for pouring the foundation. At this stage, developers underprice somewhat, in order to stimulate home sales.

Homes sold in later phases, as the project nears completion, will usually cost 10 to 20 percent more than preconstruction homes. Therefore, if you have the patience to wait, buying early can be very advantageous. Also, you'll have a choice in selecting the interior paint colors, countertops, and flooring for the home as it's being built. In addition, buying in the first phase gives you a choice of site locations, which means you're not limited to what's left.

Knowing the builder is also important. Look for a builder with experience in similar single-family home projects, not someone who used to build roads or shopping centers, for instance, and who is now trying out residential construction. Check out other projects your potential builder has completed. Drive around them and talk to those home owners and ask them whether they're satisfied with their homes.

What if this is the builder's first project? If the builder has no track record, you cannot be sure that the project will be finished. Larcenous builders have been known to disappear overnight with buyers' deposits, along with the cash from the construction loans, leaving the unfinished project mired in unpaved roads and half-built homes.

You also have to consider that you'll be one of the first residents to move into a new development. Will you be comfortable living virtually alone until your neighbors move in? And can you deal with the noise and the inconvenience of daily construction going on all around you?

Ways to Save on a New Development Home

The following are several ways to save money on a preconstructed home:

- *Buy at preconstruction prices.* You can save 10 to 20 percent if you're willing to wait for your home to be built, then live for a while in a community with virtually no neighbors.

- *Avoid most of the upgrades.* Do you really need hardwood floors or top-quality carpeting? Supplying upgrades is how builders make a large portion of their profit. For now, select standard-grade features and fixtures, and put off the upgrades till later.

- *Buy a model home.* If you can wait until the project is just about completely sold out, and you would like a home with all the features and decorations added to attract potential home buyers at a reduced price, then buy a model home. But of course, you'll have to take the model as is, and you won't have any choice as to the upgrades, options, or design features.

- *Don't assume that the builder's mortgage package is the best.* Shop around with at least three other lenders, and compare interest rates and other terms before you accept the builder's loan package.

- *Leave the addition just framed.* Delay finishing off the extra bedroom, bath, or enclosed patio. You can earn a substantial savings by just having the addition framed out to be finished at a later date.

Modular or Manufactured Homes

As opposed to "stick-built" homes, which are hand-built on site, manufactured or modular homes are produced in sections in a factory, then shipped to the building site, where the parts are assembled to form a house.

Home buyers choose modular houses for essentially one reason—they cost substantially less than stick-built homes of similar size. An average modular home with three bedrooms and two baths can cost less than $50,000, including setup, but not including the cost of the site. Larger, more plush modulars with more amenities can cost upwards of $100,000.

You have four options regarding the setup and location of a modular home:

1. You can have a modular assembled on your lot, as long as the local zoning allows it.

2. You can purchase an already-built modular by itself or purchase it along with the site it's situated on, as part of a new- or resale-home community.

3. You can purchase a modular home from a dealer, and have it set up in a planned community of your choice.

4. You can purchase a modular home and set it up in a rental community where each site is leased. Using this method, certain issues have to be addressed. For example, will you have a lease for use of the land? What is the term of the lease? What are the monthly utility costs, and is there a charge for hookups? Who pays for maintenance? If the landlord sells the land, will you have to move your home?

 NOTEWORTHY

Modular or manufactured homes set up on rented land are considered personal property rather than real estate. They are treated differently than stick-built homes, and they are not financed as improved real estate, that is, with a traditional mortgage.

Furthermore, modular or manufactured homes, unfortunately, do not appreciate like improved real estate. In fact, you can reasonably expect this type of housing to actually decline in value, whereas a well-located parcel with a stick-built house can be expected to appreciate at a reasonable rate year after year.

Financing Modulars

In order to be financed by a real estate mortgage, a modular home must be permanently set on a foundation, or erected on land owned by the new home owner. In other words, to qualify for a mortgage loan, the modular home and the land have to be considered a single real-estate entity under state law.

The same lenders that fund mortgages for stick-built housing, also have mortgages for modulars, including government-backed mortgages from the FHA and VA.

Adults-Only Retirement Community

Do you like the idea of living among folks of similar age and interests? Then an adults-only retirement community might be ideal for you. These developments are controlled by a lot of covenants, along with restrictions on parking boats and recreational vehicles on the street. The covenants may regulate the paint colors that can be used on the exterior of the house, and they generally include a rule forbidding children under the age of 18 from residing there on a full-time basis. Usually, minor children are allowed to visit for up to three months.

For example, at Del Webb's Rancho Vistoso in Tuscon, Arizona, about 4,500 adults live in a beautiful tile-roofed community, with cozy detached homes overlooking the picturesque Santa Catalina mountains. They pay annual dues of $700, which cover maintenance of the common area, the use of tennis courts and a health spa, and membership in over 100 clubs, from astronomy to zoology. Minimum age is 45, and no one under the age of 19 is allowed, except as a visitor, for a maximum visit of three months.

The Ideal House

As you can see, there's plenty to choose from when it comes time to buy a home, everything from a condominium to a detached single-family residence in a gated community. Whatever style you choose, keep in mind the three principles for maximizing value in your home investment: They are the principles of *progression*, *regression*, and *conformity*. Consider your present lifestyle, along with potential changes in your future lifestyle. This will enable you to invest over the long term, affording you more of the wealth-building benefits real estate offers. Furthermore, keep in mind the investment value of detached homes. Compared to attached residences, such as condos and co-ops, detached homes tend to hold their value better in weak markets, and they appreciate more in strong markets.

Less Is More

"Any home can be transformed into what you want it to be," says architect Dennis Wedlick, author of *The Good Home.* He urges home owners to think twice before letting space constraints make them get up and move from a home they love. "Don't give up a great neighborhood with good schools and nearby friends just to get more space."

It's better to make a wish list describing your ideal home, pretending your home isn't there. "Do it without compromise or concern for cost. Think about the features that you'd love, things that would reflect your tastes, your interests, and your style of living."

Next, have an interior designer do a quick study of your home's potential to satisfy that wish list. Then estimate all the costs of a larger home, being sure to include the cost of moving. Now make a comparison to what you'd be willing to invest to stay in your present home. "People are usually surprised at the numbers," Wedlick says.

"Remember, too," he adds, "that a renovated home in a desirable neighborhood may appreciate faster than a new property would. At least, that's the trend."

Avoiding the Most Common Mistakes Home Buyers Make

Mistake: After relocating, every available house looks like a bargain.

LESSON: When moving into a low-cost area from a high-cost area, you must reevaluate the housing market.

The cost of housing varies substantially among regions of the United States. For example, in and around San Francisco, a three-bedroom home with two baths, and a den on a half-acre lot could be valued at $500,000 or more. But the same home located in some low-cost regions, say New Mexico or Mississippi's Gulf Coast, could be bought for about $120,000.

The scarcity of available land in a particular area, determines the value of real estate.

According to *USA Today* (February 10, 2003), the most expensive places for homes, based on a 2,200-square-foot, 8-room, 4-bedroom, 2.5-bath home in communities in and around middle-income metro areas, are the following, based on an analysis of approximately 300 metropolitan areas nationwide:

San Francisco $768,100
San Jose, California $746,700
Washington $469,800
Boston $436,900
Honolulu $415,400

And the least expensive places for homes in the United States:

Hobbs, New Mexico $95,700
San Antonio, Texas $124,800
New Johnsonville, Tennessee $126,200
Rangely, Colorado $127,800
Kinston, North Carolina $129,400

PART IV

TEAM MEMBERS, GUIDELINES, AND VALUATION

Once you've got some notion of what it is you want and where to buy it, and you have determined how much house you can afford, then you're ready to discover how the home-buying process is accomplished. This part, introduces you to the people who can assist you in purchasing your home. And now that you've already been briefed on what to look for in a mortgage, this part reveals the details of the key guidelines to smart real estate investment. There is also sage advice on choosing what to buy, with precautions on how to avoid buying a lemon, or other types of loser properties. And the final chapter in this part presents the professional techniques of determining the value of residential real estate.

CHAPTER 8

Selecting Your Real Estate Team

If you're like most people who are first-time home buyers, you're not an expert on property values, taxes, or finance and real estate law. And with your life savings potentially at risk, not to mention the chance of overpaying for a home with which you'll inevitably become unhappy, all this is a lot to deal with. Time after time, I've seen naive home buyers get into situations they could have easily prevented. More often than not, what got them into trouble was inexperience with something that they, or the people representing them, should have known about, but didn't.

Yet, knowing everything there is to know about home buying isn't important. What *is* important is making sure that the people who represent and advise you are knowledgeable, so that they can help you solve the problems that invariably occur. You can hire the people who know real estate values, mortgages, real estate tax law, and escrows, in order to avoid making costly mistakes.

Building a Winning Team

To avoid making costly errors and achieve maximum success in buying a home, you need a winning team of *advisors*—not decision makers. You have to rely on your team to give good advice, so that you can make wise decisions. After all, it's your money, and it will be your home when all is said and done.

Think of purchasing a home as a game you want to win. You can't play every position on the team, so you assemble a group of competent players. Your job is to lead the players in such a way that they can advise you on how to win the game.

The following is a brief look at the players on your team:

- *Real estate agent.* A competent real estate agent will not only know property values in the area where you're interested in buying, but will have your interests at heart when it comes to negotiating on your behalf, making sure that you don't pay more for the property than you truly have to.
- *Mortgage lender.* If you're like most folks and can't pay cash for a home, you're going to need a loan. A good mortgage lender will offer a variety of competitively priced loans, and can even help you select the loan that's best suited for your particular needs.
- *Property inspector.* You need a competent property inspector to thoroughly inspect the home you intend to purchase, to ensure that you're getting precisely what you're paying for.
- *Escrow officer.* The escrow officer is the middleperson, or the neutral third party, who allocates all the funds and shuffles all the paperwork between the buyer and seller.
- *Lawyer.* Depending on where you live, you may not need a lawyer. In many parts of the western United States, the independent escrow officer handles all the essentials at a real estate closing. But if you do have any questions or doubts about the legality of your purchase agreement, be sure to hire a lawyer who specializes in real estate law.

The Real Estate Agent

A good real estate agent not only can save you thousands of dollars in a real estate transaction, but can tend to many of the necessary details, and make the process a hassle-fee experience. Conversely, a bad agent can cost you thousands of dollars, and turn what should be a good home buying experience into a nightmare.

A good real estate agent can be the backbone of your real estate team. The agent can not only be helpful in finding a home that meets your particular needs, but can also negotiate for that home in your behalf, advise you on the financing, supervise the home inspector, and coordinate the closing.

Qualities of a Good Real Estate Agent

Good real estate agents have certain qualities that give them an advantage over the ordinary agent:

- *Good agents are not part-timers working at another job.*   You need a full-time professional to give you full-time attention. Many new agents begin their real estate careers as part-timers, working weekends and after normal business hours. That's okay for them, but not for you.

- *Good agents specialize in property types and restrict themselves geographically.* When agents specialize in a specific property type within a certain geographic boundary, they become more knowledgeable about values. Agents who try to do all things for all people, and try to work outside their area of expertise, invariably deliver mediocre service.

- *Good agents will advise you.*   Instead of trying to make decisions for you, good agents will always explain your available options, so that you end up making a wise decision.

- *Good agents have contacts.*   Home buyers prefer doing business with skilled service providers whom, they know, trust, and respect and who offer competitive pricing. You benefit by using your agent's working relationships with other real estate agents, local lenders, property inspectors, lawyers, escrow officers, and insurance agents.

- *Good agents have time to serve you.*   Overburdened agents who are already busy with many other customers won't have enough surplus time to serve you adequately. If you feel neglected because of your agent's constraints, hire a new agent.

- *Good agents have carefully planned tours.*   Good agents not only have a well-thought-out tour of properties to show you, they have preinspected most properties. This way you'll be more efficient in house hunting, by being well organized and viewing only qualified properties.

- *Good agents have ethics.*   Good agents will alert buyers to problems with the location or the condition of the property.

Selecting Your Real Estate Agent

How do you go about finding a top-notch agent? Start with referrals. Ask for recommendations from friends or coworkers who are currently looking for a home or have recently bought a home. Professionals in related fields, such as insurance agents or financial advisors, can be a good source of agent referrals. While you're out house hunting, check out the agents who are holding open houses. These agents might be ideal, because you already know that they work in the community in which you want to buy.

Also, peruse the large newspaper display advertisements for the town where you would like to move. This is where many real estate offices congratulate their top-performing agents. Call one of them up, and make an appointment for an interview.

The Buyer's Agent

This is a relatively new concept, wherein the buyer's real estate agent will represent only the buyer, rather than the seller. Buyer's agents can be especially helpful when representing you in "for sale by owner" (FSBO) home sales. The commission for this type of service can vary, depending on the situation. Frequently, you can get the FSBO seller to pay at least half the buyer agent's fee. Be wary of a buyer's agent who wants to charge you a fee up front for the service of finding you the home you buy, in the beginning stages of house hunting. You should not be expected to pay anything in advance to get a buyer's agent to work for you.

Simplifying the House-Hunting Process

Make sure that the agent knows precisely what you want in a home. This includes the price range, architectural style, number of bedrooms, and location preferences. Limit yourself to viewing no more than six to eight properties per day. More than that can blur your vision and fatigue your mind. Take a camera, and make notes. Let the agent drive, so you're free to make observations, take notes, and ask questions.

House Hunting Online

Most Realtors these days have web sites that feature house listings, with photos, prices, and in some cases virtual tours of homes for sale. Advertised as the "world's largest database of homes for sale," www.realtor.com provides data on millions of listings around the United States. It will give you a good idea of price ranges by city, state, and zip code.

The Mortgage Lender

As mentioned in Chapter 3, the most expensive thing you'll likely ever buy is not your home—it's the cost of the *financing* on that home. If you borrow to buy your home, as most people do, the mortgage itself is the biggest cost item.

You need a good mortgage lender on your team. The right lender can save you tens of thousands of dollars over the life of a typical 30-year mortgage loan. See Chapters 3 and 4 for advice on choosing the appropriate mortgage alternative and selecting the best lender.

The Property Inspector

Because you don't want to inadvertently end up with a real estate lemon—a home with all kind of expensive hidden problems—you need a competent property inspector on your team. You need someone who can determine whether the roof leaks, the air conditioner's evaporator coil needs repair, or the electrical system is defective. Once you've found a home that you're interested in buying, be sure to make the offer contingent upon your approval of a home inspection by an independent contractor.

Chapter 15 covers everything you need to know about property inspections and selecting a property inspector.

The Escrow Officer

The escrow officer is a neutral third party who carries out the instructions of the purchase agreement. The escrow officer collects all the necessary documents, takes in funds and makes disbursements (loans, taxes, commissions), and remits to the seller a check for the proceeds at closing.

Because the escrow officer is technically a neutral third-party referee, the escrow officer cannot be on anyone's team. Buyers and sellers often mutually agree on the selection of the escrow holder, based on recommendations by their real estate agents. Depending on the location of the subject property, local custom determines whether your escrow is handled by a real estate broker, a lawyer, an escrow company, or the firm that underwrites the title insurance policy. Chapter 16 covers escrow and the closing in detail.

The Lawyer

The purchase agreement you sign is a legally binding contract between you and the seller. Should you have any doubts about the legality of your contract, get a lawyer on your team immediately.

The following factors determine whether you need a lawyer on your team:

- *The location of the subject property.*   In states such as Mississippi, lawyers do everything from preparing purchase contracts to closing the escrow. However, in states such as Nevada, private escrow companies do everything involved with an escrow, and rarely is a lawyer involved. Your real estate agent will know whether a lawyer is needed in your state.

■ *The complexity of the deal.*   Any time you get involved in a contract that's anything out of the ordinary, you need an attorney. Complex situations frequently arise with partnership agreements, intricate leases, or complicated titles.

■ *The absence of a real estate agent.*   If you're interested in buying a home that's being offered for sale directly by the owner, it would be a good idea to have a lawyer prepare the purchase contract and handle the work the agent would normally do. If there's no real estate agent involved, you still need someone to advise you about negotiations, inspections, contingency clauses, and the other details of the home-buying process.

If you decide that you need a lawyer, keep in mind that law is a very specialized field. In other words a corporate attorney or the lawyer who handled your cousin's divorce isn't a good choice for your real estate team. Hire a lawyer who specializes in real estate law.

Start by getting referrals. Your broker or real estate agent may have good working relationships with lawyers in your community.

A competent lawyer has the following qualities:

■ *Is licensed to practice law in your state and works full-time as a lawyer.*

■ *Has local experience.*   Because real estate law varies not only from state to state, but also from one area to another within a state, it's important to have a good local lawyer who knows the law in your area.

■ *Speaks your language.*   A good lawyer simplifies your options by being clear and concise, without resorting to technical legalese.

The completion of a successful home-buying transaction is the result of the coordinated efforts of an entire team. Each team member has certain knowledge and skills that make an important contribution to a successful and hassle-free investing experience.

CHAPTER 9

Key Guidelines to Making a Superior Investment

Anyone can buy a house or investment property, and given enough time, could likely earn a reasonable return from it. Yet, not just anyone has the skills or the strategy to buy a house or income property and make it a superior investment that yields a great return. To accomplish this feat, you need to develop a specific investment strategy, or follow key guidelines that reduce risk and maximize the value of your investment.

Introduction to the 11 Key Guidelines

The more of these 11 key investment guidelines you utilize to purchase real estate, the better chance you have of making your purchase a superior real estate investment:

1. *Buy detached single-family residences, the wisest choice.* They make superior investments. You want to avoid investing in condos, co-ops, and town homes.
2. *Buy bargain-priced or undervalued property.* This way you have built-in value and avoid overpaying for a property.
3. *Buy property that can be profitably improved.* This way you can build in value through cost-effective renovations. (Seek properties with minor defects that can easily be cured to add value to the investment.)
4. *Buy property with low-cost financing.*
5. *Buy property from motivated sellers.*

6. *Buy improved property on a sizable piece of land.*   The larger the parcel, the better.

7. *Buy property with a good location in a thriving market.*

8. *Become a great negotiator.*

9. *Buy when others are afraid to buy.*

10. *Buy during slow periods.*

11. *Buy income properties with below-market rents that can be raised.*

These 11 key investment guidelines present the greatest profit potential when you invest in residential real estate. If these qualities are inherent in the property you purchase, you can be assured that you've made a wise investment.

Buy Detached Single-Family Residences

Why should you choose to invest in a detached single-family residence (SFR)? Because of buyer demand. It's the most sought after type of residence. Americans have always had a love affair with detached homes. Even if you weren't raised in a detached home, you probably desire one, because of television shows like *Ozzie and Harriet* and *Leave It to Beaver* that idealized quality family life, or advertising campaigns may have convinced you that such homes are both desirable and representative of a successful lifestyle.

Generally speaking, this book does not recommend that you invest in any type of attached home. About the only exception would be a condominium, but only if it can be bought as a real bargain—for example, at least 25 percent below market value. (See Chapter 5 for more details on SFRs and attached residences.)

Buy Bargain-Priced or Undervalued Property

Ask yourself, "Is the property I'm buying bargain priced? And if I had to, could I sell this property tomorrow and not take a loss?" If you can answer yes to both questions, then you can rest assured that you haven't overpaid for the property, and that it has built-in value. This quality is important, too, because you would at least want to get out of the property what you paid for it, including any costs to sell it.

How to Know If a Property Is Bargain-Priced.   In order to make sound real estate investments, you must evaluate potential acquisitions accurately. You have to recognize a bargain when you see it. Knowing how to precisely determine value, then, is the real nuts-and-bolts skill of investing in real estate. Conversely, by not using proper appraisal techniques, you could fall prey to one of the greatest perils in real estate investing—paying too much for it. (Chapter 10 covers determination of value in detail.)

Yet you can easily overcome this pitfall by understanding property values in your local market. Once you become familiar with local market values and are fully informed about recent sales prices, you will become more efficient at spotting bargain-priced real estate.

You can begin educating yourself by doing some research. Obtain a multiple-listing service (MLS) book, which covers all property listed for sale in the area, from your friendly realty agent. Look up recent sales, and especially take note of the price per square foot of both improved and unimproved real estate.

The price per square foot of living space is the most important factor in quickly determining the value of improved real estate. From this information alone, you can usually decide whether a property deserves further attention. For example, if you already know that you can sell a particular home at $65 per square foot, then you can be assured that if you buy it at $60 per square foot or less, you will have definitely made a wise investment.

In addition, you should become familiar with unimproved land values. Knowing the value of a vacant standard-sized residential lot, or a half-acre residential lot, could prove to be very useful during your house-hunting treks.

Besides researching the MLS book, check out open houses on weekends, and read through the local real estate classified ads.

Remember, before you buy, think about selling—could you resell it tomorrow for what you paid for it today?

Buy Property That Can Be Profitably Improved

Does the property have curable defects that can be fixed to enhance its value? One of the best ways to add value to your investment is to make selective, cost-effective renovations. Some of the easiest problems to correct are cosmetic. Often, the sellers just never bothered to properly clean and maintain the property. Frequently, all that's needed is fresh paint, new carpeting, hardwood floor refinishing, and new landscaping. (See Chapter 18.)

Buy Property with Low-Cost Financing

Does the property you're interested in buying have good financing available? One form of good financing would be an existing low-interest assumable loan, or perhaps the sellers will carry back a low-interest loan for their equity in the property. If no seller financing is obtainable, can you originate new financing on good terms? Could you arrange to have the sellers accept FHA or VA financing on the property? If so, you could buy the property using any one of the high-leverage owner-occupied investment strategies discussed in Chapter 3.

Buy Property from Motivated Sellers

Why do you want to buy from motivated sellers? Because a motivated seller is more inclined to be flexible. A motivated seller (often referred to as a "don't wanter") is someone who, because of certain circumstances, is prepared to sell below market value, at favorable terms to the buyer. Such circumstances might include an upcoming divorce, a death in the family, a job relocation, a vacant rental property with associated landlord headaches, financial problems, or another home purchased and ready to be moved into. If you have any combination of these factors, the seller will be extremely motivated, and may be prepared to look at just about any offer.

Conversely, an unmotivated seller can be a real stick in the mud. Unmotivated sellers are inflexible, because there's nothing pushing them to sell. They have a fixed price in mind, and come hell or high water, nobody will ever get the property for less. With so many motivated sellers around, there's just no reason why you should have to deal with an unyielding seller.

Buy Improved Property on a Sizable Piece of Land

Why are you better off with more land? First, you must understand that the improvements on the land—such as the house and garage—have value, but these improvements eventually wear down and become obsolete. It's the land itself that endures and appreciates in value.

Simply put, the more land you have, the more flexibility for expansion you have, which makes your property more desirable, which in turn makes it more valuable. Not long ago, I discovered that the best bargains were to be found investing in homes on large parcels of land. In particular, I began specializing in middle-class homes built on lots that were at least a half-acre in size. The reason was that I could get more for my money, particularly more land. I found that the sellers of these half-acre ministates usually overlooked the precise value of the land. In other words, frequently I could buy a 1,600-square-foot home on a half-acre for about the same price as a similar tract home on one-fourth the amount of land.

It's often difficult to find a bargain among tract homes, because they're all so much alike. Therefore, they are easy to appraise. Everyone within the tract knows what each home is worth because all the properties are about the same.

LANDLORD TALE

Mike and Barbara retired, sold their home, put their furniture in storage, and bought a 34-foot motor home. They traveled full-time throughout the United States, visiting friends and family. Eventually they tired of the travel, and bought a new home along the Mississippi Gulf Coast. They planned to move all the furniture in, and sell the motor home. Unfortunately, they didn't plan on it being difficult to sell. They tried putting it on a recreational vehicle (RV) lot on consignment, but it had no slideouts. New RVs are financed with no money down, but old ones require a down payment. No one wanted a motor home without slide-outs. When they took it off the lot, they had to pay storage fees.

The problem was that they didn't have enough land to park the motor home on. They ended up having to pay $50 a month to store it, when they could have kept it on their property had they had more land.

Conversely, half-acre miniestates are more diverse. Most uninformed owners of these properties tend to underestimate the value of the land, and therein lies the opportunity for the wise investor.

Lack of sufficient land also inhibits the growth of a property. Many potential home owners desire more land so they can later add on to the house. Obviously, if there isn't enough land, expansion of the home will be limited; but, more important, the more land you have, the better off you'll be when it comes time to convert the property to higher use. For instance, if the home you own can eventually be converted to commercial usage, and the land area isn't large enough, the amount of new office space you develop, not to mention the required parking area, will be limited to the small confines available. (Chapter 19 discusses the concept of *land banking*—investing in a home to eventually convert it to a higher commercial use—in more detail.)

Over the long term, especially after 30 or 40 years, the primary worth of the property you purchase will not be in the improvements—rather, it will be in the land itself. The more land that you have, the more useful and desirable it will be, and the more your property will be worth.

Buy Property with a Good Location in a Thriving Market

Chapter 5 discusses the characteristics of a good neighborhood in detail, along with what to avoid. Briefly, here's what you should look for in a good location:

- *Sound economics.* You wouldn't want to live in a neighborhood with a lot of "For Sale" signs. That could be a sign of layoffs, indicating that a local corporation is relocating or going out of business.

- *Low crime rate.* If you want to know the crime rate in a particular area, call the local police department, visit its web site, or check the neighborhood reference library.

- *Quality schools.* Even if you don't require them, it may be important to the buyers should you decide to sell.

- *Amenities.* Being in a good location means that your property is in reasonable proximity to shopping and entertainment.

- *Pride of ownership.* This is representative of a neighborhood full of well-maintained homes with manicured landscapes.

If the property you're interested in buying has these characteristics, you can be assured that the chances are very good that it has a good location in a thriving market.

Become a Great Negotiator

Making a superior investment can be as simple as being a good negotiator. To be in a strong negotiating position, you need to be in a situation in which you don't have to buy. Good negotiators are patient, and are willing to walk away if they cannot get a good deal. They know that many other available properties are on the market. (See Chapter 14 for more details on how to negotiate a winning deal.)

Buy When Others Are Afraid to Buy

Historically, real estate values tend to be cyclical. Their trend is generally upward, although at times—when the economy is in a recession, unemployment rises, and the general consumer outlook is gloomy and somber—demand for housing can seriously decline, with fewer home buyers in the marketplace. Subsequently, the supply of homes for sale increases, while their price tends to fall. Yet, for the shrewd investor, this situation presents a great opportunity. If everybody else is afraid to buy that means you don't have as much competition, and you can choose from a larger inventory of homes for sale at reduced prices.

Buy during Slow Periods

With few exceptions, real estate markets experience predictable busy and slow periods. Just as it wise to buy when real estate prices are depressed, it likewise can be worthwhile to buy during those typical slow and inactive periods.

For instance, the holiday season from Thanksgiving through February is typically a very slow period in most real estate markets. There are fewer potential home buyers in the dead of winter. (Many northern snowbirds are vacationing in the warm South, while others are busy celebrating the holidays with family.) Furthermore, in the colder, northernmost regions of the United States, these slow periods can extend to April. In the warmer year-round places, such as the desert Southwest and Florida, home-buying activity revs up as early as February.

It's advantageous to buy during these slow periods, because there are fewer buyers to contend with. And those who have their properties up for sale during these slow periods tend to be more motivated to sell.

However, this is not to recommend that you look for good buys or expect to find superior investments only during these slow times. In fact, most knowledgeable realty owners sell their property during the most active period of March through early November—which means that in most markets, most of the time, there will be fewer properties to buy during the slow and inactive periods.

Buy Income Properties with Below-Market Rents That Can Be Raised

This, of course, is not a key guideline for buying a home, but it is essential to making the purchase of income property a superior investment. If you can raise rents to market levels within 6 to 12 months, you not only increase your net income without cost, you also substantially increase the property's value.

By following these investment practices, you have a very good chance of making your real estate purchase a superior real estate investment. Now that you have a grasp of the key guidelines for profitable opportunities, you can supplement them by learning another very important skill that could save you a lot of time and money—how to spot a real estate lemon.

How to Spot a Real Estate Lemon

You've probably heard the horror stories. A couple of unwitting home buyers, after committing to a huge mortgage and putting down their life savings, move into what promises to be their ultimate dream home—only to spend their free time battling against a leaky roof, pet odor, and a cracked foundation.

Unfortunately, they've got a real estate lemon.

Problems, of course, vary from lemon to lemon, and, the property inspector will often alert you to trouble before you buy. Unfortunately, more and more home buyers are walking into bottomless money pits without thinking twice.

"People fall in love with homes, but don't get the facts about them. It's like a blind date," says Richard Collier, CEO of Choice Point, which issues CLUE reports. "They have no idea what they'll get."

Ideal dream house or not, you might consider buying another home if the inspection report flags problems with the home's structure or foundation, roof, mold, or pet odor.

Here's what it can cost you:

The Leaky Roof

A roof replacement could cost between $5,000 and $20,000, according to Nancy Knott, a Realtor in Rancho Bernardo, California. When you take a tour, keep an eye out for signs of leaks. Ask how old the roof is. And have your home inspector tell you the roof's life expectancy.

The inspector should check the shingles for wear and tear, says Richard Matzen, president of the American Society of Home Inspectors. If water or snow can pool on the roof, for example, you may need a replacement sooner than you think. Each type of roofing comes with its own wear cycle. Cedar shake or shingle roofs, for example, often have a shorter life cycle than other types of roofing, and can be maintenance-intensive if the wood is cheap.

Jim Hastings, a Realtor in Las Vegas, Nevada, says the roof on his own home, bought two years ago, was 30 years old—a good life span for a shake roof. He knew he could get another 6 to 10 years before he'd have to replace it, but also knew he would need to make sure it was properly treated for it to last.

The Cracked Slab

You might be unaware of what a cracked slab is, but you know it cannot be anything good. It isn't: A cracked slab is a crack in the foundation of your home, Knott said. Ignoring a shaky foundation for many years could lead to eventual collapse.

Cracks come from unstable soil beneath the slab, Matzen explained. Soils may be unstable for different reasons: Along the Pacific Rim, homes may have seismic problems. In the northern and northeastern states frost and frost heaves can lift frozen soil like an ice cube in a tray—and can break a weak foundation in the process.

Moldy Walls

Mold itself has been around for thousands of years. But public concern about mold contamination—and mold claims submitted to home insurers—have skyrocketed over the past few years, according to the Insurance Information Institute.

"Wall mold is common on the West Coast, and in desert states like Arizona and Nevada," Hastings says.

"Years ago, we'd see mold in the house from a water leak, in the corner of the shower, and it was no big deal," says Hastings. "But now there are molds that causes health problems—allergies, or dizzy spells."

Caught early, mold usually can be removed with bleach and water. But if the home is not maintained and the mold becomes hazardous, it must be removed professionally, or *remediated*, Hastings says, to avoid health risks. That could cost $500 to $15,000, depending on its severity.

If your inspection reveals any discoloration on your walls, the inspector will order a mold test, which costs about $300. That will confirm whether you need professional mold removal.

Pet Odors

Rhonda Richardson, a Realtor in northern Virginia, says buyers often underestimate the odor that pets leave in homes, even very clean homes. New owners may need to have carpets replaced and floorboards bleached to remove odors, especially if cats lived in the home years before you.

Any real estate agent worth his salt will have sellers clean their carpets professionally before putting a home up for sale and that often will temporarily overshadow the smell. Then they move out, and you move in. After some moisture and closed-house conditions—say, a few days of rain—the odor could resurface with a vengeance.

The cost of replacing carpeting and flooring can run up to $8,000.

Wood Rot

When you buy a home, your inspector will also check how much wear and tear its wood components—such as outdoor decks and many window structures—have

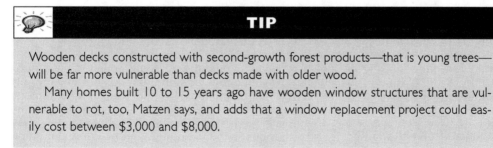

TIP

Wooden decks constructed with second-growth forest products—that is young trees—will be far more vulnerable than decks made with older wood.

Many homes built 10 to 15 years ago have wooden window structures that are vulnerable to rot, too, Matzen says, and adds that a window replacement project could easily cost between $3,000 and $8,000.

endured, Matzen says. "Decks, for example, deteriorate over time and eventually become unstable and unsound. Replacing one costs between $15,000 and $30,000."

A pressure-treated, well-built wood deck can last up to 30 years. A deck built incorrectly, with a species of wood vulnerable to rot, could be out in five to seven years.

Avoiding Problems

"To avoid a real estate lemon, request from the seller a CLUE report on the home. (You can't get one unless you're an insurance professional or you own the home, so you'll have to ask the seller for it.) The report will show you every insurance claim filed on the house over the past five years. Reports are available for 90 percent of the insured homes in the United States," Collier says.

"It takes the mystery out of what the buyer is really buying, and out of obtaining insurance," Collier explains. "If you want to insure the home, and it has too many claims, you may have difficulty getting insurance at a reasonable price."

Finally, if your home inspector does pull up a list of expensive potential problem areas on that house you "must have," don't be afraid to play hardball. "If the [inspector] finds structural problems, I would inform the home owner in writing of the issue and the cost of repairs. The owner can then fix the problem, reduce the expected price, or do nothing," says Kurt Reuss, president of Contractor.com.

If the owner does nothing, go on to greener pastures. This is no time to sink hard-earned money into a bottomless money pit.

CHAPTER 10

Appraisal—How to Determine Value

To be successful buying a home or investing in income property, it's important that you learn to evaluate potential investments accurately. You have to know how to recognize a bargain when you see it.

The best way to learn how to evaluate properties is to review the appraisal methods the professionals use. The following material will assist you in making accurate appraisals on your own, reducing the risk of overpaying when you buy.

The Four Methods of Evaluation

The four methods addressed in this chapter are the *reproduction cost approach*, the *comparable sales approach*, the *capitalization* (income) *approach*, and the *gross-income multiplier approach*. The final opinion of value on a given subject property is determined by weighing the values from each method to arrive at a range of value.

Reproduction Cost Approach

The reproduction cost approach to appraisal determines value in three steps: First, it takes today's cost of replacing all improvements on the property. Second, it deducts a depreciation allowance to determine the current appraised value of the improvements. Third, it adds the current appraised value of the improvements to the land.

As an example, say the subject property is a 10-year-old custom home on a half acre. It has 2,000 square feet of living area, plus a 400-square-foot garage. Additional amenities include a sprinkler system and a swimming pool. Table 10.1 shows a simple replacement cost evaluation.

Now you have to add in the cost of the land. If comparable vacant half-acre lots in that area are selling for $60,000, then you can add this figure to the total cost less depreciation of $138,420 (Table 10.1) to arrive at a final opinion of value at $198,420.

Note that if the subject property needed to have certain items replaced or repaired, those costs would also be reflected in the depreciation allowance.

The Comparable Sales Approach

The comparable sales approach, also referred to as the *market data approach,* is the most common method of appraisal used today. This approach compares the subject property with similar properties that have recently sold in the same area. The valuation of the subject property is adjusted up or down according to certain amenities, such as square-footage differential, quality of construction, inclusion of a garage or pool, and individual location. It is used primarily for evaluating single-family homes and condominiums where a number of similar properties are available for comparison.

Selecting Comparable Properties

A simple application of the comparable sales approach would be to compare the subject property with three similar properties in the same area that have recently sold and that essentially have no meaningful differences. For instance, assume

TABLE 10.1   Simple Replacement Cost Evaluation

Item	Cost
2,000 sq ft (living area) × $65/sq ft	$130,000
400 sq ft (garage) × $22/sq ft	8,800
Cost of pool	14,000
Cost of sprinkler system	1,000
Total cost of improvements	$153,800
10% depreciation for wear and tear since the property is 10 years old	−15,380
Total cost less depreciation	$138,420

that all three comparables sold for $120,000 to $124,000, and had the same square footage and lot size. The subject property is similar in quality of construction and lot size; however, it has a 300-square-foot den and a swimming pool, which the comparables do not have. Therefore, based on this information, the subject property is worth $122,000 plus the value of the additional amenities of a den and swimming pool. You determine that at today's construction costs, a 300-square-foot den would cost $65 per square foot, for a total of $19,500. You also determine that a swimming pool would cost $14,000. So your final opinion of value would be $122,000 + $19,500 for the den + $14,000 for the pool, or an appraised value of $155,500.

Comparing Cost per Square Foot of Living Area

The accuracy of the comparable sales method depends primarily on your ability to locate recently sold properties that are similar to the subject property. Ideally, the comparable properties need to be situated in the same neighborhood and be similar in size, age, amenities, condition, quality of construction, room count, and floor plan.

When you find at least three comparables that have sold within the past six months, you can estimate the value of the subject property by comparing the price per square foot of living area.

For example, you locate three comparables. Comp A has 1,650 square feet, Comp B has 1,750 square feet, and Comp C has 1,890 square feet. These homes sold for the respective prices of $114,675, $122,300, and $129,450. To calculate the selling price per square foot of living area, you divide the selling price of each home by the number of square feet.

$$\text{Comp A } \frac{\$114,675}{1,650 \text{ sq ft}} = \$69.50/\text{sq ft}$$

$$\text{Comp B } \frac{\$122,300}{1,750 \text{ sq ft}} = \$69.89/\text{sq ft}$$

$$\text{Comp C } \frac{\$129,450}{1,890 \text{ sq ft}} = \$68.49/\text{sq ft}$$

If the subject property you're evaluating has 1,800 square feet of living area, then based on comparable square footage costs, you can determine that it will likely sell in the range of $68 to $70 per square foot, or $122,400 to $126,000.

Estimating value based on comparable sales price per square foot will suffice when you need a quick, off-the-cuff estimate. However, to do a more precise appraisal, you need to compare the subject property to the comparable properties on a feature-by-feature basis.

Adjusting for Differences

Once you find three comparables, you have to adjust their values up or down to compensate for the amenities that the subject property may or may not have. Table 10.2 shows an example of the adjustment process.

Your quick estimate based on the average cost per square foot revealed a range of value of $122,400 to $126,000. However, by making precise adjustments in the example in Table 10.2, you arrive at a more accurate range of value of $115,000 and $129,000.

Explaining the Adjustments

The purpose of making adjustments is to equalize the value of the comparables to that of the subject property. You accomplish this by adding or subtracting the value of features to or from the value of the comparables to make them equivalent to the subject property. In other words, you want to know what the comparable would have sold for had it been precisely like the subject property. For example, consider the –$4,000 adjustment to Comp B for sales concessions (Table 10.2). The $124,000 sales price in this deal included the seller's custom-made drapes and a storage shed. Since these are not usually included in a real property sale, the sales price had to be adjusted downward to make it equal in value to that of the subject property, whose sale does not include these amenities.

TABLE 10.2   Adjustment Process

Item	Comp A	Comp B	Comp C
Sales price	$120,000	$124,000	$131,000
Features			
Sales concessions	0	–4,000	0
Financing concessions	–6,000	0	0
Date of sale	0	4,000	0
Location	0	0	–10,000
Floor plan	0	3,000	0
Garage	5,000	0	8,000
Pool, deck, patio	–4,000	–6,000	0
Indicated value of subject	$115,000	$121,000	$129,000

The following are explanations for several other adjustments in Table 10.2:

- *Comp A financing concessions at –$6,000.* In this sale, the sellers carried back a 95 percent mortgage (5-percent down) on the property, which they sold at a 7.5 percent rate of interest. Because investor financing at that time required a 25 percent down payment at an 8.5 percent interest rate on the mortgage, the value of the favorable owner financing must be deducted from the sales price.

- *Comp A garage at + $5,000.* Since the subject property has a double-car garage while Comp A has only a single-car garage, you have to add $5,000 to Comp A to equalize it with the subject property. In other words, had Comp A been built with a two-car garage, it would now be worth $5,000 more.

- *Comp B floor plan at $3,000.* Unlike the subject property, Comp B lacked convenient access to the kitchen from the garage. The garage was built under the home, which meant the owners had to carry groceries up a stairway into the kitchen. If Comp B had a better garage design, it would have likely sold for $3,000 more than it did.

Now you might want to know how you arrive at precise dollar amounts for each of the adjusted features. Simply put, there is no easy answer. As you gain experience in real estate, you get a feel for what certain things are worth. While you're out looking at property, don't be afraid to ask a lot of questions. Find out about construction costs and lot values. As you're viewing different properties, make a list of features that make a difference. Ask the Realtor or a building contractor what they think the added feature is worth. Then weigh their opinions against your judgement to arrive at a value for a particular feature.

Capitalization Approach

The capitalization approach to appraisal, also referred to as the *income approach*, is primarily used to determine the value of income property. It uses the net operating income (NOI) of the subject property, which is then "capitalized" to arrive at fair market value.

To determine NOI, first calculate the gross income of the property at 100 percent occupancy, then deduct all operating expenses, including allowances for bad debts and vacancies. Now the resulting NOI has to be capitalized to arrive at fair market value.

The rate of return on invested capital is called *capitalization*, or the *cap rate*. It is defined as the rate of return—expressed as a percentage—that's considered reasonable to expect for an investment. The appraiser arbitrarily determines a cap rate, of 8 to 12 percent that must be adjusted based on the going rate for that type of property. The appraiser determines the cap rate within the 8 to 12 percent range by considering the risk of the investment, the type of property, and the quality of the income.

For example, an investor who was considering investing in a high-risk area (high-crime slum neighborhood) would expect a higher rate of return on the investment. Therefore, a cap rate of 12 percent would be selected. The same investor, would expect a lower rate of return on an investment in a low-risk prime area of town, especially since there would be more appreciation in the prime area. Thus, an 8 percent cap rate would be selected. For an in-between area (average), a 10 percent cap rate would be chosen.

Figure 10.1 shows an example of an income and expense statement that will help you in appraising income properties.

For a better understanding of the income and expense analysis, each numbered item is defined as follows:

1. *Gross annual rental income.* This is the total annual rent the property would earn at 100 percent occupancy.

2. *Other income.* This item is reserved for additional income other than rent.

3. *Vacancy and credit losses.* This is established by the going rate for similar properties in the neighborhood. The national average is 5 percent, with good areas about 3 percent, and bad areas as high as 10 percent.

4. *Trash removal.* This is the total annual cost to remove trash from the property.

5. *Property taxes.* This is the actual real property taxes for the current year.

6. *Insurance.* This is the total amount for all necessary forms of insurance. If the insurance is part of a blanket coverage for several properties, then you must allocate the expense for each separate property.

7. *Utilities.* This is a figure for a full year's operation, including gas, water, and electricity.

8. *Business license.* Certain cities require a business license to operate apartment buildings. Use the actual cost for the entire year of operation.

9. *Advertising.* This includes the total annual cost of newspaper advertising and the cost to make rental signs for the property.

10. *Resident manager.* The total cost of employing the resident manager goes under this item. If you use the services of a management company, that cost can also be included under this item.

FIGURE 10.1   Sample income and expense statement.

Description: 18-unit apartment building (9 1-BR, 9 2-BR)		
9 1-BR @ $500 per month rent		$ 4,500
9 2-BR @ $650 per month rent		5,850
Gross monthly rent		10,350
Net laundry equipment		360
Gross monthly income		10,710
Annual gross income		128,520
1. Gross annual rental income ($10,350 × 12)		124,200
2. Other income (laundry: $360 × 12)		4,320
3. Less vacancy and credit loss (5%)	$ 6,210	
Less annual operating expenses:		
4. Trash removal	480	
5. Property taxes	18,000	
6. Insurance	4,200	
7. Utilities	5,220	
8. Business liscense	35	
9. Advertising	480	
10. Resident manager ($650 × 12)	7,800	
11. Reserve for placement	6,210	
12. Supplies	240	
13. Total operating expenses including vacancy and credit losses	$48,875	−48,875
14. Net operating income		79,645
15. Less loan payments (P&I)		−62,200
16. Gross spendable income (cash flow)		17,445
17. Principal payment (equity buildup)		4,200
18. Gross equity income		21,645
19. Less depreciation		−21,200
20. Real estate taxable income		$ 445

11. *Reserve for replacement.*   This item covers a reserve fund for all repairs and replacement. These include furniture, drapes, carpet, and all major equipment (elevators, water heaters, pool equipment, and so on). A fair estimate is 5 percent of gross annual rental income.

12. *Supplies.*   Rent forms, cleaning supplies, and all miscellaneous items are included in this category.

13. *Total operating expenses.*   This item includes a summation of all operating expenses before loan payments. As a rule of thumb, annual operating

expenses as a percentage of gross annual income should be in a range of 37 to 51 percent, with 40 percent being average.

14. *Net operating income.* This figure is the result of deducting total operating expenses from gross annual income. This figure represents what the property would earn if purchased for cash, free and clear of any loans. This item is also used to determine capitalized value by dividing a suitable cap rate into net operating income.

15. *Loan payments.* This figure includes principal and interest. The principal portion of the payment is added under Item 17.

16. *Gross spendable income.* This figure is the result of deducting annual debt service from NOI, or the actual cash (cash flow) you'll have left over after expenses and debt service.

17. *Principal payment.* This is equity buildup, or that portion of the loan payment that applies toward the principal of the loan.

18. *Gross equity income.* This figure is the result of adding annual equity payments to the gross spendable income.

19. *Depreciation.* As a general rule, 80 percent of the property's cost can be depreciated for income tax purposes; the remaining 20 percent is allocated to the land, which cannot be depreciated.

20. *Real estate taxable income.* This figure is the result of deducting depreciation from gross equity income.

The income and expense statement is very important, because the numbers it reveals predict how much you're going to earn. As discussed earlier, total operating expenses are usually in a range of 37 to 51 percent. Newer buildings fall within the lower range, while older buildings are in the higher range, owing to the higher maintenance costs inherent with older, less efficient equipment.

The NOI in Item 14 of the income and expense statement is the figure that will be capitalized in order to determine appraised value.

Based on an average cap rate of 10 percent and an NOI of $79,625 (see Item 14), the result is an appraised value of $796,250. But now take notice of what happens to the appraised value when different cap rates are applied to the same NOI.

If you apply a cap rate of 8 percent to the same NOI, you get the following results: $79,625 ÷ 0.08 = $995,312. And if you apply a cap rate of 12 percent to the same NOI, you see the following: $79,625 ÷ 0.12 = $663,541.

Note the substantial difference in appraised values using different cap rates—a range from a high of $995,312 to a low of $663,541. In other words, to earn an 8 percent return using an NOI of $79,625, an investor would have to pay $995,312 for the property; to earn 12 percent, the investor would have to pay $663,541.

Finally, look what happens to the appraised value of the subject property when you simply raise the rents $50 per month on each of the 18 units. The end result is adding $900 per month, or $10,800 annually, to gross collectable income. And presuming that total operating expenses remain the same, at a 10 percent cap rate you actually add $108,000 in value simply by raising the rents $50. This is why it's so important to invest in income properties that are underrented, because you're actually buying built-in value.

Gross-Income Multiplier Approach

This method of determining value cannot be classified as a true professional approach to appraisal, yet brokers and investors often find it useful as a quick off-the-cuff calculation to see whether a property deserves further attention. The gross-income multiplier offers only a ballpark estimate. It does not reflect net income or expenses, nor is it reliable in determining true value.

You'll often see newspaper advertisements for income property that state "8 times gross" or "5.7 times gross." This means that the sales price of that particular property is 8 or 5.7 times the gross income (i.e., income before deductions for expenses). For example, if gross income is $30,000, then the selling price would be $240,000 at 8 times gross, or $171,000 at 5.7 times gross.

Similar to the capitalization rate, the gross-income multiplier is determined by the appraiser within a range of values, taking into consideration the going rate for the area. This going rate is normally 4 to 12, the lower number being for the less-desirable locations.

If the gross income equals $30,000 per year, you have the following valuations using different multipliers:

Area	Multiplier	Value
Worst	4	$120,000
Average	7	210,000
Best	12	360,000

Now that you're familiar with the four methods of appraisal, it's time to make some important conclusions.

Conclusions

The number-one priority in making an accurate appraisal, is to know the market where you plan to invest—not only the prices properties have sold for; you should also be informed regarding asking prices. Without adequate knowledge of the market, you'll find it impossible to precisely determine value. Start by doing your homework. Obtain a multiple listing service (MLS) book from your friendly real estate agent and read it over. Analyze recent sales.

The most important factor in quickly determining the value of improved property is the price per square foot. From your research with the MLS book, determine the price range per square foot that property in your area sells for. This information is often all you need to determine whether a property deserves further attention. For example, if you know that you can sell a house at $65 per square foot, you know it's a solid buy if you can get it for $50 per square foot or less.

Besides studying the MLS book, you can also become familiar with local values by checking out open houses on weekends, and by reading through the local real estate classified ads.

The greatest risk of investing in real estate is paying too much for it. Carefully analyze the market before you buy. Well-informed investors know a good buy when they see one, and conversely, are fully aware if a property is overpriced.

THE SOURCES

So far this book has discussed what to look for in a realty investment and how to finance and appraise it, along with the strategic how-tos of maximizing the value of your investment. This part focuses on where to find your house. A supply of available investment properties can be found by surfing the Internet, scanning the local newspapers and your realtor's multiple listing service, locating the countless HUD and VA repossessions, or seeking out a lender's bargain-priced foreclosures and bidding at special auctions. These special sources are presented in the hope that among them you will find your dream home (your diamond in the rough, so to speak), or your ideal secondary real estate investment.

CHAPTER 11

Where to Find Your Diamond in the Rough

Sources of potentially good realty investments are almost boundless; you only have to know where to look. Nevertheless, if it was easy to locate and purchase bargain-priced real estate, everyone would be doing so. Since it is not, you need perseverance to locate and buy the property that's right for you.

On average, two-thirds of all the real estate for sale is listed with a Realtor. But you also have a wide selection from other sources, such as properties for sale by owners (FSBOs), HUD repossessions, special auctions, and various other types of foreclosure properties.

Newspaper Advertisements

You'll find homes and multiunit buildings listed in the classified section of your local newspaper under the column "Real Estate for Sale." Start by circling with a pen the ads for properties that appear interesting, then cut them out and staple them to the left-hand margin of an 8.5- × 11-inch piece of plain paper. Now you have adequate space to make notes adjacent to the stapled-down advertisements.

With FSBOs, you will have to deal directly with the owners. Begin by calling the numbers in the cut-out advertisements. Inquire into the available financing, if any, and the down-payment requirements. Ask about the square footage, lot size, condition of the property, and reason for selling. Get as much information as you can. Then, if the property still sounds promising, make an appointment with the owner to visit it.

Working with a Realtor

A top-notch real estate agent is a priceless asset. Competent agents look out for your interests. They can make properties available you would not otherwise have access to. When you do locate the property that deserves an offer to purchase, your agent will present the offer and help to negotiate the final agreement with the seller. Once a satisfactory agreement is reached, the agent will follow the transaction through its normal channels, securing any loose ends that might otherwise jeopardize the final closing.

To work effectively, the agent needs to know exactly what you're looking for. Therefore, give your agent the specifics of precisely what you want in a property. For instance, a single-level three-bedroom, two-bath with about 1,800 square feet of living space. It should also be a fixer-upper priced in a range from $120,000 to $150,000. Now the agent has specific guidelines as to what it is you're looking for. And with this information at hand, the agent can prepare a list of properties that fit your specifications.

An agent has access to the multiple-listing service (MLS), which covers every property listed for sale with a Realtor in your area. It's the agent's responsibility to keep abreast of what's on the market and to be looking for property you will be interested in. Furthermore, the agent possesses the key to the lock box that opens the door to all the MLS properties.

Real estate agents who belong to the MLS have access to the MLS book, which is normally published every other week, maintaining up-to-date information on all listed properties. It's an invaluable tool for potential home buyers and investors. As often urged before, once you get to know an agent, ask to borrow last week's MLS book so you can study the listings. (Technically, lending out MLS books to nonmembers is against MLS rules; however, it's done all the time.)

Once you have a recent MLS book, go through it carefully, noticing properties of interest. On a separate sheet of paper, note the address and the MLS page number. Then, later, when you call on or drive by the property, you can make notes on the reference sheet. Also, important information regarding recent sales prices is usually listed in the back portion of the MLS book, and this information will help you to get a feel for values in the local market.

Dealing with the FSBO

As explained earlier, the FSBO (pronounced "fizzbo") is a property that's for sale by owner. The owners are attempting to sell their property without the assistance of a real estate broker, usually to save the cost of a sales commission. These sellers are at a distinct disadvantage in the marketplace, because they don't have the exposure of the multiple-listing service, nor do they have the professional assistance of many Realtors seeking buyers for their property. Historically, about 85 percent of FSBOs end up being converted to contractual listings with realty agents. Sellers of converted FSBOs often find that the commission they wanted to save ends up being money well spent, when they get the assistance they need to finally sell the property.

If you come across an inexperienced FSBO seller and you're unprepared, without purchase contracts or disclosures, it would be a good idea to seek professional help. Consult with an experienced real estate broker or attorney for assistance in getting the property under contract and following it through all the way to closing.

If you're interested in a particular FSBO and you've been working with a Realtor, have the Realtor contact the seller. If the seller is unwilling to pay your Realtor a commission, then you should pay it. A 3 percent commission would be an equitable fee, and is what the Realtor would have earned under a typical listing agreement.

Internet Shopping

Modern home buyers and real estate investors not only scan MLS books and read newspaper advertisements, they also surf the Internet to look for properties. Thousands of real estate-related web sites now list properties for sale. Internet surfers can access the Realtor's multiple-listing service at www.realtor.com.

There's also a growing industry of network providers who make available specialized listings of everything from foreclosure properties to FSBOs. You can find virtually all the real estate-related information that once only was available from newspaper ads, Realtors, public records, and other sources. (See Appendix B for a listing of useful web sites.)

Federal Government Auctions

Besides VA and HUD repossessions (covered in Chapter 13), each year the federal government auctions off all types of seized and surplus real estate, including homes, apartment buildings, office complexes, multiacre estates, and undeveloped land. The most active sellers are the Internal Revenue Service (IRS), the Government Service Administration (GSA), and the Federal Deposit Insurance Corporation (FDIC).

You can find a list of available properties, along with the required sales procedures, at the following web sites:

Federal Deposit Insurance Corporation, www.fdic.gov/buying/owned/real /index

Government Services Administration, http://propertydisposal.gsa.gov /propforsale

Internal Revenue Service, www.gov/auctions/irs

Sheriff's Sales

A sheriff's sale (or judicial sale) involves legally mandated property sales that are the result of foreclosures, property tax liens, civil lawsuit judgments, and bankruptcy proceedings.

When property owners reach a certain stage of delinquency on a mortgage, the lender and the circuit court of the county notify the owners that they can redeem their delinquency by making the mortgage payments, along with any due penalties of interest. If the owners do not pay, they are then considered to be in default of the loan, which means the mortgaged property will go to a sheriff's sale. These sales are conducted by order of the circuit court, and are held in designated municipal buildings or in title company offices.

Interested buyers are required to bring a cashier's check for 10 percent of the price of the property being acquired. Therefore, if a property is going to be offered at $60,000, but you could bid as high as $90,000, you'll need a cashier's check for $9,000. The balance of the amount owed must be paid in full within 24 hours of the sale. Typically, the sale will need to be confirmed in front of a judge within four weeks of the sale, which gives the owners in default one last chance to redeem the property. Therefore, the successful buyer of the property in default does not own it until the judge's confirmation of the sale.

Bear in mind that property at a sheriff's sale is sold strictly as is, and you have to be wary that you're not assuming obligations to pay many years of delinquent property taxes or other liens attached to the property. You have got to know exactly what you're getting, which means you have to know how to research the title before you buy.

Attend a couple of sheriff's sales before you become an active participant. This will give you a chance to see how they are conducted and become familiar with the procedures before bidding yourself.

Probate and Estate Sales

Probate and estate sales offer the bargain hunter another great opportunity to purchase undervalued real estate. When property owners die, their property is often sold to satisfy the mortgage lender and other creditors.

Probate Sales

To purchase real estate through probate, you submit a bid through the estate's executor, who is commonly an attorney. All bids are then reviewed by the probate judge assigned to the estate. Depending on state and local statutes, the probate judge can then choose a bid for approval, or reopen the bidding if the opening bids prove unsatisfactory.

Bidders at probate sales need a lot of patience and perseverance, due to the common delays and detailed legal procedures. Judges exercise a lot of discretion in deciding whether to accept a probate bid. I know of a probate sale that took place in a neighborhood of $180,000 homes. The probate administrator listed the house for sale at $145,000. Such a reasonable price attracted a wide array of bids, from a low of $135,000 up to a high of $149,000. Seventy days later, the probate judge reviewed the bids, announced the high bid of $149,000, and then reopened the bidding to solicit additional offers. In the end, the judge accepted a bid of $159,000 from a bidder who wasn't even present at the first round of bidding. When it was all over, the successful bidder did end up with a bargain-priced property—presuming that the property was in good condition and didn't need a lot of repairs.

Unlike forced sales, which are usually held on the courthouse steps, at probate sales prospective buyers are usually allowed to enter and inspect the subject property before submitting a bid. To find out more about probate sales in your area, make some inquiries with the clerk of the county court, or talk with a probate lawyer. In addition, peruse the announcements of upcoming auctions in the classified sections of local newspapers.

Estate Sales

In special situations, it's not necessary to have a probate sale. You may be able to buy an estate's assets directly from the executor of the estate or the heirs. Experienced buyers who are familiar with estate sales follow the obituary notices in the newspapers and will contact the executor of the estate, then attempt to purchase the property before it's listed with a Realtor. To make a successful proposal under such circumstances, it is recommended that you assume a compassionate demeanor.

Bargain-priced property can often be found at estate sales, because the heirs simply want to cash out and be done with the whole ordeal. That's because they usually need money to pay off creditors, estate taxes, or a mortgage. This is especially true when out-of-town heirs are anxious to liquidate a vacant property, inasmuch as they are unwilling to patiently wait for a top-dollar buyer.

Auctions

Quite often, especially during recessionary times, sellers decide to liquidate their properties through private auctions. Such a time occurred in California during the mid 1990s, when banks and savings and loans pooled their real estate owned (REO), and jointly auctioned off hundreds of properties at a time. New-home developers also frequently liquidate their closeout inventory with an auction, so they can devote their time and effort to the next new housing project. At other times, a home builder in financial difficulty might use an auction to stimulate home sales in order to avoid bankruptcy.

Preparing for an Auction

It is recommended that you attend an auction just for the experience, to see how auctions function. It's very interesting to watch the professional auctioneers and the bidders contend with one another.

Here's how you can properly prepare for an auction:

- *Have an established maximum bid price.*   Keep your maximum bid price in mind, and don't get caught up in the captive frenzy that auctioneers like to create. You're looking for a bargain—not market value. Don't let the auctioneer's boosters bamboozle or intimidate you into bidding higher.

- *Be sure to thoroughly inspect the property.*   Before the auction, the auctioneers will schedule open houses for the properties to be sold. If you're unable to attend, contact a Realtor and request a personal showing. (Most auctioneers cooperate with real estate brokers.) At times, auction properties sell dirt-cheap because they're dilapidated old structures waiting to be torn down. Or they may suffer from other types of incurable defects. Never bid on property at an auction unless you or your inspector have thoroughly looked over the property.

- *Carefully appraise the property.*   Evaluate the recent selling prices of at least three comparable properties in the area of the subject property. Don't rely on list prices. The only way you can acquire a bargain and avoid overpaying is to have precise knowledge of property values in the area you're interested in.

- *Review the accompanying paperwork.*   Before the auction begins, ask to see the important documents that pertain to the property—the lot survey, the property tax statements, the legal description, and the purchase agreement you'll be required to sign.

- *Come with a sufficient deposit.*   Eligible auction bidders are required to show proof of funds (amount varies, but 10 percent of the successful bid price in the form of a cashier's check is common) and register with the auctioneer before the auction begins. Registrants are then issued bid cards which make them authorized bidders. Bids made without an authorized bid card will not be accepted.

- *Learn what type of deed the successful bidder will get.* Under a warranty deed, the seller guarantees clear title, subject to specific exceptions. Other kinds of deeds transfer fewer warranties. Before you accept a deed, make sure you're aware of its limitations, such as easements, encroachments, or recorded liens. Your best protection is to buy title insurance. And if for any reason the property's title is uninsurable, get an opinion of title from a reputable real estate lawyer.

- *Get all the details of the sale.* Find out if financing is available at the sale. Frequently the auctioneers will have financing prearranged on some or all of their properties. If this is the case, get the details of the terms and what it takes to qualify. Should you be required to arrange your own financing, find out how much time you're allowed to do so. Private auctions differ from government agency property auctions, in that payment in cash is not required. And find out whether the properties are being offered under absolute terms or subject to a reserve price. Under absolute terms, there is no minimum bid requirement: The property is sold regardless of how low the highest bidder's offer might be. Under a reserve price, the highest bid must exceed a pre-arranged minimum price, or the property is removed from sale.

How to Find Auctions

Many auctioneers advertise future auctions in local newspapers and occasionally in national newspapers, such as the *Wall Street Journal*. Also, part of their advertising strategy is to add the names of those who register to their mailing lists. Auction companies strive not only to attract the maximum number of prospective buyers, but also to allure huge crowds in order to instill a festive mood of anxious anticipation and excitement.

The Yellow Pages list local auctioneers. Nationally known auction companies, such as Hudson and Marshall, J.P. King, NRC Auctions, and Ross Dove and Company, hold large-scale local auctions. Even if you don't intend to bid, it's a good idea to enjoy the experience of a large-scale auction. Then, if later on you do decide to bid at an auction, you'll know what to expect.

Lease/Purchase Option (for Investors)

Consider leasing a home while the owner gives you an option to purchase it. To acquire the best bargain on a lease/purchase option, don't look exclusively to sellers who advertise them. It's more difficult to find a good deal here, because the sellers are trying to retail their properties. Rather, seek out people who are trying to rent their vacant properties. Or look for FSBO sellers in the "Homes for Sale" classified ads of your local newspaper. After you contact them, make a lease/purchase option proposal. Most often, the best lease/purchase sellers are those who never considered the notion until you proposed it.

In the following situation, Suzanne Brangham accidently stumbled into her investment career with a lease/purchase option experience. Perhaps you can benefit from her successful experience. From her book *Housewise* (p. 39), here's her story:

> While searching for the ideal career, I was also looking for a place to live. The building was making a painful transition from rental to condominiums. Units were for sale or rent. But sales were practically nonexistent.
>
> With my head held high, preliminary plans and a budget tucked under my arm, I decided to make the manager an offer he couldn't refuse.
>
> I told him that in lieu of paying the $800-a-month rent that was being asked for a two-bedroom, two-bath unit, I would renovate the entire apartment. I would agree to spend $9,600 for labor and materials, the equivalent of a full year of rent payments. Along with a 12-month lease, I also requested an option to buy the unit at its $45,000 asking price.

After three months, Brangham was on her way to owning the unit. She purchased the renovated condo at the predetermined option price of $45,000. Then, on the same day, she sold the condo to a buyer for $85,000. She ended up netting $23,000, after deducting renovation costs, closing costs, and the Realtor's sales commission.

Today, after investing in 23 homes and 71 properties over the past 20 years, Brangham has not just reached a pinnacle of financial independence, but is a nationally known speaker and best-selling author. In *Housewise,* she reveals stories from her career and her renovation endeavors. It's a wonderful book, loaded with profit-making ideas about buying and renovating fixer-uppers.

CHAPTER 12

How to
Buy Foreclosures

If you're interested in owning distressed real estate, you'll have the choice of investing in any one of three phases through which foreclosure property may evolve.

Reasons for Foreclosure

What exactly is *foreclosure?* A definition appropriate for present purposes would be as follows: It is a lawful method of enforcing payment by taking and selling the secured property when a loan is substantially delinquent. Foreclosure is the termination of rights of an owner of real property that is secured by a deed of trust or mortgage, applicable when payment of the debt was not made when it was due.

Why do so many home owners allow their homes to be foreclosed on? Believe it or not, the federal government is the inadvertent culprit in the majority of single-family dwelling foreclosures. Due to federal home assistance programs, such as FHA-insured loans and VA-guaranteed loans, which offer very lenient terms, some recent home owners don't have much to lose if they cannot meet their mortgage obligations and are foreclosed on. Under these government-backed programs the buyers merely have to come up with nominal closing costs, and they can often move in for an investment of less than $1,000. All that's required is a fair credit rating and steady employment. (This is not to criticize these helpful

---

NOTEWORTHY

Due to the huge expanse of the United States, complicated further by the fact that half the states use a mortgage as a security instrument when lending money on real estate, while the other half utilize a deed of trust, it's impossible to set down the standards of practice for the entire nation in a book of this nature. Although the terms are very similar, and for the most part laws regarding foreclosure and real estate are somewhat uniform nationally, it is sound judgment to consult a trusted real estate attorney or professional in this field to answer specific questions regarding your area. Furthermore, for the purpose of clarity, this chapter will essentially refer to a *deed of trust* and the foreclosure proceedings regarding it, instead of continually describing both it and a mortgage, when each instrument is mentioned. For all practical purposes, the instruments are very similar. The only major difference is their method of enforcement during foreclosure proceedings.

---

housing assistance programs. They are definitely a boon to many families who normally could not afford adequate housing. The point is merely that a lack of adequate home-owner equity causes the majority of foreclosures.)

In most cases it takes years for buyers of this type to build up equity in the home. If poor financial times come along within two years of the purchase, they feel they don't have that much to lose, since they bought the home with such a small down payment. Their attitude might be that they have simply paid rent during that period, or that they have plenty of time to catch up on the payments. If the loan is government backed, they can often get away with missing loan payments for up to eight or nine months before foreclosure occurs, because it takes two to three months just to get the default recorded. During this period they'll receive late notices, payment demands and a variety of collection devices. Only if they totally ignore these will a default be recorded.

By that time the minimum amount of equity acquired in the property will have been consumed by the delinquency charges. As time passes, the actual foreclosure proceedings will be held, and they will have likely moved away, leaving the house for that particular government agency to take over. This abandonment, as unappealing as it may be, can be your gain.

The Three Phases of Foreclosure

The first phase is the default period. The second phase is the actual foreclosure sale. The third phase occurs if the sale is unsuccessful, and the property reverts back to the lender and becomes real estate owned (REO).

The Default Period

During this first phase, foreclosure proceedings are initiated with a notice of default, after the owner has been sent numerous requests for payment and written threats of eventual foreclosure, should the delinquency not be immediately corrected. The notice of default is recorded at the request of the lender by the trustee, which, in effect, gives notice to the public that the loan is in default. The actual recording of the notice takes place at the county recorder's office in the county in which the property is located. It denotes essential data pertaining to the trust deed, the amount in arrears, the address of the property, and the date of recording.

In the state of California, the trustor (owner of the property), has 90 days from the date of recording the notice of default to reinstate the loan (to make the loan current by paying all payments in arrears, including any late charges or other deficiencies). The law requires the lender to accept the trustor's reinstatement money during this 90-day period.

If the trustor fails to reinstate the loan within the reinstatement period, the lender has the right to notify the trustee to publish a notice of trustee's sale on the ninety-first day. This notice states that the subject property will be sold at public auction to the highest bidder at a given date and place in that county. The actual date of sale will be at least 21 days after the 90-day reinstatement period.

During this 21-day period, referred to as the *publication period*, the lender has the right to refuse reinstatement of the loan, and can demand payment in full of the entire unpaid balance. Often, lenders will allow reinstatement during the publication period, depending on the history of the loan, or how the current market interest rate compares with the rate attached to the loan in arrears. If the rate on the loan is far below the current market rate, the lender may wish to proceed with the foreclosure sale and relend the proceeds out at a higher rate.

It is during the 90-day default period that the alert investor can enter into negotiations with the troubled owner and acquire the property through various means, as is detailed later in this chapter.

The Foreclosure Sale

The second phase is the actual foreclosure sale, and it occurs if the borrower is unable to reinstate the loan. The sale will be a public auction held by the lender, or an agent of the lender, at which the property will be sold to the highest bidder. Proceeds from the sale will be disbursed to all lien holders in order of the priority of their recorded loans. This particular phase of the foreclosure process requires that the successful bidder pay the full bid price for the property in cash (or by cashier's check).

The REO Phase

The third phase in the foreclosure process occurs only when the auction fails to attract a buyer at the minimum bid price or higher. The property then reverts to the lender, the party that actually begins the bidding with the minimum acceptable bid. If there are no other bidders, the property is placed on the lender's books at the cost of the outstanding loan, including all late fees, trustee fees, and costs associated with the foreclosure sale.

In most cases, of course, the lender is a bank or savings and loan. The property is now included in the lender's portfolio of real estate owned holdings.

It is at this phase of foreclosure that the distressed property offers a variety of opportunities to the wise foreclosure investor. Because of my experience in directly managing over $6 million worth of foreclosure property for a major California savings and loan during the mid-1970s, I can now offer you some advice from the inside looking out.

Advantages of Buying REO Property

There is one aspect of REO property that makes it a superior investment compared to buying at the other two stages of foreclosure. In the process of acquiring the property, the bank will clear it of all outstanding liens, clear the title, and pay the back taxes, if any. The lender owns it free and clear. If you can acquire REO, it will be free of all liens.

There are other advantages to investing in REO. You can usually purchase it with a small down payment, and occasionally for virtually no money down. Furthermore, you can usually finance your purchase at interest rates that are below market rates, because the lending institution itself is also the seller, and is usually eager to unload the property. It's often possible to defer the first principal and interest payment for one to three months after acquiring title to the property. And in some cases, it may be possible to accomplish some refurbishment while you're in escrow. Finally, the bank will usually handle most of the closing costs, since institutional lenders usually have escrow facilities available in house. Taking these advantages, of course, will depend primarily on your relationship with the person responsible for disposing of the REO.

Dealing with REO Managers

To be successful at investing in REO, it's necessary to find a technique for dealing with the bankers who own it. This can be difficult because, surprisingly enough, there's a lot of public interest in the purchase of foreclosure property, and many potential buyers are constantly inquiring over the phone, although the majority are unsuccessful.

Typically, an inquiry from an uninformed solicitor takes the form of a phone call to the bank or savings and loan, asking if there are any foreclosure properties available. So many people phone in, the banks now usually give a stock reply: "Sorry, nothing available."

REO will usually be sold through an established real estate broker, or directly to known buyers, or even to personal friends of the banker. Thus, if you want to invest in REO, it's your job to approach the REO department in person, and to meet its manager. Establishing such a personal relationship at a lending institution is the only viable method of getting into the REO business.

Besides giving me the opportunity to manage several millions in foreclosure property, one of our most profitable investments was a 20-unit apartment building acquired from an REO department. At first glance, it did not appear so desirable. Seven of the 20 units were vacant, and in dire need of repair. The exterior walls were inscribed with a variety of grafitti, highlighting key members of local neighborhood gangs who nightly spray-painted their memoirs in assorted ghastly colors. Due to the numerous vacancies, complicated by the fact that other tenants hadn't paid rent in quite some time, this particular REO department was anxious to sell.

The lenders had earlier foreclosed on this building with an outstanding loan balance of approximately $110,000, which they now agreed would be the selling price. We made a full-price offer, agreeing to $11,000 down, with the balance financed for 30 years at 8.5 percent interest. The seller accepted, contingent on our buying the property in as-is condition, in which the seller does not warrant anything, and will do no repairs whatsoever. Because we knew that when the property was refurbished, with the deadbeats evicted and the vacant units filled with good paying tenants, it would be worth twice what we paid for it, we were anxious to take possession of this potential gold mine. Within two months of the closing on this 20-unit building, once the vacant units were refurbished and occupied, we began clearing $1,000 a month in cash flow. Not bad, considering such a small down payment of $11,000.

Opportunities like this are few and far between, although they do exist. But they can only be found by the specialist who is continually seeking these hidden opportunities.

To cite another example, another time while I was managing foreclosures, an interesting and timely event occurred. One day, a gentleman named Fred walked into my office and inquired if we had any property for sale. Earlier that morning I had been informed that we had just taken back, through foreclosure, a run-down 16-unit building—and what a catastrophe it was. One of the tenants had just called to complain that heavy rains were coming through the roof, and that the entire ceiling in her apartment was about to cave in. The beauty of his timing was that Fred, who seemingly appeared out of nowhere in my office on that rainy morning, just happened to be a roofing contractor.

I told Fred about the available 16-unit building, which was presently being inundated by a major storm. He said he'd drive out and take a look at it, and see what he could do. Later that day, he returned and said that there was a three-inch-wide by 15-foot-long gap in the roof, and water was gushing into the building. He had laid a polyethylene cover over the gap, then masked it down, which would temporarily keep the water out.

Because the building would obviously require much repair, and we would prefer not to own it, I offered it to Fred for what the company had in it, an outstanding loan balance of $72,000. He accepted, and both parties were very satisfied with the transaction. My company sold a real loser, and by doing so was able to avoid sinking a lot of money into a dilapidated building. But Fred had the opportunity to make something of the property by investing a little money and some elbow grease. Besides, the savings and loan I worked for was not in the business of investing in real estate. It's primary function was to take in deposits, then relend those deposits to borrowers at a profit.

The point is that profitable opportunities do not simply grow on trees, waiting to be picked like ripe plums. You have to make a concentrated effort to locate and develop these opportunities. Otherwise, those who are making the effort will buy those profitable opportunities right out from under your nose, while you're waiting around watching the plums grow.

Buying from Distressed Owners

Every year in almost every community, hundreds of property owners end up in some kind of financial difficulty. Whatever the reason, whether it's job loss, divorce, accident, illness, or other difficulty, it inevitably renders people unable to make their mortgage payments. If they fail to resolve their problems when default is inevitable, they end up facing foreclosure on their property.

It is at this point, during the default period, that the shrewd investor not only can help the troubled owners salvage their credit record and part of their home equity, but can also acquire a bargain. With time running out and lacking money to alleviate the pressure, distressed property owners may be willing to accept a fast sale—one that salvages their credit and gives the investor a property priced at less than market value.

Owners Must Be Approached Sympathetically

Property owners who are facing foreclosure have to be dealt with in a certain way. You have to understand that over the past few months they have had to contend with all kinds of financial difficulty, including phone calls from annoying bill collectors and bothersome mail threatening foreclosure on their home. To make matters worse, they've likely been pestered by countless fore- closure sharks who recently attended get-rich-quick foreclosure seminars. These troubled owners are probably very depressed, perhaps out of work, and living with the shame of failure. Due to this distressing situation, they are going to be difficult to deal with.

Nevertheless, to be successful in dealing with these distraught owners, you have to approach them sympathetically. Be sensitive to the problem at hand, with the objective of developing a mood of mutual assistance.

You should refrain from using the phone until after actually meeting with the owners. This will avoid the potential for being brushed off easily over the phone. A personal visit not only is more businesslike, it will also give you the op- portunity to look over the home.

Begin your approach with a simple introduction. Tell them who you are and why you're there. Mention that you have discovered through your sources that their property might be for sale. If the property is in fact for sale, you can imme- diately get the details. However, should the troubled owners not currently have the property up for sale, a different approach has to be used.

Timing Is Important

It's important that you understand that investment in foreclosure property is a patient business. There's much continuing effort and analysis of pertinent data required, in order to keep abreast of available opportunities.

Time is on your side, as the investor. Time works against the troubled own- ers facing foreclosure. The pressure is on them to remedy their troubled situa- tion, or else they will lose their property along with their good credit rating. You want to remind the property owners that you're interested in making a good deal for yourself, while at the same time helping them realize some cash and salvage their credit rating.

Keep in mind, too, that under the stress of foreclosure, owners often dis- guise the truth about certain matters. Understandably so, as they are facing the loss of home and property. Therefore, it's imperative that you verify all details of what the troubled owners say. While you're in their presence, it's essential that you keep the dialogue going to find out as much as possible about their financial condition, as well as the condition of the property.

Should the troubled owners miraculously remedy their financial condition and bring the delinquent payments up to date, be happy for them. But at the same time, continue to keep in touch with them, because now they are faced with an additional problem—how to keep up with the existing house payments, plus paying back the additional funds they borrowed to remedy the initial crisis.

Chances are, if you continue to keep in touch with them, the opportunity to make a deal on the property will arise once again.

The following bits of dialogue are suggested conversational openers that you can use to stimulate negotiations with the troubled owners:

"If you'll allow me to make a complete financial analysis of the property, I can be back within 24 hours with a firm offer that will solve your present financial dilemma."

"By assisting you during these troubled times, I can help myself at the same time."

"I can operate much faster than a real estate agent, plus save you a costly sales commission."

"I completely understand how you feel. By allowing me to acquire your property, you can be assured that the lender, or anyone else, cannot profit from your hard luck."

"My purpose in being here is to offer you cash for your equity which you would lose in a foreclosure sale. Therefore, by dealing with me you can salvage your good credit, and drive away much better off and start all over again."

"Please allow me to see the documents on your home. Do you have the deed, the title policy, and the payment records?"

"Be careful that you do not let other people know that we are speaking about a deal. If Realtors and lenders get involved, it could make our deal very messy."

It's important that the troubled owners be made aware at the onset of negotiations that time is of the essence. Because they are in the midst of a foreclosure proceeding, take care that the deal is completed before it's too late.

Often, during the initial stages of negotiating with the owners, they might mention that they're arranging new financing on the property. They somehow believe that the current situation can be remedied by acquiring additional funds. The thing for you to remember is that when a property is in foreclosure, the owners will most likely be unable to acquire additional financing. It's improbable that a lender would fund an additional loan with the current mortgage loan in default. If the owners cannot make payments on the first loan, they probably won't be able to make payments on another loan, either. If by chance they are able to get a loan, they're probably only postponing the inevitable foreclosure.

Should the troubled owners state that they're arranging another loan, advise them as follows: "Okay, if you feel supplemental funds will ease your distressed situation, then by all means do it. But if you cannot arrange the loan, or if you have problems later, please call me so that I may make an offer for your property and assist in rectifying your credit."

The point is to leave the owners with a positive view of you, as an investor who wants to help, so that if they get into a distressed situation, they know who to call.

As a private investor, you can act more quickly and offer more results to the distressed owners than anyone else. A Realtor who gets involved in such a transaction requires a sizable commission, which is a needless expense when you, the private investor, purchase the property.

Probable Difficulties You'll Face with Owners in Default

The enticing scenarios brought to us by the get-rich-quick-in-foreclosures promoters exaggerate the opportunities attainable. They would have us believe that most troubled properties have substantial equity with easy-to-obtain nonqualifying assumable mortgages. All you have to do to acquire the property is give the owners a few thousand dollars and reinstate the past-due mortgage payments. The seller deeds you the property and moves out. You can then either rent out the acquired property, or fix it up and sell it for a profit. According to the so-called foreclosure experts, regardless of which strategy you choose, buying foreclosures will make you rich. Unfortunately, it's just not that simple. It's what they don't tell you that gets the naive foreclosure investor into trouble.

In reality, when you talk with owners facing foreclosure, you're more likely to uncover a cesspool of difficulties that have to be overcome with investigative skill and creativity. The following are some of them:

- *No equity in the property.* Many owners facing foreclosure owe more on their mortgages than the properties are worth. For a deal to work under this situation, you have to persuade the lender to agree to a *short sale*. In a short sale, the lender agrees to reduce the mortgage owed, in order for you to receive a fair profit in exchange for bringing all the past-due mortgage payments up to date, and taking over the loan.

- *Scarcity of nonqualifying assumptions.* Lenders stopped making nonqualifying assumable loans in 1987. Thus, they're difficult to find.

- *Restrictions on qualifying assumptions.* VA and FHA mortgages can be assumed only by owner-occupants with decent credit. If you intend to rent the property or immediately sell for a profit, neither the VA nor the FHA will approve the assumption.

- *Multiple creditors.* Check to see if the owners have to contend with the claims of more than one creditor. If more than one creditor is involved, such as through a tax lien, a recorded judgment, or a *lis pendens,* you may be required to settle up with all of them to gain clear title. (A *lis pendens* is a recorded document that gives legal notice that a specific action affecting the property has been filed in court.)

- *Salvage equity through bankruptcy.* In some states home owners can file for bankruptcy, and exempt all or part of the home's equity from the claims of creditors.

- *Estimating repair costs.* Keep in mind that owners facing foreclosure have likely neglected property maintenance because if they'd had any money, it likely would have gone toward making the loan payments.

Prequalifying the Property

Before going ahead with a feasibility study, you have to prequalify the property. Check the property's potential for profit by answering the following questions:

- Is there a significant amount of equity in the property?
- If applicable, will the lender agree to a short sale to reduce the loan balance?
- Will the lender allow you to assume the mortgage? If so, at what interest rate? Can you be an investor, or must you be an owner-occupant? If assumption is not permissable, will you have to pay a prepayment penalty, or can it be waived?
- Can the sellers convey marketable title that's free of consequential clouds?
- Will the property owners avoid filing for bankruptcy?
- Are you able to accurately estimate the cost of repair and renovation?
- Is the potential margin for profit sufficient to justify your investment of money, time, and effort? Use the cost estimate worksheet in Figure 12.1.

Evaluating the Property

In order to determine whether the property has any potential as a worthwhile investment, you have to determine whether the market value after improvements, less the acquisition cost, plus the cost of all repairs and renovations, result in a sufficient profit.

After you've completed the cost estimate worksheet, is the profit potential (the difference between A and B) enough to offset your risk? If the answer is yes, you've found a distressed property that's worth investing in.

FIGURE 12.1   Cost estimate worksheet.

Address _____

Cost of acquiring the property

    Purchasing the deed $_____

    Delinquent taxes   _____

    Bonds and assessments   _____

    Delinquencies on first loan:
    _____ months @ $_____   _____

    Total late charges and fees   _____

    Advances   _____

    Pay off second loan (include all delinquencies,   _____
    advances, and fees)

Preliminary cost estimates

    Title and escrow expenses   _____

    Loan transfer or origination fee   _____

    One month P&I, taxes, and insurance   _____

Total cash to purchase   _____

    Balance of all loans after purchase   _____

    Other encumbrances   _____

Total property cost (before repairs)   _____

Cost of repairs needed

    Paint   _____   Plumbing _____   Roof   _____

    Electrical _____   Termite   _____   Fencing   _____

    Landscape_____   Floors   _____   Carpeting_____

    Wallpaper _____   Fixtures _____   Hardware_____

Total cost of repairs   _____

    A. Total property cost   _____

    B. Market value after repairs and improvements $_____

Profit potential $_____

Finding Owners in Default (Prefiling)

Property going into foreclosure almost always has that particular unkempt appearance—a look of neglect. You can spot it a mile away. It's the only house on the block with a dried-out, unmowed lawn with debris scattered about. It may have a broken window or two, and it probably needs a coat of paint. It stands out in the neighborhood like a man wearing brown shoes with a black tuxedo. These indicators often signal an owner facing foreclosure.

By driving through neighborhoods, you can keep an eye out for these properties. You may discover an owner whom you can negotiate with, before the foreclosure sharks learn of the prize and begin competing with you.

Finding Owners in Default (Postfiling)

After the mortgage lender has recorded the default, you can learn the names and addresses of the owners in the following ways:

- See the clerk of the county courthouse and ask to see (or get a copy of) the list of foreclosure filings. (Typically, the county clerk will provide only legal descriptions, not street addresses. You may have to refer to a plat map, or ask the clerk how to translate the legal description into a usable address.)
- Research special subscription services that report court filings, such as legal newspapers.
- Peruse the legal notices in your local newspaper.
- Surf the Web under "foreclosure filings" for your county.

Keep in mind that the minute the default enters the public records, anyone who has any interest in distressed real estate will soon learn of it. And that's when you'll have to deal with your competition, especially if it's a worthwhile property to invest in.

CHAPTER 13

How to Buy HUD Homes and VA Repossessions

HUD Homes

HUD homes are repossessed properties that were once insured by the Federal Housing Administration (FHA), a division of the Department of Housing and Urban Development (HUD). Nationwide, the number of outstanding FHA mortgages runs into the millions. As mentioned in Chapter 3, the FHA insures loans funded by various types of institutional lenders. If FHA borrowers fail to repay these loans, the lender can initiate a foreclosure sale. Instead of maintaining the foreclosed property in its REO portfolio, the lender turns in an insurance claim to HUD. Then HUD reimburses the lender what is owed, and HUD takes over ownership of the foreclosed property. Finally, HUD puts the property, including all the others it recently acquired, on the market for public sale.

Investing in HUD repos can be a very rewarding experience; however, you have to be aware of certain shortcomings. You have to keep in mind that you're dealing with the federal government, which means you need patience. HUD requires all kinds of special forms, contracts, and procedures. If you're interested in purchasing HUD property, it is recommended that you deal directly with a Realtor who is accustomed to selling it.

Who Can Buy a HUD Property

If you have the cash or can qualify for a mortgage, you can buy a HUD home. HUD employees and relatives of HUD employees are eligible, but must receive written approval from the director of HUD's Office of Single Family Asset Management in order to purchase a HUD-owned single-family property.

Owner-Occupants versus Investors

HUD favors owner-occupants over investors in two ways: (1) Owner-occupants have first choice, and (2) only owner-occupants are offered FHA low- or nothing-down insured financing. For now, the FHA has refused to offer investors FHA insurance on HUD properties.

Owner-Occupants Have First Choice.   During the first five days the property is on the market, HUD accepts bids only from home buyers who intend to occupy the premises. Should the property remain unsold, for the next five days HUD allows both owner-occupants and investors to bid. But the owner-occupant bidders have the edge. An investor can win the bid only if no owner-occupant submits an offer, even if the investor submits the highest bid. Only during the third selling period does HUD not give an advantage to buyer status.

Owner-Occupant Certification.   To discourage investors from falsely claiming owner-occupant status, HUD enforces stiff penalties and procedures. All owner-occupant buyers are required to sign a purchase contract addendum that certifies that they will occupy the property as their primary residence for at least 12 months. Furthermore, all Realtors who submit owner-occupants' bids must also sign a certification that they're not knowingly representing an investor. Penalties for false certification can be as high as $250,000 fine and two years in federal prison.

HUD Property Is Sold As Is

HUD properties are sold as is, without warranty. This means that HUD will not pay to correct any problems. But even if a HUD property needs fixing up—and not all of them do—it can still be a real bargain. For example, HUD's asking price will reflect the fact that the buyer will have to make improvements. HUD might offer special incentives, such as allowances to upgrade the property or cover moving expenses, or a bonus for closing the sale early. And keep in mind that on most sales, the buyer can request that HUD pay all or a portion of the financing and closing costs. Your real estate agent will have details. Have the home professionally inspected before you make an offer, so you will know what repairs may be needed before you submit your bid.

Finding a HUD Property

HUD properties can be found in several ways, including cruising the neighborhoods looking for HUD's "For Sale" signs, scanning the local newspaper for HUD's weekly advertisements, or visiting HUD's web site, www.hud.gov, or one of the many other web sites that list HUD properties and buying information.

Buyer Incentives

During slow and inactive periods, HUD will often make its terms of sale more lenient in areas where unsold properties have accumulated.

Reduced Down Payments. Typically, owner-occupants with FHA-insured financing are required to make a down payment of 3 to 5 percent. But sometimes HUD offers special low- or no-down-payment terms to stimulate sales. For instance, several years ago all HUD-owned FHA-insurable properties throughout the state of Georgia could be purchased with a down payment of only $300. To find out about special offerings, check with a HUD-approved Realtor in your area.

Other Incentives. Besides low-down-payment specials, local HUD offices often try to stimulate sales with other types of buyer incentive programs. For instance, in Boston, HUD offered a purchase price credit of 5 percent on certain specified properties, a $250 bonus to buyers who had been preapproved for a loan, and a $675 bonus if the settlement closed within 45 days. In Indianapolis, HUD offered a $2,000 early closing bonus (less than 30 days) to owner-occupants and investors. And in Chicago, HUD offered a rebate of up to $1,000 to renters who purchased a HUD home for owner occupancy.

Notably, the best bargains with the most incentives are available when there's an oversupply of HUD properties during slow markets. But when sales are strong in a given area and HUD has few properties available, it will usually reject bids at less than the property's list price.

Purchasing a HUD Property

Start by finding a participating real estate agent. Your real estate agent must submit your bid for you.

Normally, HUD homes are sold during an *offer period*. At the end of the offer period, all offers are opened, and the highest reasonable bid is accepted. If the home isn't sold in the initial offer period, you can submit a bid until the home is sold. Bids can be submitted any day of the week, including weekends and holidays. They will be opened the next business day. If your bid is accepted, your real estate agent will be notified, usually within 48 hours.

If your bid is successful, your real estate agent will help you through the paperwork process. You'll be given a settlement date, normally within 30 to

60 days, by which time you'll need to arrange financing and close the sale, or forfeit your earnest money deposit, or pay for an extension of your sales contract.

HUD will pay the selling agent's commission, but only if you make this a condition of your offer. HUD always pays the listing agent's commission. HUD will pay a total sales commission of up to 6 percent.

The Bid Package

Unlike the typical purchase agreement, HUD requires an explicit submission package. Buyers must use only HUD-approved forms and documentation. Each of the required forms and pertinent documents must be completed fully and accurately. Furthermore, the submitted bid package must arrive at HUD's regional office during the posted offer period. Because of HUD's notorious inflexibility, it is recommended that you work with conscientious realtors who are familiar with HUD's requirements.

Bid Rules

Although HUD's bidding rules and procedures are quite extensive, here is a condensed version of the most important ones:

Net Return to HUD.   HUD accepts the bid that yields the largest amount of net proceeds, not necessarily the highest offer.

As an example, say a property is listed for $90,000 on an insured-sale basis. Two bids for the same property arrive simultaneously. The following example shows how HUD determines which offers nets the largest proceeds:

Bidder 1: Selling Broker Buying for Own Account

Bid price	$90,000
Deduction (credit report)	−50
Net proceeds to HUD	$89,950

Bidder 2: Owner-Occupant Buyer

Bid price	$93,500
Deduction (commission, load fees, and closing costs)	−7,800
Net proceeds to HUD	$85,700

In the preceding example, although Bidder 2 offers a higher price for the property, the largest net proceeds come from Bidder 1. Bidder 2 asks HUD to pay a total reduction of $7,800, which includes a 5 percent sales commission, various loan fees, and closing costs. Bidder 1 asks HUD to pay only for a credit report; notably, the bid it does not ask HUD to pay for any other expenses. Also, Bidder 1 improved the advantage by waiving the selling commission, even though the bidder is a real estate broker. Please note that HUD's owner-occupant preference period must have elapsed for the investor-broker's bid to be considered.

To help prospective bidders increase the net proceeds of their bids to HUD, some Realtors voluntarily cut their selling commission. If your Realtor doesn't volunteer to reduce the commission, you should request that he or she do so. Such a reduction, especially when submitting a low bid, could be the difference that makes your bid the winner.

Earnest-Money Deposits.   Typically, HUD refunds the earnest-money deposit when bid-winning owner-occupants' mortgage applications are rejected. In an effort to avoid this problem, many HUD offices require that bidders submit letters of preapproval from lenders along with their bids.

Regarding cash-sale as-is properties, both owner-occupant and investor bidders who fail to close will generally forfeit their deposits. The only exceptions to this policy are situations of "great hardship" that must be petitioned and are reviewed by HUD on a case-by-case basis. It is recommended you get preapproval for a mortgage before you submit a bid to HUD.

Settlement Period.   Usually, successful bidders are required to close their purchases within 45 days after notification that HUD has accepted their bids. At HUD's discretion, however, buyers may be given one or more 15-day extensions to close, if they consent to pay an extension fee of $10, $15, or $25 per diem, depending on the sales price.

No Occupancy before Closing.   Buyers are prohibited from working on or occupying a HUD property prior to closing.

HUD's Right to Reject an Offer.   HUD reserves the right to reject any offer, bid, or purchase contract that is incorrectly drafted, or that is submitted as the result of an incorrect listing or other error.

Contract Revision.   Should a Realtor have reason to revise a purchase contract offer already submitted, that Realtor must deliver a letter of request to HUD. Said letter must be signed by the buyer, declaring the reasons for the revision, and must include a revised purchase contract, complete with attachments. After a review by HUD, the Realtor will be informed as to whether such revisions will be permitted.

Bid Cancellation.   Bidders can cancel their bids by submitting a written request outlining the reasons for the cancellation through the selling Realtor. The

Realtor must forward the request to HUD along with other relevant information. HUD decides on a case-by-case basis whether to refund the earnest-money deposit; see earlier discussion.

Procedures after Closing.   After closing, all material used to board up the property is relinquished by HUD and becomes the property of the buyer. Regardless of the type of sale, HUD does not remove such material from the property. However, the lockbox or padlock is to be returned to the HUD Area Management Broker by the selling broker, as a condition of receiving a commission check.

VA Repossessions

VA repossessions are properties that are foreclosed on by institutional lenders, when buyers fail to make payments on VA-guaranteed loans. Under the loan guarantee, the lenders are repaid and the property is given to the VA, which then offers it for public sale.

Similarities to HUD Procedures

The following VA rules and procedures are similar to those of HUD:

- Bidders must submit their bids through a VA-approved Realtor. In other words, you cannot submit a bid to, or negotiate with, the VA.
- The VA markets its properties through a sealed-bid process. Bidders can submit multiple bids either as owner-occupants or investors.
- The VA sells all its properties strictly as is, without any warranties whatsoever.
- The VA charges buyers who choose its financing a 2.25 percent guarantee fee.
- The VA guarantees a marketable title and allows buyers to obtain a title policy.
- The VA accepts the bid that yields it the highest net proceeds, not the bid with the highest price.
- The VA accepts bids only on VA forms and documents. Each of the required forms and pertinent documents has to be completed fully and accurately; otherwise, the VA can deem the bid invalid.
- The VA advertises its properties through a combination of newspapers, broker lists, and Internet web sites, such as www.va.gov.

- The VA requires that an earnest-money deposit of 1 percent of the purchase price be held on all properties. All earnest-money deposits will be made payable to and held by the broker, unless otherwise directed by the VA. If the purchaser is the successful bidder, the earnest money will be immediately deposited in the broker's escrow account; Otherwise, it will be refunded immediately.

- The VA may decide to retain the earnest-money deposit if a bidder fails to close a winning bid for any reason other than failure to obtain financing.

- Similar to HUD purchase contracts, VA purchase contracts do not include a contingency for a property inspection after submitting a bid. Bidders are, however, allowed to inspect a property prior to the bidding.

- Buyers will receive a vacant property at closing. When necessary, the VA will evict holdover tenants or home owners before listing a property for sale.

Advantages for Investors

Although many of its rules and procedures are similar to those HUD, the VA has two distinct rules that favor investors:

1. *Owner-occupant bidders do not receive preferential treatment over investors.* The VA will accept the bid that results in the highest net proceeds regardless of whether the bid is from an investor or an owner-occupant.

2. *The financing offered by the VA has very advantageous terms.* You can usually purchase a VA property with a total out-of-pocket cash investment of less that 6 percent of the selling price. Moreover, the VA utilizes more lenient qualifying standards. Prospective buyers of VA property are not required to show a *perfect* credit history; it only has to be *acceptable*.

If you review a property that interests you, contact a real estate broker participating in the VA acquired sales program. (For a listing of the VA's repossessed property, see www.va.gov). Note that you do not need to be a veteran to purchase a VA repo, and you may also obtain VA financing on any property purchased.

Besides great financing with very lenient terms, many investors find the program worthwhile for the following reasons:

- VA financing is assumable, which means that when you sell the property, the buyer can take over the existing loan. This can be a great benefit in periods of high interest rates, as a lower rate on your VA loan makes your property very attractive.

- Because you'll have a small amount invested with corresponding high leverage you should have an accelerated return on investment.
- Even if you have to pay near market value for a VA repo, most such properties should rent for enough to provide a positive cash flow from the first day of ownership.

Generally, VA repos can be a great source of real estate and advantageous financing for anyone who takes the time to research the VA's list of local properties. It is recommended that you take the time, and make the effort to investigate this viable opportunity.

PART VI

THE MIDDLE GAME

This part gets down to the real nitty-gritty—how to negotiate a winning deal, including how to get a thorough house inspection and have a hassle-free closing without unnecessary costs. Along the way you'll learn about the smart things to do with your home after you buy it, including protecting it (getting insurance), and the legal and tax ramifications of your purchase are described. Chapter 18 closes this section with advice on the dos and don'ts of renovating a home.

CHAPTER 14

How to Negotiate a Winning Deal

Negotiation is an ongoing process of give and take between buyer and seller to arrive at a compromised price. The seller, of course, is trying to get as much as possible for the home. The asking price not only reflects certain add-ons made over the years, it's also likely to be padded somewhat to allow for negotiation. Meanwhile, the buyer is, of course, trying to pay as little as possible. The final negotiated price will be somewhere between the two extremes. Unless you're prepared to pay the full asking price at the seller's stipulated terms, you have to be prepared to bargain for a better price that's also acceptable to the seller.

Secrets of Successful Negotiating

The following are proven techniques that should help in your negotiations with the seller:

- *Know the property's value.* Knowing the market value of the house will help in reducing the seller's expectations. You or your agent can show the sellers recent comparables to make your case that the asking price is too high.
- *Establish the maximum price you're willing to pay.* Establish an absolute maximum objective price, then target a price somewhat below that maximum. This way you avoid overbidding for a property.

- *Whoever first speaks—loses!* Whenever you're in face-to-face negotiations with a seller, always let the seller open the negotiations. Why? Because the opening price, could be substantially less than what you were prepared to bid. For example, say you find a nice house that interests you. It's a FSBO, priced at $149,500, but you think it would be a good buy at anything below $140,000. You make an appointment with the seller, and after thoroughly touring the house decide to make an offer. Instead of waiting to see if the seller opens negotiations, you go ahead and open your big mouth with an offer of $135,000. Then, to your surprise, the seller quickly accepts.

  Well, by speaking first, you just made a terrible mistake in the art of successful negotiating. Because in all likelihood, if you would have just waited a little longer, you would have heard the seller say "I won't take anything less than $132,000." So, by not waiting to hear what the seller had to say, you just cost yourself $3,000.

- *Never expose your hand.* Never let anyone know how much you want the property, or how much you're willing to pay for it. If the agent, who ultimately works for the seller, knows this, the agent can use it against you. Example: The buyer is bubbling over with anxiety, and can't wait to buy. The seller's agent sees this, and advises the seller to be firm with the price, because the buyer is sure to bid higher.

- *Keep your emotions in check.* If you believe that this particular house is the only one for you, and that you'll never find another like it, you can forget about negotiating effectively. You have to think rationally. And keep in mind that there are other houses out there that will suit you just as well. You'll just need to take the time to search for them.

- *Be flexible.* You don't want to lose a good buy over something as paltry as a few hundred dollars. Set limits on your negotiations, yet don't be so inflexible that you can't compromise. Using phrases such as "take it or leave it" or "never in a million years" will most definitely stop fruitful negotiations dead in their tracks.

- *As you increase your bid, ask for something more.* Each time you have to counteroffer with a higher bid, ask for more concessions. These can be the inclusion of any personal property in the home you're trying to buy—for

---

TIP

Be sure to include a "subject to inspection" clause in your written offer to purchase. This contingency gives you a way to get out of the contract should your inspection prove the property to be unacceptable.

instance, power tools, lawn equipment, vacuum cleaner, lawn furniture, chandeliers, or appliances. Continue to ask for more as your bid rises.

Your Initial Offer

Where do you start negotiations? Some people say 10 percent below the asking price is a good starting point. But that won't be a good place to start if the property is overpriced to begin with.

Before you make an offer, make sure that you know the property's fair market value. Have your agent show you some comparables that have recently sold. Once you have a good idea of what similar homes in the neighborhood have sold for, you can compare prices to what the sellers are asking. If your evaluation is higher than the seller's asking price (which rarely happens), don't immediately jump to any conclusion that you've found a super bargain. Examine the property again. Perhaps there's something you overlooked—the location, an incurable defect, anything. However, if everything seems normal, then go ahead and make an offer. The sellers could have simply underpriced their property. So go ahead and buy it before the competition sets in.

You're more likely to find that the sellers' asking price is higher than your estimate of fair market value. They most likely not only allowed room for negotiation, they also want to be repaid for that expensive kitchen modernization they did last year. You have to take the position that not all upgrades will add to the resale value of a home.

Real estate traditionally sells at about 5 percent below its asking price. This doesn't mean, however, that you should make all your offers at 5 percent below the listed price. The 5 percent figure only represents an *average*, which means that some properties sell for 10 percent below the asking price, while others may sell for exactly the listed price.

Incidentally, certain properties have been known to sell for more than the listed price, especially when more than one interested party gets involved, and a frenzied bidding war begins. Usually, the only party that benefits from this is the seller. Try to avoid getting involved, because the competition makes it too difficult to negotiate a good buy. Why bother with competition when other potential bargains are available? You only need to locate them.

It's customary to presume that the sellers' asking price includes a margin for negotiation. You don't want to offer full price unless you know that the sellers are firm on their price, and that the property is well worth the asking price. Conversely, a ridiculously low offer may not be taken seriously. Your objective is to make an offer that has a reasonable chance of being accepted, or, at least of stimulating a counteroffer.

How much should you offer? From your homework, you should already have an established maximum price in mind and know what similar homes in the area have sold for. Therefore, assuming that the listed price is reasonably close to fair market value, make an offer of about 10 percent below the asking price.

Bargaining to reach agreement is what negotiation is all about. Unless you're prepared to pay the seller's asking price in cash, you'll be bargaining for price and terms. As a general rule, if the seller is firm on price, negotiate the terms. If the seller is firm on terms, negotiate the price. If the seller is firm on neither, negotiate both. If the seller is firm on both, start looking for another investment (unless, of course, the asking price is just too good to pass up, which is unlikely).

Never Make an Oral Offer

Purchasing real property is a substantial undertaking, with a great deal of money at stake. For the sellers, it is likely to be the largest transaction they have ever participated in. You can't expect to look the sellers in the eye and say, "I'm interested in buying your home, but $140,000 is way too much. I'll give you $110,000." Not only are you asking the sellers to substantially reduce the price of their home, but you have yet to clarify the details of the transaction, such as the terms of the down payment and financing, and when to take possession. It's just not practical to handle all these details face to face.

Other Considerations

Consider what you can offer the sellers in terms of a down payment. A total cash down payment is not always necessary to consummate a purchase. Personal property items, such as vehicles, boats, recreational vehicles, and appliances, can often be used instead of cash. If the sellers are nearing retirement age, they might consider taking a boat or RV for their equity in the property. Or, instead of looking for cash, they might be looking for income, which means you could offer a secured mortgage for their equity.

The important thing to remember is that cash is a valuable asset; it's working capital, and without it you're out of business. And remember the principle of leverage. The less you have invested in the property, the more leverage you'll have, and the greater your return on investment will be.

Counteroffers

Frequently the sellers will find your initial offer unacceptable, and in most cases they will propose a counteroffer. Once a counteroffer is proposed, the initial offer is terminated.

Your second offer should still be below your established maximum price, an amount you feel is still a bargain in case the seller accepts. At each phase of bidding, it's important that you mention to the agent the flaws of the house—that the carpeting needs to be replaced throughout, and that the kitchen needs remodeling—and relay to the sellers that you're not as committed to the house as they are. You can just as soon look for other homes that might be more suitable, with owners who are more motivated to sell.

The procedure of offer/counteroffer is important, because it brings out the flexibility of both buyer and seller. Always remember your maximum price, and don't waste your time if you're confronted with an inflexible seller. However, if the property remains an excellent buy, then continue to pursue an agreement. Quite often, especially when a good buy is at hand, a property is sold right out from under a negotiating buyer who persists in demanding excessive concessions from the seller.

Contingency Clauses

Certain contingency clauses must be written into the offer. A *contingency* is a certain specific event (such as getting a loan) that must be satisfied in order for the sale to go through. Think of contingencies as escape clauses cleverly inserted into your purchase contract to protect your interests.

Inspection Clause

If the property you're purchasing is a multiunit building, it's just not practical to inspect the interior of every unit before buying. The seller cannot be expected to disturb every tenant just to satisfy the whims of a prospective buyer. Therefore, the seller can exhibit a typical unit to you, then allow you to examine the remaining units once a contract is agreed on.

Thus, an inspection clause should be worded in such a way that allows you to inspect all units before closing. This clause might say, "This offer is contingent upon all rental units essentially being in the same condition as the unit already inspected."

New Loan Clause

If you're purchasing a property you intend to originate a new first mortgage on, you need a contingency clause that voids the purchase contract in the event that you cannot get the loan. This clause would be similar to the following: "This offer is contingent upon buyer acquiring a new first mortgage in the approximate amount of $_____, at prevailing rates and terms within 16 working days of acceptance of this offer." If you can't acquire the new first mortgage, this contingency clause voids the offer, and you get the deposit back.

Contingency clauses can cover almost anything, and you do need to limit your liability. However, keep in mind that the sellers, or their agent, will attempt to eliminate excessive contingencies, because they tend to complicate an otherwise simple closing.

Amount of Earnest-Money Deposit

To protect the seller, you must deposit *earnest money*, demonstrating the seriousness of your offer. Any amount from $500 to $3,000 would be appropriate.

The recommended deposit is $500, so as to limit your liability. If you're forced, for whatever reason, to default on the transaction, you need to keep your losses to a minimum. If the sellers accept your offer, they will probably require a larger deposit to secure the transaction and protect their interest.

CHAPTER 15

Protecting Your Home

The House Inspection

Before calling in a professional house inspector, do your own inspection. By doing so you avoid the aggravation and cost of bidding on a house, and hiring an inspector, only to learn that repairing the house is not feasible because it's not worth the investment. Call a professional home inspector only after you've made an offer to purchase, that offer is accepted, and you have a sales contract signed by the sellers.

The Seller's Disclosure

If you find a particular house interesting, be sure to ask the real estate agent for the seller's disclosure. By law, most states require the seller to provide an accurate assessment of any material defects in the property. When you read the disclosure you'll find one of three things. First, you may find that the seller has no knowledge of any material defects in the property. Second, you may find that there was a problem, such as termite infestation, and that it has been solved. Or third, you may find that there is a problem that requires attention.

Read the disclosure carefully, as it may reveal a problem area that should be inspected. If you find an existing problem that has not been repaired, you can negotiate to reduce the purchase price accordingly.

Should you find a problem after the closing that was not listed in the seller's disclosure, you have the legal right to recover damages from the seller, according to state statutes where you reside.

Home Inspection Checklist

Hiring a home inspector can ease many uncertainties, or it can uncover costly problems and save you thousands of dollars on the price of the home. A professional home inspector licensed by the American Society of Home Inspectors (ASHI) charges about $250, depending on location. Once you've found a home that you're interested in buying, be sure to make the offer contingent upon your approval of a home inspection by an independent contractor. The following items should be included in the inspection:

- *Electrical.*   Newer homes have 100-200-ampere service, which is adequate to handle modern appliances (microwave ovens, dishwashers, and clothes dryers). Older homes usually are equipped with 60-ampere service, which could be adequate if the house is small and the clothes dryer, range, and furnace operate on gas. Also, rooms with only one electrical wall outlet are underserved. Look to spend at least $1,000 for new service, plus $60 and up per additional wall outlet.

- *Interior plumbing.*   Turn on the water and begin looking for leaks. Check for stained ceilings, drips under sinks, leaks around toilets while flushing, and puddles in the basement. Older homes may have galvanized steel pipes (check by using a magnet; they are gray in color) or brass pipes, either of which will eventually have to be replaced. Newer plumbing systems shouldn't give you any trouble. The cost of replacing the old plumbing can be $2,000 or more, depending on the complexity of the house.

- *Roof.*   On shingled roofs, look for missing or curled shingles as evidence that a new roof is needed. On asphalt roofs, if the granular composition surface is worn off or stains are present on the underside of the overhang, it won't be long before a new roof is needed. Replacement of an asphalt or shingle roof on the average-sized home costs upwards of $2,000, and the new roof will last about 20 years. The more expensive clay tile or wood shingle roofs start at about $4,000 and can last 40 years.

- *Air conditioning.*   Check the compressor to see whether it's running smoothly. The large intake pipe should cool quickly after the unit is turned on. If it doesn't, you could have a coolant leak.

- *Heating.*   Be sure each room has a heating outlet.

- *Walls and windows.*   In colder climates, look for storm windows. Cracked plaster is common in older homes; however, in newer homes it means the house is settling. Look for deteriorated caulking around window sills and window frames; it will allow heat loss.

- *Foundations, basements, and underflooring.*   Water stains on the basement walls and floor indicate previous water leaks or flooding. Also look for white dust, which is the residue of salts washed out of the concrete. Because of the instability of the underlying earth, Florida homes should be checked to be sure the concrete slab is supported by pilings. Saggy or squeaky floors can be checked by examining the floor trusses underneath.

Check for large cracks in the following areas: foundation, exterior retaining walls, interior walls, fireplace, chimney, concrete floors, and sidewalk. A large crack is one that you can stick your finger into.

- *Termites.* Tunnels in the wood are a sign of termites. They are a particular problem in the southern states, the Midwest, and California.
- *Septic tanks and wells.* You can tell if the septic tank is functioning properly by mixing dye with running water. If the colored dye bubbles to the surface of the ground, the septic system will have to be replaced. If the house uses well water, run the water for an hour during the inspection. If the water runs dry, the well yield is too low, and your family will have to practice careful water conservation if you decide to purchase the home.

Calling on a Professional Inspector

How do you go about finding a competent home inspector? Two things you do not want to do: Never ask the seller for a recommendation, and never use the Realtor's recommendation, either. The reason you don't want a referral from a Realtor is that even the most competent home inspector might avoid making too many waves, for fear that the sale will fall through. If the Realtor loses a sale because the home inspector finds too many faults in a home, the Realtor might never recommend the inspector again. Get referrals from friends or business associates who have recently used an inspector. Also check the Yellow Pages of your local phone book under "Building Inspection Services" or "Home Inspection Services."

Before you hire a property inspector, it is recommended that you first conduct a simple phone interview with several of them. The following are pertinent questions:

- *Are you a full-time professional property inspector?* The only acceptable answer to this question is yes.
- *How many property inspections do you perform each year?* An active property inspector will perform 100 to 250 inspections a year. It's important that the inspector you hire be familiar with the area where the home to be inspected is located, to ensure that the inspector is familiar with local codes, local building regulations, and local problems (such as mud slides, floods, tornadoes, or earthquakes).
- *Do you carry insurance for errors and omissions?* Errors-and-omissions insurance protects the home owner should the property inspector make an error or overlook a problem.

- *Are you certified or licensed?*   Qualified property inspectors usually have experience in some related field, such as engineering, construction, or electrical work. Membership in ASHI or other professional associations for property inspectors indicates some knowledge of property-inspection procedures.

- *How thorough is the property inspection?*   Check to be sure that the inspection covers all the property's major mechanical and structural components, from the foundation to the roof. Don't accept anything less.

- *What kind of inspection report do I get?*   You need a detailed written description of the property's mechanical and structural condition. It has to be written in plain English, and it must fully explain the implications of its inspection.

For the name of a home inspector in your area, contact:

American Society of Home Inspectors
932 Lee Street, Suite 101
Des Plaines, IL 60016
(847) 759-2820
(800) 743-ASHI
www.ashi.com.

Evaluating the Problems

After receiving the inspection report and noting the property's defects, you need to put the problems in perspective. You need to recognize which ones are serious and which are not. Certain kinds of defects may cause you to walk away from what appears to be a great bargain, because of the high costs involved. You may decide that other types of problems can be easily cured, making the property appear to be a worthwhile investment. Once you're aware of the property's faults, the following items should be helpful in deciding whether to buy.

Red Flags

Any of the following serious items should be enough to keep you from buying:

- Location in a floodplain. (You can find out if the property is located in a floodplain by checking with the U.S. Geological Survey, which has mapped most floodplain areas in the United States. Be wary of property that is low lying or located near a stream or river. Mortgage lenders require federal flood insurance on all mortgaged property that lies within a floodplain.)

- Unsafe or inadequate supply of drinking water
- Malfunctioning independent sewer system (septic tank or cesspool)
- Uncontrollable flooding in the basement
- Cracked foundations or uneven settling
- Evidence of recent mud slides or earth movement in hillsides at the back of the property

Yellow Flags

The following items indicate discretion, because potential problems and costly repairs are inevitable:

- Stains on the ceiling, indicating roof leaks
- Exterior paint that's cracked or bubbling
- Pests (roaches, mice, or termites)
- Sump pump in the basement, indicating past flooding
- Evidence that a new roof is needed
- Signs of deterioration on gutters and downspouts
- Inadequate electrical service

Green Flags

The following items only indicate a remediable problem and should not discourage you from going ahead with the purchase:

- Appliances in disrepair (dishwashers, microwave ovens, built-in ranges, and so on)
- Leaky faucets
- Hairline settling cracks in the foundation
- Dirty carpets, peeling wallpaper, and gaudy decorating

You have to be especially wary of any defects that involve the foundation, electrical system, or roof. Any defects in these areas can be prohibitively expensive to repair. Yet when you buy a resale property you have to expect some deferred maintenance—just figure it into your purchase price. Keep in mind that you cannot expect perfection. When you finally choose a property to purchase, don't let an aggressive property inspector spoil a deal for you. Just avoid properties with serious defects, and don't be afraid to refurbish and clean up those properties that only need a little mending and some tender loving care.

Insuring Your Home

The purpose of insurance is to protect yourself against financial catastrophe. You spend a relatively small amount of money to protect yourself against losing a great deal more. If, for example, your home and all its possessions burn to the ground and they're not insured, you would likely lose at least $100,000.

You need to have the following types of insurance in place before you take possession of your home.

Home-Owners' Insurance

The most basic home-owners' policy protects your home and belongings from many perils, including fire, vandalism, theft, lightning and windstorms. It is recommended that you shop around for home-owners' insurance, just as you would for a home and a mortgage loan. Rates and coverage vary substantially. Ask friends and associates for referrals.

Note that there are three packages available, with HO-1 being the most basic and HO-3 the most comprehensive. The basic policy covers 100 percent of the replacement value of your home. (Don't consider anything less than 80 percent of the replacement value.)

It's important that your coverage be equal to the cost of rebuilding the home at today's prices. That cost should be based on the square footage of the home. It should not be based on what you paid for the home or the amount of the mortgage.

 TIP

Should you ever have to file an insurance claim, it's a good idea to have complete documentation covering all your personal property. Maintain a file folder of receipts for major purchases, and keep a written inventory of your belongings. Also make a videotape of all your personal belongings. Then, be sure to keep this documentation in a safe place somewhere outside your home (such as a safe deposit box). A videotape and a file folder of your belongings won't do you much good if it all goes up in smoke during a fire!

Your standard home-owners' policy will also protect you against lawsuits that may arise from accidents that can happen to others while they're on your property. You should carry liability insurance equal to a minimum of twice the value of your assets.

On a typical home-owners' policy, coverage of personal property, such as clothing and furniture, is often set at 50 to 75 percent of the coverage on the dwelling. This standard coverage is actual cash value, which deducts for depreciation. If you want to be insured at full replacement value, you may want to purchase the extra coverage as a rider (add-on provision).

Flood Insurance

Home-owners' insurance does not cover flood damage. Your home-owners' policy will likely protect you from water damage if a pipe bursts in your home, but it won't cover you against flooding from a storm or from storm drains around your property. You need special flood insurance, especially if you live in a low-lying flood-prone area.

The federal government offers flood insurance through the National Flood Insurance Program, administered by the Federal Emergency Management Agency (FEMA), 500 C Street SW, Washington, D.C., 20472, www.fema.gov. FEMA flood insurance (202) 566-1600, can be purchased through most insurance offices.

Lowering Your Insurance Costs

There are many ways to save money on home-owners' insurance. Ask your insurance agent about the following methods:

- *Can you raise your deductible?*   The *deductible* is the amount of loss the policyholder is responsible for covering before the insurance begins to pay. You can save 10 to 40 percent on the premium cost by increasing your deductible.
- *Have a security system installed in your home.*   You can lower your home-owners' insurance by 10 to 15 percent with the installation of a home security system.

TIP

If you think that you need flood coverage, regardless of whether it's required by your mortgage lender, it's best to acquire the policy when you purchase the home. Note that there's a waiting period after you submit the application, which means that you can't get insurance just when you learn that a big storm is headed your way.

- *Nonsmokers are less of a fire risk.*   If all members of your household are non-smokers you can usually get a reduction in the cost of a home-owners' policy.

- *Being a loyal customer pays off.*   If you have been a steady customer for at least three years, you may receive special consideration. Many insurance companies offer a 5 to 10 percent discount if you remain a customer for a specified term.

- *Use the same carrier for both car insurance and home-owners' insurance.* Many companies will give you a 5 to 15 percent reduction on that two-policy package.

Title Insurance

What does title insurance do? It assures mortgage lenders and home owners that the property in question has a valid (marketable) title. The title insurance company protects the home owner and lender against loss or damage from anyone who may make a claim that threatens the ownership of the property. Title insurance covers your risk of loss from past claims on the title, such as unpaid property tax liens, that may exist at the time your policy is issued.

You have a choice of two different kinds of home-owners' title insurance. A standard title-insurance policy is less expensive because its coverage is limited. It's limited to certain off-record risks, such as defective records in the chain of title and recorded mechanic's liens, tax assessments, judgments, and other defects that a title search of public records can uncover. Extended title-insurance policies provide the same coverage as a standard policy, but they also provide additional coverage for off-record risks that could be revealed through an inspection of the property, as well as defects such as unrecorded mechanic's liens, contracts of sale, and leases. For instance, only an extended title-insurance policy could protect home owners against a faulty land survey.

The good news is that title insurance doesn't have to be paid every month: Unless you refinance your mortgage, it is a one-time fee that you pay at the close of escrow.

CHAPTER 16

The Closing and Escrow

Once your mortgage has been approved, all buyer's and seller's contingencies are met, and the purchase agreement has been signed by both parties, you'll be notified of a closing date. Then all funds, documents, and instructions relevant to your transaction will be delivered to a neutral third party—the escrow officer designated in the purchase agreement. The actual delivery of the funds, documents, and instructions to the designated escrow holder is what comprises the escrow. Depending on local custom in your state, the escrow may be handled by an escrow company, a lawyer, or a title company.

The escrow officer handles all the necessary paperwork and money details between you and the seller. It is the escrow officer's responsibility to review and prepare documents related to the transfer of title, and ensure that they are properly signed, delivered, and made a matter of public record; to satisfy your lender's funding instructions; to request a title search; and to give a thorough accounting of your money to you and the seller.

Your escrow will hopefully go smoothly from the opening to the closing. However, should your escrow officer receive conflicting instructions from you, the seller, and the lender, processing of the escrow will be held up until a resolution is agreed on by all parties. Disagreements over whether personal property (such as a chandelier or an appliance) should be included in the purchase price are a common holdup.

Reviewing Closing Costs and
Your Closing Statement

To ensure that you're properly prepared for the closing, you should pay special attention to the following three items.

Closing Costs

In addition to your down payment, you will be obligated to pay certain costs at closing, which usually total 4 to 6 percent of the home's sales price. These items will show up on your closing statement (some charges may not apply to your transaction, depending on which region of the country you live in).

- *Loan origination fee.*   Expect to pay 1 or 2 points of the loan amount to originate a new mortgage.
- *Loan commitment fee.*   Expect to pay 1 point if you want to lock in a guaranteed interest rate at closing. If you accept the going market rate at closing, you won't have to pay this fee.
- *Escrow fee.*   This fee covers document preparation, notary services, and transaction packaging.
- *Appraisal.*   This is a cost the buyer customarily pays when originating a new mortgage loan.
- *Credit report.*   This is a cost every borrower pays to initiate a new loan.
- *Title insurance.*   A title policy, usually issued by a title-insurance company, ensures payment to any claimant in case of disputes involving the title to the property. The cost is usually paid by the seller; however, the cost is sometimes split between buyer and seller.
- *Recording fee.*
- *Termite report.*
- *Prorated taxes.*

In addition to the closing costs paid by the buyer, the seller is also obligated to pay certain closing costs:

- *Sales commission.*
- *Certain fees.*   These include escrow, recording, reconveyance, and trust fund fees.
- *Title insurance.*
- *Points (discount) on government-backed loans.*

- *Prepayment penalty.*
- *State or local revenue stamps.*
- *Transfer taxes.*
- *Prorated rents, taxes, and interest.*
- *Impound account.*
- *Documentary stamps.*

Preliminary Title Report

Soon after escrow is opened, you should receive a very important document from your title company—the preliminary title report. This report reveals who presently owns the subject property, along with any liens against it. The preliminary title report also reveals third-party restrictions and interests that limit the use of the property, such as condominium covenants, conditions, and restrictions (CC&Rs), and utility company or private easements.

The purchase agreement should be contingent on your approval of the preliminary title report. Review it carefully. If there's something in it that you don't completely understand, don't be afraid to ask your Realtor or escrow officer to explain it. You have the right to reasonably object to certain liens or restrictions that you don't want on the property, and to ask the owner to have them removed before the close of escrow. For instance, it would be reasonable to ask the owner to pay off all loans secured by liens and judgments against the property. However, asking the owner of a condo to remove the CC&Rs would be unreasonable because they are an integral part of the property.

Final Closing Statement

On closing day you'll receive the final closing statement, which is a complete accounting of all money related to your purchase. All the money that went through escrow will appear as either a credit or a debit:

- *Credits.* These are items deposited into your escrow, such as your initial deposit, the down payment, and your loan. Other items that show up as credits are property taxes and corrective repairs by the seller.
- *Debits.* These are items paid out of escrow on your behalf. Debits include such items as the final selling price of the property, loan origination fees, and the property inspection fee.

The final closing statement is a very important document that needs to be safely kept in your home file folder. You'll need it to establish your initial cost basis to figure your capital gains when it comes time to sell. And it will come in handy when it's time to do your annual income taxes. Certain expenses—prepaid interest, points, and property taxes—paid at closing are tax deductible.

Taking Title to Your Home

If you're single, your choices are simplified, because you take title as a sole owner. However, under coownership you have three choices of ways you can take title. Which one is best for you depends on your particular circumstances. The following are the forms of coownership, along with the advantages of each.

Joint Tenancy

Under joint tenancy, each owner has the right of survivorship. In other words, if one spouse dies, the ownership of the property automatically transfers to the surviving spouse without going through probate. Under this form of title you also have a tax advantage called a *stepped-up basis* on your spouse's half-ownership of the house. Here's how it works. For example, say you and your spouse bought a house for $150,000. Then, just after your spouse's death, the house was appraised for $250,000.

For tax purposes, your new cost basis is $200,000 ($75,000 for your half-share of the original purchase price, plus $125,000 for your spouse's half of the house's value at time of death), since no capital gains tax is applied to the $50,000 appreciation of your spouse's half.

Please note that the coowners do not have to be married to take title under joint tenancy. Furthermore, there must be a minimum of two coowners in order to take title under joint tenancy.

Community Property

Taking title as community property is restricted to married couples. Community property coownership has the advantage over joint tenancy of greater tax savings, in that both halves of your home get a stepped-up basis on the demise of your spouse.

If the same example as was used for joint tenancy, as the surviving spouse your cost basis is the entire $250,000. One hundred percent of the capital gains from the date of purchase to the time your spouse died are excluded from taxation.

Community property has another advantage over joint tenancy in that you can bequeath your share of the property to whomever you wish.

Tenants-in-Common (Partnerships)

When you hold title as tenants-in-common or in the form of a partnership, you do not get a stepped-up basis on the death of a coowner. Although this is an obvious disadvantage from a tax point of view, this form of title does have some legal advantages. Under this form of coownership, you don't need the permission of the coowners to sell or bequeath your share of the property. Moreover, coowners are not required to have equal ownership interests in the property; which is ideal for investors who just want a small piece of the pie.

Attending to Closing Day Tasks

The following are a few other details that will need your attention on or just prior to closing day:

- *Utilities.* Make sure the sellers have the orders to disconnect the electrical and water service in place. This way you can have a reconnection order put in your name on the day of the closing.
- *Fuel.* If the house is heated by fuel oil, check how much fuel remains. If it's a sizable amount, reimburse the seller for what's left in the tank. If gas is the fuel, have the gas company read the meter on the day of closing and send a final bill to the seller. Then you can open a new account in your name.
- *Walk-through inspection.* It's customary to do a walk-through inspection of the property within 24 hours of the closing. Note any problems that were not there on your last tour of the property. You're entitled to have the seller remedy such problems by either writing you a check for the cost of repairs or reducing the sale price.
- *Money.* On or about the day before closing, the escrow officer will phone you to inform you what your closing expenses will be. You will need to bring to the closing a cashier's check for precisely that amount. It would also be a good idea to bring your checkbook to the closing, just in case something else comes up.

Dealing with Buyer's Remorse

Buyer's remorse is a nasty psychosis that frequently strikes home buyers right after they take possession and move in. Buyer's remorse is primarily a terrible sinking feeling that you paid much too much for your property, but it's compounded by other anxieties—that you're stuck with the world's worst mortgage loan, that you could lose your job, and that neighborhood property values will surely decline in the years to come.

You have to understand that these anxieties are a normal reaction to life's uncertainties. You're not alone, because nearly all home buyers go through a similar traumatic experience. The remorse and fear will go away.

In time, you'll learn (just as the countless home buyers who went before you did) that you have the ideal mortgage, that your job is secure, and that property values in the neighborhood will remain stable.

But what about that fear that you paid too much for your home? Don't let it secretly gnaw away at you. You have to openly confront it. Knowledge overcomes fear. The faster you acquire the facts you need, the less you'll suffer. If you did your homework and studied real estate values in the neighborhood, you should know what is overpriced and what is a good value. When you follow the principles in this book, you'll gain the confidence and know-how to get the best mortgage loan and negotiate a good deal.

With knowledge you have nothing to fear.

Celebrating

After the closing, it's time to celebrate. You have earned it. You're now a proud home owner. Now you get to enjoy all the benefits of being a home owner—such as the value appreciation, the built-in wealth-building benefit of paying down the mortgage every month, the tax deductions, and the freedom from paying rent.

If this is your first home purchase, you've really got something special to commemorate. This would be a good time to kick back and smell the roses. Enjoy your property for what it's worth. Tomorrow you can start thinking about all the wonderful things you can do to the home. Then, too, you can set up a file folder for all your important home-related documents. If applicable, file for a home owner's tax exemption at your local county tax collector's office. Note that a copy of the recorded deed should be mailed to you within six weeks of the closing.

For now, enjoy your new home.

CHAPTER 17

Wise Things to Do after You Buy

This chapter is all about how to become a financially happy home owner, and how to avoid the many pitfalls new owners often fall prey to. There is also advice on how to evade the many solicitations that are headed your way. Unfortunately, as a new home owner, you are now entered on countless mailing lists, since your home purchase is a matter of public record. And to make matters worse, some newspapers publish the buyers' and sellers' names, the purchase price, and the address of the property.

Rebuild Your Cash Reserve

If you're like most new home owners, you used up most of your cash for the down payment. Ideally, you should have on hand a ready cash reserve equivalent to at least three month's salary. Keep the ready reserve in a bank money-market account.

To rebuild your financial reserves, you will need to go on a financial diet, which means spending less than you earn. Much easier said than done, you say, especially with all those gorgeous home-improvement stores out there beckoning you with their 24-hour sales. For now, pass on the home-improvement stores, restaurants, and shopping malls until you get back on your feet financially. (See Chapter 2 for more ways to save money.)

Plan Your Allocation for Furniture and Future Renovations

Before you go making renovations or buying furnishings, live in the house for a while, take the time to smell the roses, and then make a plan for what you want to do. You should stay on top of your spending and saving too, so that you can eventually buy a second property. Take your time in converting your new home into a virtual palace, and enjoy the moment, because it's not every day that you buy a new home.

Consider Electronic Mortgage Payments

Making the mortgage payments on time should be a home owner's top priority for two important reasons. First, if you make your payments late, most lenders will charge you 5 percent of the mortgage payment as a late fee. That works out to an annualized interest rate of 60 percent. Second, late charges show up as derogatories (blemishes) on your credit report. And you need good credit if you plan to finance any future real estate investments.

If your mortgage lender has an automatic payment service, you can sign up for it and have your monthly mortgage payment automatically deducted from your checking account. Should your mortgage lender not offer such a service, you can establish it yourself through one of several home-banking services, such as CheckFree [(800) 297-3180; www.checkfree.com] or with bill-payment software, such as Quicken.

Avoid Premiums for Mortgage Insurance

As mentioned earlier, soon after you buy a home, your mailbox becomes a target for all sorts of solicitations trying to get you to sign up for mortgage disability insurance and mortgage life insurance. Most of these solicitations will come from your mortgage lender, and other advertisements will likely come from insurance companies that add the names of new home owners to their mailing lists.

Such policies are often highly overpriced. They do not give the insured an appropriate amount of benefits. The amount of disability and life insurance protection you carry should not be predicated on the size of your mortgage. If you have a family that is dependent on your income, it's more cost effective to buy low-cost high-quality term life insurance. Similarly, long-term disability insurance coverage is suitable if you're solely dependent on your income.

Ignore Prompts for Faster Mortgage Payoff

You may receive solicitations that tout thousands of dollars in interest savings if you pay off your mortgage sooner than scheduled. In exchange for a monthly fee, this service converts your 12 monthly mortgage payments into 26 biweekly payments, each of which is half of your present monthly payment. The end result is that instead of making 12 months' worth of mortgage payments every year, you'll be making 13. The added payment each year will actually result in reducing the repayment schedule on a 30-year mortgage loan down to approximately 22 years—a reduction of about 8 years.

There are two fundamental problems with this type of service. First, you pay for an unnecessary service. In other words, you can make this added-payment conversion without the service and its fees. Second, prematurely paying off your mortgage may not be such a good idea. True, you save eight years of interest, but look at the alternatives. You could put the extra money into a tax-deductible IRA. And you wouldn't want to prematurely pay off the mortgage loan if doing so would leave you short of cash. You need at least three to six months' worth of income in reserve in case you lose your job. Otherwise, you would have to use high-interest credit cards to cover monthly expenditures while you search for a new job.

Refinance Your Mortgage If Rates Fall

There are two basic rules of thumb for refinancing, to make sure that the lower monthly payments offset the total added cost:

1. *Rule 1.* You must continue to own the refinanced home for at least three years to benefit from the reduced monthly payments.
2. *Rule 2.* The refinanced rate of interest must be at least two points below the original rate.

Rule 2 would apply when the market rate is 8 percent and the existing fixed rate on your mortgage loan is 11 percent. Since your rate is 11 and you could refinance at 8 (a difference of 3 points, which is more than the recommended 2 points), it would benefit you financially to refinance. However, if the market rate is 8 percent but your existing rate is 9 percent, it would not be practical (costwise) to refinance, because the differential between the two rates is only 1 point.

Briefly, the savings in monthly payments of the new loan should, over three years, at least equal the cost to acquire it. In other words, if the refinancing will save you $100 per month, and it costs you $2,800 to acquire it (loan origination fee, and so on), then it will take you 28 months to recover the cost. Which, in this case, is less than the recommended 36 months. See the tables of monthly loan payments at selected interest rates in Chapter 4 (Tables 4.2 and 4.3).

Know the Difference between Improvements and Repairs

It is wise and in your best interest to keep track of all the receipts related to the upkeep and improvements made to your home or rental real estate. When you sell your home, the IRS allows you to exclude from taxation that portion of your profit that is due to capital improvements.

For tax purposes, the IRS allows home owners to add the cost of improvements (but not the money spent on maintenance) to the original purchase price. For example, suppose you bought a house for $100,000, and it appreciates over the years so that (after paying the selling costs) your net selling price is $180,000. Thus, your capital gain is $80,000. But the IRS allows you to add the value of the capital improvements that you make to your home to your purchase price.

The difference between capital improvements and maintenance is as follows:

- *Capital improvements* are things that you do to your home that permanently increase its value and lengthen its life. These may include such things as adding a deck to the backyard, building a patio, landscaping, acquiring new appliances (as long as you leave them when you sell), installing a new water heater or roof, adding on or remodeling a room, and so on.
- *Maintenance and repair expenses,* on the other hand, are those kinds of fix-up items that are required from time to time. These include such things as painting, repairing a toilet or leaky pipe, repairing a leaky roof (not replacing it, which is an improvement), paying someone to mow the lawn, and the like.

Ignore Homestead Solicitations

You may get an offer to homestead your home if you pay the solicitor upwards of $100. *Homesteading* is the procedure of filing with the county recorder a legal document known as a *homestead exemption,* which protects all or part of your equity from lawsuits. If you reside in a state where you need to file a homestead exemption, by all means do so. Simply call the county recorder's office and ask how to do it. The procedure is not difficult (and in some states, not required) and it's not worth paying someone else to do it.

Take Time to Enjoy Your New Home

Buying a home, especially if it's the first home you've ever owned, is a big achievement in life. It's very likely that 30 years from now, your home will have developed into one of your most valued assets. But for now you should cherish this moment, and enjoy the fruits of your labor.

When you buy a home within your financial means, and are frugal with your spending while living in it, your home should not rule your finances and your need to work. In other words, your home should not own you. You should own the home.

And always remember that as a proud home owner, you have the privilege at day's end of returning to your appreciating investment—to that wonderful parcel of earth that belongs solely to you.

CHAPTER 18

Fixing Up the Fixer-Upper

When I started in this business, my only training in fixing things up was an eighth-grade class entitled Shop 101. As a novice real estate investor, I hired most of the necessary repair work out until I learned how to do it myself. If I didn't learn by watching, I learned by reading. I recommend the *Complete Do-It-Yourself Manual* (Reader's Digest, 1973).

Sometimes it's not even necessary to fix a house up. Frequently a house may need only a slight alteration, or something added to make it more appealing, which in turn will make it more valuable. For instance, in 1986 we purchased a lovely 2,200-square-foot custom home on the southwest side of Las Vegas that actually didn't need any fixing up, but there were certain things about it that had to be changed. The living room had a dreadful-looking sunken carpeted floor, and instead of wood baseboards along the room's perimeter, the carpeting came eight inches up the walls. We decided the living room carpet, including the gaudy carpeted baseboards, had to go. The rest of the house was rather plain, as it lacked any distinctive decoration. The walls were all painted in a variety of off-white colors, with no wallpaper whatsoever.

The first thing we did was pull out that living room carpet and lay in dark oak floors. Wow! The wood was magnificent, and it made a great first impression when you came through the front door. Next, we put solid oak, laid at a 45-degree angle, on two walls in the living room near the entry. Then we stained the oak to match the tone of the oak flooring. The finishing touch was to encase both archways in the living room and adjacent dining room with solid oak molding, stained and varnished to match the gorgeous new oak floor.

We did the whole project ourselves, and it was truly a pleasure. My neighbors were impressed, and everybody loved all the woodwork. But the final pleasure came when we lease/purchase-optioned the house for a handsome $20,000 profit four months after we bought it. I am convinced to this day that we would have never have made as much, nor had such a great response, had we not added all that woodwork to that once very plain home.

Is Renovating a Home Suitable for You?

Renovating a home can be murder. Just ask Sarah Graves. The mystery author is renovating her 200-year-old Federal-style home in Eastport, Maine. In her latest book, *Unhinged*, she has some good advice for future renovators. In an article in *USA Today*, Graves was asked: "What are the hardest projects for you? Floors? Plaster?"

> Stripping windows, doors and woodwork of the (multiple) coats of lead paint someone else slapped onto them. But here's a tip: You know those miracle strippers you can buy that say they will make the paint just peel off? Only in the fine print it says for tough jobs you might need two applications? Well, you'll be a much happier camper if you plan on three coats, maybe even four. Also, if you feel yourself going into a trance, it's probably not from the calming effect of honest work. It's the poison fumes seeping in through your respirator. Get fresh air.

Graves was also prompted to give one other piece of advice to wannabe renovators:

> I've always liked fixing things, and my husband has always liked building things and been good at it. And he has a very good eye for color and design. If you have some of those traits, you might enjoy, and be able to survive rehabilitating an old house.

Finding a Fixer-Upper

What is a fixer-upper? Generally speaking, it's a property that needs work but has great investment potential. The potential of a home in move-in condition has already been realized, but a fixer-upper buyer can create value through sweat equity (adding value by doing the renovations oneself).

Investors who buy fixer-uppers need to look beyond the mess; they need vision to see what needs to be done to make a home beautiful. Moreover, they need the financial resources, and the courage, to take on the risks involved in renovating a home. If you think you might fit that mold, here's a sampling of what you could expect after converting your unpolished gem into a exquisite diamond:

- You will have substantially increased the home's value in excess of the cost it took to make the improvements.

- You will be living in a better neighborhood and a nicer home for a lot less than you could otherwise afford.

- The home will be renovated the way you like it, instead of reflecting someone else's concept of style and taste.

Developing a Market-Sensitive Improvement Strategy

Unfortunately, there are no rules carved in stone on how to create value when you buy a property. Features that one person likes, another may despise. What's popular in a Manhattan high-rise condominium may be out of place in Southern California. Likewise, certain amenities treasured in the desert Southwest would be inappropriate in the New England states. Features that suit you may not appeal to the lifestyles and tastes of most people. Money invested to remodel a kitchen in Detroit might pay back $2.00 for each $1.00 invested, while in Cleveland, returns for the same renovations might be only $0.50 per $1.00 invested.

With so many variables in the mix, how do you appease the lifestyles and tastes of the prospective tenants and buyers who inevitably will inspect your real estate? In order to create value in a fixer-upper, you have to learn to create features that people will pay for. To do so, you must first put your own personal taste aside. Instead, do what successful home builders do—they carefully research the market to determine precisely what home buyers want.

For starters, you can ask local realtors what home buyers and tenants want in a home. You can also tour new home developments and take note of their floor plans, decorating themes, and countertop and floor covering materials. While you're touring the models, ask pertinent questions as to what features and amenities are selling the best, and which ones are rarely chosen.

You should also visit open houses, to look for ways other property owners have improved and decorated their properties. Visit the major home-improvement outlets in your area, and talk to the people working there. While you're in the store, enhance your creative impulses by looking over all the home-improvement guides.

Improvements to Consider

When you're out searching for a viable fixer-upper to create value through sweat equity, you must analyze properties in a certain way. You must curb both your enthusiasm and any negative reactions. Disregard your first impressions. Rather, judge the property on its potential for profitability. Based on what you've gathered from market research, could you invest $10,000 to earn a return of $20,000?

Two-for-One Rule

One rule of thumb for evaluating whether a property is worth fixing up is that every dollar invested in renovation should yield at least two dollars in increased property value. For example, if you buy a house and spend a total of $4,000 renovating it you should be able to realize at least $8,000 gain in value.

Many of the properties you'll look at will be run down and dirty condition. Obviously, they have been given little care and attention recently. Often the landscaping is overgrown, trash is strewn about, and a window or two might be broken. The house might need paint. Yet this shabby condition presents great opportunities for the investor with foresight. All you have to do is determine precisely what it will cost to trim, clean, and renovate the property, then double it (the two-for-one rule). Add to that the cost to buy the property, then decide whether you can actually add any value. In other words, after renovations are complete, will the property be worth at least what you paid for it plus double the cost of renovating it? If the answer is yes, then it's likely a good investment and a prime prospect for renovation.

Here are some of the more practical improvements to make a property more appealing and boost its value:

- Thoroughly clean the property.
- Decorate the drab and mundane.
- Revamp a bad floor plan.
- Create a view.
- Eliminate a negative view.
- Reduce noise.

Thoroughly Clean the Property

Whether you intend to rent or sell the property, it's very important that it be thoroughly cleaned before you show it to any prospects. Why? Because a spotless unit will not only rent or sell more quickly, it will also attract a better quality of tenant at a higher rent. But many property owners seem to take the attitude, "Why should I give the tenants a meticulously clean property? They'll only leave it dirty anyway." Yet such an attitude will only earn you an objectionable result. When a property is not carefully maintained, first-rate renters and buyers are repulsed. They would rather live elsewhere. It is the people who tolerate units with soiled carpets, grime-layered stoves, and dirty windows who are apt to use your property as a cesspool. Kitchens and bathrooms are especially important. Make a special effort to remove stains on bathtubs, sinks, toilet bowls, countertops, and mirrors.

When you demonstrate cleanliness in your units, you'll achieve three positive things: You'll attract a better grade of tenant, earn a higher rental rate, and display to your tenants the measure of cleanliness you expect. And because cleaner units attract better tenants, you can get a better price if you sell, because investors pay more for properties with better tenants, because better tenants mean less trouble, lower risk, and reliable rental income.

Decorate the Drab and Mundane

Often, when it comes to appealing features and good taste in home decor, it's the simple little things that count the most. In 1987, we owned a big, plain, ranch-style home made of stucco with a beautiful red-tile roof. But it was lacking something. Looking at the house from the street, I knew the front elevation needed some dressing out, yet I was unsure of what to do about it. So I drove around the neighborhood viewing the other homes. Finally, I came up with what was missing—dormers around the front windows.

I rushed down to Home Depot and bought three sets of wood dormers. I installed them adjacent to the windows, then painted them dark brown. Against the beige walls they looked great, and they really added pizzazz to what was once a very plain looking house.

Perhaps you can enhance the appeal of your units with more modern color schemes, wallpaper patterns, or other special touches. Adding ceramic tile to an entry or kitchen floor can really dress out what would otherwise be a drab-looking home. Special moldings too, such as chair rail in the dining room or kitchen, can create a special flair or ambience. Try replacing drab or dull light fixtures with decorative fixtures. Remember to keep it simple. Adding just the right amount of creativity or flair can make what was once mundane very appealing.

Revamp a Bad Floor Plan

My friend Mike bought a four-bedroom home that had been on the market for 15 months. It went unsold for so long because it had four very small bedrooms without a sizable master bedroom. The first thing he did after taking possession was to combine two small bedrooms into one large room. Mike was able to capitalize on the past owners' nearsightedness and use available living area more effectively.

Perhaps you can use space more effectively in your properties. Could you convert an attic or a basement to additional living area? Or could you enclose a porch or patio, or build a studio apartment and rent it out? While looking at properties to buy, you should be constantly asking yourself, "How can I create more usable space, or make changes to create appeal that will generate more rent from these units?"

Gary Eldred, author of *Investing in Real Estate* (Wiley, 2003, p. 170) says:

Consider "rightsizing" the living area within the units. "Rightsizing" the living area means reducing the size of large rooms by adding walls or separate areas, or perhaps combining small rooms to make larger areas. In other words, every storage and living area within a house or apartment should be proportionate to market tastes and preferences. When floor areas are perceived as "too large" or "too small," you can't get top rents or a top price. By rightsizing, you better fit the space to buyer or tenant needs.

In another sense, rightsizing can pertain to making units themselves larger or smaller. Several years ago a Manhattan investor noticed that two-bedroom apartments were a glut on the market, and rent levels were severely depressed. On the other hand, those few buildings that offered four-bedroom apartments had long waiting lists. So he bought a building of two-bedroom units at a steep discount, combined the apartments into four-bedroom units, rented all of them immediately at premium rent levels, and then sold the property for twice the price that he had paid 18 months earlier.

Create a View

Quite often, builders use poor judgment in capturing the view potential of their sites. If you can find properties that fail to take advantage of a picturesque view of the ocean, a lake, the mountains, a park, or other dramatic surroundings, you may have found a great way to make the property more appealing and add to its value.

Eliminate a Negative View

Many properties lack appeal and suffer in value because their windows look directly onto another building, an alley, or a dilapidated old fence. Your objective is to convert a negative view to a positive view by either removing it or somehow camouflaging it. Could you relocate a window? Could you camouflage the view by planting shrubbery or leafy trees in front of it? Could you build decorative fencing?

My grandparents had a backyard in Detroit, that overlooked an alley with a two-story commercial building on the other side. My grandfather built a tall wooden fence adjacent to the alley, then planted tall shrubs along it, with sprawling ivy growing all along the fence. It turned out to be a much prettier view than looking at that dirty old factory.

Reduce Noise

Excessive noise is a real turn-off to both home buyers and tenants. Noise causes excessive turnover among your tenants. If you're considering buying a multiunit building or an attached home, be sure that you test the soundproofing between units. If you can hear a toilet flushing, a television, or people talking, be cautious. Unless you can overcome the noise problem, you'll have to deal with the neverending problem of tenant turnover.

People will pay a premium for peace and quiet, and they discount heavily for noise. Consider more wall insulation, soundproof windows, block walls, earth berms, trees, and shrubs.

Required Improvements and Repairs

Whether your intent is to rent or sell your properties, always market them in A-1 condition. This means that whenever you show your property, all systems have to be in working order, and the property must be spruced up, showing no signs of wear or abuse. Otherwise, the prospective tenants or buyers will be critical of the obvious problems and will discount from value anything in disrepair.

Air-Conditioning and Heating

For a prospective tenant or buyer, there's no bigger turn-off than an inadequate cooling or heating system. Be sure that both systems are working effectively. Change the filters on the furnace and air conditioner before showing the property. If the prospects find dirty filters they could presume that the filters have not been changed regularly, and thus suspect that the system itself could be damaged. In addition, be sure to clean heating and air-conditioning ducts and registers.

Electrical

Be sure all light bulbs are working properly. Pay special attention to any fluorescent bulbs that appear weak or are slow in coming on. Check the fuse box or circuit-breaker panel to make sure it's in good working order. Electrical outlet covers that are charred or burned should be replaced. An electrical outlet should never have many adapters or extension cords plugged into it. Such a condition makes it obvious that there are insufficient outlets, and it's also a fire hazard.

Plumbing

Check all faucets for leaks and drips. Replace the washers in faucets that drip. All the drains should drain rapidly. Be sure the floats work properly to automatically shut off the fill valves in toilet tanks. Toilet seats that are stained or in disrepair need to be replaced. Check for leaks around the perimeter of bathtubs and shower stalls. Use caulking compound to repair cracks or seal obvious leaks. In the northern latitudes, be sure to insulate water pipes that are exposed to weather. Eliminate stains from previous leaks. Stains are like waving a red flag in the face of prospects warning them of a plumbing problem.

Appliances

All appliances that are to be included in the rental or sale should be clean and completely operational. Notably, refrigerators should be kept defrosted and ovens should be kept clean while the property is being shown to prospects. Should tenants occupy the property, make sure they know to keep all the appliances and their living units clean for showings.

Walls and Ceilings

Color schemes should be light earth tones and neutral colors that will blend with your prospect's furniture. Avoid vivid dark colors. Repair all cracks in plaster and wallboard with spackling, then repaint. Try to attain a bright, cheerful ambience.

Windows

Windows that are painted shut are a real turn-off to prospective tenants and buyers. All windows that open should do so easily. Replace all cracked or broken glass. Repair all broken pulleys and damaged frames or window sills. Replace all broken or torn screens.

Doors and Locks

All doors should open and close freely, without squeaking or being too tight. Hinges that squeak need to be oiled. Doors that are too tight can be planed. Replace any damaged screening on the screen doors. Since home security is important to most people, it's a good idea to replace old worn or broken locks with a better grade of lock.

Landscaping

Well-maintained grounds will definitely enhance the appeal of the property. Remember curb appeal—the front yard is the first thing the prospects see when they drive up to the house. So keep the leaves raked and the lawn mowed. Trim the shrubs and remove any dead or unattractive bushes and trees.

Storage Areas

All storage areas, including the basement, have to be cleaned. Items you don't need can be sold at a garage sale or thrown away. This chore will be necessary before the tenants or buyers take possession anyway, and it will give the property a more spacious look.

Roofs

Clear the roof and the gutters of all debris. Inspect the roof for any missing tiles or shingles and replace accordingly. Shingles typically last 20 years, wood shakes 30 years. If the roof is not repairable, don't be afraid to replace it with a quality, long-lasting roof. Avoid going the cheapest route just to save a few dollars. Remember, real estate is better as a long-term investment, so you must also think long term with your improvements.

Hiring a Contractor

You'll probably ask yourself many times whether to do the repairs yourself or to hire the job out when you buy a fixer-upper. That decision is based on whether you have adequate fix-up funds. If you have plenty of cash and are in a big hurry to invest in more property, then hire the work out. But if you're like most of us, always scraping for a buck and wanting to earn some sweat equity, then you'd be wise to do most of the work yourself. Personally, I enjoy the work. I usually hire out only the specialized work I'm incapable of doing. (This usually entails laying new carpet and certain specialized electrical work.) When I do hire the work out, I make a point of watching what's being done and asking plenty of questions—because next time I'll do the job myself.

If you decide to hire a contractor, follow these guidelines:

- Discuss the job you want done with at least two contractors, and get written bids for the work.
- Get references from your neighbors. Ask them if they can recommend someone. Good craftspeople build their businesses on their reputations. Satisfied customers will be your best guide.
- Get at least three references from the contractor, and check them out. Call each reference and ask whether there were any problems; if there were, did the contractor correct them? Also check whether there were any extra charges and whether the work was completed on time.

Doing It Yourself

The best fixer-uppers are those that simply need cleaning up, plus a little added cosmetic work inside and out. Avoid those old clunkers that require significant repair and renovation.

No-No Improvements

Nearly all real estate investors have developed a list of repairs to avoid. Acclaimed syndicated columnist Robert Bruss says "Smart fixer-upper home buyers and investors look for properties with the right things wrong." To Bruss, the "right things wrong" include cosmetic improvements such as painting, landscaping, carpets, and light fixtures. On his list of no-nos are roofs, foundations, wiring, and plumbing.

Although Bruss is certainly right, there are certain exceptions. I know of a foreclosed house that sat on the market for over a year because of foundation problems. The house itself was in good shape, but the foundation was crumbling, and no one would underwrite a mortgage. It was situated in the midst of $100,000 homes, yet it was offered for $15,000 cash, with no takers. Eventually, a fellow who happened to be a professional house mover came along and bought it. He then jacked up the house 12 feet, poured a new foundation, sat the house back down on its new foundation, and resold the completed project for a $42,000 profit. (With a new foundation he had no trouble selling the property with FHA-guaranteed financing.) Not too bad for three months work.

Painting the Interior

Latex paints are recommended for the interior, because they are easy to apply, can be thinned and cleaned up with water, dry quickly, and have little or no odor. Flat latex is best for walls and ceilings. Semigloss or enamel finishes are preferred on doors, window trim and baseboards, and bathroom and kitchen walls. The semigloss or enamel finish will take more scrubbing and abuse than flat paints.

An off-white color like antique white or beige is recommended. If you keep all your rentals painted in a standard color, you'll work more efficiently, avoiding partly filled cans of a variety of paint colors. Off-white makes a room appear larger, blends nicely with most furniture schemes, and looks clean.

Careless painting wastes time and can be a very messy experience. Proper preparation is necessary for a good job that will last the years. Your first step to purchase all your paint and supplies. You can save money by purchasing five-gallon cans of paint instead of single gallons. Next, wash the walls and woodwork with soap and water. (Paint adheres better to a clean, nonglossy finish.) Fill all cracks and holes with spackling. Let it dry and sand it down. Remove all fixtures, electrical plates, and switch covers from surfaces to be painted. Then cover everything with dropcloths to protect the furniture and the floor. Apply paint to the ceiling first, then the walls starting at the top; finish up with the trim and semigloss work.

Landscaping

With most fixer-upper properties, you will need to dress up the front of the house to make it more appealing. Keep in mind that first impressions are lasting ones. If a prospective tenant drives up to inspect your property and the grounds are shabby, the prospect is likely to just keep going without further inspection. However, if your lawn is well-maintained and tidy, the entire property will definitely deserve further attention.

Remember, you will probably hold your investment for an extended period of time. Therefore, it makes sense to invest in a sprinkler system to water at least the front yard, if the property doesn't already have one. A complete system, including the grass seed, can be installed for less than $600. If you decide to do the job yourself, materials will cost less than $160.

It's important to keep the grounds properly maintained. Invest in a timer to turn the sprinkler system on and off, so your tenant won't be left with the responsibility of watering the lawn.

General Fix-Up Tips

Wall-to-wall carpeting gives your units a special glow of warmth and luxury. Before you go overboard, however, you must consider expenses versus return on investment. You can keep carpeting expenses to a minimum by using linoleum in the entry area, hallways, bathrooms, and sometimes the dining area. Linoleum lasts much longer than carpeting and is significantly less expensive.

When you do purchase carpeting, a gold or beige shag of good quality is your best value. These colors match almost any furnishings and show stains less than others. Furthermore, it's best to stay with one standard color for all your units, in order to take advantage of quantity discounts. Shag carpeting has the advantage of being easier to patch than other types, although it's more expensive to begin with.

The carpeting industry is highly competitive, and you will find a large number of suppliers to choose from. Shop around and get the best price. And consider using the moonlighters of the industry, who will often install carpeting for less than the cost of a package deal from a large supplier.

Finally, save all old drapes, carpets, curtains, and furniture. These items come in handy on any future rentals.

Summary

When it comes to fixer-uppers, the best opportunities for creating value come from concepts and improvements that most people overlook. Owing to lack of imagination, most potential buyers see things they don't like, but they're unable to envision creative solutions. You can't expect to easily find a $150,000 house reduced to $100,000 just because it needs new carpet, paint, and a thorough cleaning. Fixer-uppers with such simple problems, tend to sell with lesser discounts, because almost anyone can renovate them. You need to look for those properties where other buyers say, "No way, let's look for something else" the minute they walk through the front door.

Study what successful home builders and developers are doing in the marketplace. You should always be thinking, "What can I do to overcome the defects and improve the appeal of this property?" and "How can I make improvements that add value?" In other words, you need to put your creativity to work.

As you gain more experience in real estate, you'll learn that a little money can buy a lot. Yet, you have to be selective in the property you buy, bargain properly, make improvements that pay, and find quality tenants (or pyramid your profits from one sale to another). So get started now. By starting small, always adding value and generating more income, continually investing that additional income into more property, and repeatedly saving and adding value to your other investments, you can quickly build a magnificent net worth.

PART VII

THE END GAME

This part introduces several profitable holding strategies you can utilize to maximize your investment yield as you prepare to invest in more real estate. Then you'll learn all the how-tos of managing real estate without hassles, with advice on avoiding the most common mistakes landlords often make. In later chapters you'll learn about the ins and outs of selling your home for top dollar, and how to be tax-wise with not only your home, but all your realty investments. There are even some tips on how you can "retire on the house."

CHAPTER 19

Profitable
Holding Strategies

After owning a particular property for awhile, you may have investment money at your disposal and decide that it's time to look for another real estate investment. You have several options and many decisions to consider. For instance, if you buy a second house, should you move into it and rent out the home you're now living in? Or should you stay put and rent out the second house? This chapter addresses these questions and offers several profitable options for your consideration, so that you can choose the strategy that best suits your needs, ability, and long-term goals.

But first, in order to work efficiently and maximize the value and profitability of your realty investments, you need to understand this preeminent rule—*Real estate is a better long-term investment than a short-term one.* If you follow this key guideline, and utilize the proven long-term investment strategies illustrated in this chapter, you'll have a great chance of accumulating more than just the ideal home. Your home can be the financial foundation for the acquisition of more income properties, which eventually can fund your retirement.

Why Real Estate Is a Better Long-Term
Investment Than a Short-Term One

Over the long haul, you'll make more money holding on to your realty investments, rather than "flipping" them (selling them quickly), because if you sell them, you'll have to find another property to invest the proceeds from the sale.

Essentially, after you buy improved real estate you have two basic options—you can hold it as a long-term investment, or you can try to sell it for a profit. If you buy a property and immediately sell it for a profit, you immediately realize the gain, of course. That's the good news. But to keep your money invested, you now have to find another property to buy. You also have to consider the costs of liquidating the property, including the sales commission. And you'll probably have to pay taxes on the capital gain from the sale.

But, if you hold improved real estate as a long-term investment, look at the advantages you derive:

- *It's a great hedge against inflation.*   Improved real estate, on average, will appreciate at 1.5 times the rate of inflation. If you buy a property and sell it quickly, you don't get to enjoy this great benefit.

- *Time is on your side.*   As time passes, your rental income can be increased while your monthly expenses remain relatively constant. This means that a property that generates little or no cash flow when first purchased can later provide a source of income.

     Many property owners who have been fortunate enough to hold on to their properties for a long time are able to live off the net rental income, especially after the mortgage is paid off. The lesson: *Buy all the income property you can when you're young, then enjoy the benefits when you're older.*

- *It has a built-in wealth builder.*   You gradually accumulate wealth as you pay down the mortgage every month. For instance, when you first buy a house you might owe $120,000 on the mortgage. But gradually, as you make regular payments of principal and interest, your equity accumulates, and eventually you pay the loan down to zero.

- *It's a great tax shelter.*   For home owners, the mortgage interest and property taxes are deductible against federal, state, and local income taxes. A husband and wife, in most cases, can sell their home for a profit of up to a $500,000, with the entire gain exempt from taxes. In addition, property owners can shelter some of their rental income from federal, state, and local income taxes. Also, through home equity loans, refinancing, or installment sales, borrowers can extract cash out of their realty holdings with little or no payment of income taxes.

- *You can refinance to your benefit.*   As the value of your properties increases, you can refinance your loans and invest the proceeds in more real estate. The situation becomes even more favorable when interest rates on fixed-rate mortgages decline, and borrowers are able to refinance at a substantially lower rate of interest (Figure 19.1). The reduction in the cost of debt service produces more net income on rentals. Here's what occurs when interest rates

FIGURE 19.1   Average 30-year mortgage rates from 1987 to March 2003.

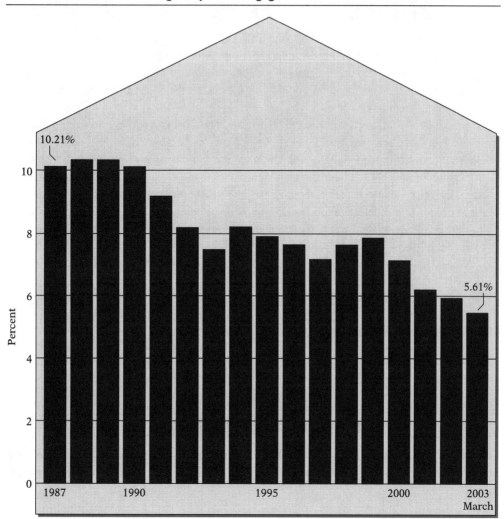

(*Federal Home Loan Mortgage Corporation*)

decline and you refinance a $120,000 loan originally funded at 9.5 percent to the lower mortgage rate of 6.0 percent:

Monthly P&I at 9.5 percent before refinancing $1,093
Monthly P&I at 6.0 percent after refinancing   719
Savings per month, or increase in net income $ 374

LANDLORD TALE

Although I don't recommend selling your real estate holdings, the man in this tale did pretty well with his quick turnover sales. I met him when I was managing foreclosures in California in the late 1970s. He generally made a living as a house mover. He also purchased repossessed foreclosed properties for 10 cents on the dollar, and made a small fortune reselling them at full price.

How did he do it? First, you have to remember that California is prone to earthquakes, so lenders were adamant about the quality of the foundations under the homes they loaned money on. In the Pasadena area, there were many older, very nice homes but some of them unfortunately had been built on foundations that were defective by modern standards. Eventually, many lenders had repossessed some of these homes through foreclosure. And because of the defective foundations, no one, including the FHA, would offer financing on them. Thus, lenders would try to sell these homes at ridiculously low cash prices just to get rid of them.

Well, along came the house mover. He would buy a house that would normally sell for, say, $50,000 for $5,000 cash. After he took possession, he'd jack the house up, spend another $5,000 to pour a new foundation, lower the house back down, then sell it for a huge profit. With the new foundation, FHA-insured financing was no problem. (Today those homes are likely worth over $150,000.)

Long-Term Holding Strategies

Owners of an individual home, such as a detached single-family residence or a condominium, can use several strategies to attain higher yields on their investment:

- Renting the home
- Leasing the home with an option to purchase
- Selling the home on installment

Renting the Home

Bear in mind that to get the most out of your realty holdings, you have to think long term. Properties you buy today, especially with a small down payment, are unlikely to be highly profitable at first. But as time goes on, your expenses should remain relatively fixed while rents and values gradually rise. This means that a property on which you initially break even will, after a few years, show a substantial net income and subsequent greater value.

As an example, let's say you buy a house with a small down payment and rent it out for $800 per month. Your total expenses on the house are also $800 per month, which, except for equity buildup, essentially represents a breakeven situation. One or two years later, you could rent the same property for $900 per month, and presuming your expenses remain fixed, you'd receive $100 per month in positive cash flow.

In a similar situation, assume you have a second loan on the property that you'll pay off after eight years. Once it's paid in full, you're that much further ahead in net income. But more important, you've paid off the second loan with money you earned from your tenants.

If you decide to rent the property, you have to choose either a long-term lease or a month-to-month rental agreement. The long-term lease (one year or more) has one primary advantage—it secures the tenant over a long term, essentially limiting turnover and somewhat assuring a stable flow of income over the term of the lease. (I say "somewhat assuring" because you cannot entirely guarantee that a long-term tenant won't move out without regard to lease obligations.)

A long-term lease has two primary disadvantages. The first is that it restricts the salability of the property, because the lease takes priority over the buyer's occupation rights should you sell the property before the lease expires. (The lease and all rights belonging to it are conveyed if the property is sold.) The second disadvantage is that a long-term lease agreement restricts the amount of rent you can charge. In other words, you can't raise the rent until the lease's term expires.

Under a month-to-month rental agreement, about the only disadvantage is that your tenant is obligated only to occupy and pay rent in monthly increments. The advantages are that a short-term rental agreement does not limit the salability of the property, and you're entitled to raise the amount of rent after each 30-day period.

Simply renting out your property is definitely a proven method of realizing a reasonable yield on your investment. However, there's another method that offers tremendous returns with fewer hassles: a lease with an option to purchase.

Leasing the Home with an Option to Purchase

A lease with an option to purchase (lease/purchase or buy option) is a month-to-month or yearly rental agreement in which the tenant has a leasehold interest in the property with an important added feature—the tenant has an option to purchase the property at some future time. The option to purchase is a separate part of the rental agreement that specifies the price and terms of the purchase contract. Under a typical lease/purchase option agreement, the owner (optionor) of a property gives the tenant (optionee) the right to purchase the rented property at a specified price and terms within a set period of time.

In addition to rent, the tenant pays the owner a specified option fee, which is applied toward the established purchase price. For instance, say you own a house and rent it for $800 per month. But instead of simply renting it, you offer the tenant a lease/purchase option, and the tenant pays you an additional $200 per month (the option fee) in addition to the monthly rent. Now, instead of collecting $800 per month, you collect $1,000 per month. The additional $200 per month in option fees is applied toward the established purchase price of the rented property.

The lease/purchase-option strategy can be a lucrative tool in real estate investing. It works. It has a broad market appeal, because many potential home buyers like the idea of making their down payment on the installment plan. You would be surprised at how many potential home buyers earn enough income to afford to buy a home, but don't have an adequate down payment to purchase a home under other methods of financing.

Aside from being more profitable, the lease/purchase option has a number of other advantages over renting:

- Lease/purchase-option tenants take better care of the occupied property than renters. They tend to make improvements to it and care for it better than if they were merely renting the property.
- Should the optionee fail to exercise the option within the term of the agreement, the optionor would forfeit all option fees already paid.
- The owner saves a sales commission on the sale, because there's no need to hire a Realtor to find a buyer.

Lease/Purchase Option Example

Consider this actual lease/purchase deal my wife and I negotiated in Las Vegas several years ago:

Purchase price	$96,000
Down payment	$10,000
Cost to renovate	1,200
Total investment	$11,200

The price was $96,000. We put $10,000 down and assumed an existing $40,000 loan at 8 percent interest. The balance of $46,000 was carried back by the seller in the form of a purchase money mortgage at 9 percent interest. Payments on the two loans were $400 and $485 per month, respectively, while the payment for taxes and insurance was $90. Therefore, total monthly payments including taxes and insurance were $975.

After spending $1,200 renovating the property, we rented it out with a purchase option agreement. The tenant had a one-year option to purchase the property at a price of $115,000. The tenant paid monthly rent of $1,075, of which $225 per month was applied to the purchase price. At the end of the one-year term, the tenant exercised the buy option, and in doing so paid a $5,000 down payment. This amount consisted of a $2,300 cash payment, plus $2,700 accumulated in option fees already paid ($225 monthly × 12 = $2,700). The balance of $110,000 was financed at 11.5 percent on a wraparound mortgage for 20 years.

The wrap was a new all-inclusive loan that kept the other existing assumable loans intact. We continued to pay on the underlying existing loans at $885 per month, while the optionee paid us 11.5 percent on a new wraparound at $1,173 per month. Thus, we earned the difference ($1,173 − $885 = $288) of the amount paid on the underlying loans and the amount paid on the new wraparound loan.

In addition, we also earned another $230 per month in principal payback, the amount by which the existing underlying loans were paid down each month. Consequently, we ended up earning $288 per month in cash flow, plus an additional $230 in equity buildup, resulting in $518 per month in gross equity income before taxes.

Now let's take a look at the numbers and examine why purchase options are so lucrative.

To calculate return on investment, you divide the total amount invested by the annual return on investment. In the preceding example, the annual return is $6,216 ($518 × 12). Dividing this amount by the total investment of $11,200, which is the renovation cost plus the down payment ($1,200 + $10,000), the result is a 55.5 percent return on investment. This is the return on investment after the first year. But for the first year you also have to figure in the additional gain of the $2,300 down payment received. Therefore, $6,216 + $2,300 = $8,516 ÷ $11,200 = 76 percent return on investment in the first year.

Such a phenomenal return is the result of a number of factors. The first is that the two underlying low-interest-rate loans were wrapped with a much higher all-inclusive loan. The second factor is that the property was sold for $19,000 more than what was paid for it.

Figure 19.2 shows the lease/purchase option agreement we used on that Las Vegas property.

Put Everything in Writing

The exact terms of the option must be spelled out in the agreement. That way there will be no doubt or further negotiation between the parties. The buyer and seller will know exactly who is responsible for what, and for how much.

FIGURE 19.2   Sample lease/purchase option agreement.

This option is made and entered into this 1st day of April 1989, by and between Andy Seller, herinafter called Landlord (owner), and Fred Buyer, herinafter called Tenant.

Subject property is a single-family residence located at 3450 Arby, Las Vegas, Nevada 89107.

Landlord hereby agrees to grant an option to purchase to Tenant based on the following terms and conditions. Provided that Tenant shall not then be in default of leased property, tenant to have option to purchase subject property at a price of $115,000 for one year beginning April 1, 1989, and expiring March 31, 1990.

Tenant agrees to pay a monthly option fee of $225 during the term of the option, which will be applied toward the purchase price. Tenant further agrees to pay a down payment, including paid option fees, of $5,000 to exercise this option. Tenant agrees to finance the balance owing of $110,000 secured by a wraparound mortgage in favor of Landlord at 11.5 percent per annum for 20 years at $1,173.08 per month.

Tenant agrees further to pay all taxes, insurance, and mortgage payments into a trust account for disbursement to all parties concerned and pay for such a trust account.

Tenant also agrees to purchase subject property in "as-is" condition.

Landlord agrees to have all loans, taxes, and insurance current at time of execution of this agreement.

Landlord and Tenant agree to split all normal closing costs, except Tenant is to pay for title insurance.

Landlord further agrees to apply all security deposits and cleaning fees under the lease agreement toward down payment upon execution of this agreement.

The parties hereto have executed this option on this date first above written:

By: _____ Landlord By: _____ Tenant

An option to purchase can be as creative as the buyer and seller want it to be; however, it should be kept relatively simple to avoid any misunderstandings. Should your tenant require a longer term on the option, you essentially have two methods of determining the selling price for that extended period. After the first year, you could set the option price at the existing price plus 1.5 times the Consumer Price Index (CPI). The other alternative is to arbitrarily fix a selling price at which the tenant can buy the property during a specific term, such as $100,000 after one year, $110,000 after two years, and $120,000 after three years. (I prefer using 1.5 times the CPI because the CPI measures inflation, and over the past 20 years real estate values, on average, have increased at about 1.5 times the rate of inflation.)

Structuring the Option Agreement

The option agreement should spell out any arrangements that might be considered unclear. For instance, the cleaning and security deposits, which have been prepaid, can be applied toward the down payment. The exact disposition of all the appliances (washer, dryer, and refrigerator) must be spelled out. If the appliances are to be included in the selling price, say so in the agreement; otherwise, spell out the price you require for such items.

Another consideration is the rate of interest to charge the buyer on the wraparound mortgage, if applicable. It makes good business sense to be fair and reasonable. Bear in mind that you'll be competing with conventional lenders, because you are, in effect, acting as a conventional lender when you wrap existing loans, which in reality creates a new loan. Then, as a rule of thumb, charge a rate of interest comparable to what conventional lenders are charging.

But since a wraparound mortgage is subordinate to the original mortgage, you do not charge a loan origination fee. This means substantial savings to the prospective buyer. This is an important selling feature that deserves further attention. Conventional lenders add a variety of incidental charges to the cost of originating a new loan. These include the credit report, typically $75; appraisal, $300; and 1 to 2 percent of the loan proceeds in points; plus the inconvenience and the time to complete the required paperwork. Therefore, remind your potential buyers of the convenience and cost savings they receive under the lease/purchase option method.

When the time comes for the tenant to exercise the purchase option, you can open an escrow account, so a neutral third party will carry out the provisions of the agreement according to procedures common for your area of the country. Once the escrow is closed, however, it's important to open a trust account for the protection of both you and the buyer. Most title companies will also operate a neutral trust.

The purpose of the trust is to act as a neutral third party that will take in the buyer's funds, make all disbursements (loans, taxes, and insurance), then send you a check for what's left over. This assures you and the buyer that everything is taken care of. You don't have to worry about the taxes or insurance being paid, and the buyer doesn't have to worry about the existing underlying loans being paid.

Finally, as part of your tools of the trade, you'll have to purchase a book that covers interest rates and associated monthly loan payments. Such books consist of tables to calculate monthly loan payments for specific terms and interest rates and are available in most bookstores.

Selling on Installment

Instead of renting or giving your tenant a purchase option, you also have the alternative of selling the property on installment. Please note that this method is appropriate only if underlying low-interest assumable financing is already built in. Say, for example, you purchase a property with an existing 8 percent mortgage which you assume, and the seller takes back a second mortgage at 9 percent. You could resell the property and allow your buyer to assume all this built-in financing. But instead, why not make a profit on the financing and sell on installment?

If you sell the property outright, you're totally cashed out. Now you have to find a place to invest the proceeds from the outright sale. However, you can earn a substantial profit by wrapping the existing financing with a new loan at a higher interest rate for 20 or 30 years.

Summary

Choose your niche according to what you like to do, or what you do well. If you're a carpenter, then remodeling is likely your forte. Same for people who like to paint or wallpaper. A person who knows how to pour concrete would be ideal for replacing faulty foundations under older houses. If you're a patient person, a land-banking investment strategy could suit you (see Chapter 23).

And keep in mind the benefits of long-term ownership of real estate—appreciation and changes in interest rates produce great opportunities. Declining rates mean you can refinance and earn more net income on your rentals. As time passes, you have several ways to retrieve your accumulated equity to invest in more property that will earn even more income. Before you know it, you'll have acquired a magnificent portfolio of income-producing real estate.

CHAPTER 20

Property Management

Anywhere you go in the world today, the richest citizens invariably are the landlords, the owners of improved real estate who rent to others. Some of them may have earned their riches elsewhere, but to protect and shelter their gains, they usually find real estate investment to be the wisest choice. Properly managed, a well-selected piece of income property is the closest thing you'll ever find to a thriving, self-generating money machine. That's what this chapter is all about—how to get the most out of your property with the least amount of difficulty.

Being a successful landlord is no accident. Mostly it's a matter of education, of learning how to do things the right way. The skills of collecting rent, showing vacancies, qualifying prospective tenants, handling maintenance, and keeping records don't require hard work. Performing them efficiently, however, does require that you take the time to apply yourself and learn how it's done.

Successful property management is about managing people. This includes overseeing a resident manager if you own a multiunit building, or properly handling tenants of single-family rentals. Whatever the case, you must manage people, and they manage your property for you. Then most of your management duties can be handled over the phone.

I like to refer to this approach as the "lazy person's guide to simple and efficient property management." This chapter shows you how to avoid the normal nuisances—the ones the inexperienced rental owners face every day, but don't know how to handle appropriately.

Bad management is not only a drain on your finances, it's an active drain of your time and energy. It can turn a potentially good investment into an unwanted nightmare. However, when you do things the right way, not only will you make the most from your investment, you can just about put your real estate holdings on automatic pilot and go fishing.

Showing and Renting Vacant Units

This section presents a step-by-step procedure for filling a vacant unit with a good, qualified, paying tenant. Your unit might be the greatest rental in the city, but a vacant house or apartment will remain unoccupied indefinitely if the public doesn't know it's available. Of course, if you rent the unit to an undesirable deadbeat, you'll soon wish the unit were vacant! The surest way to financial suicide, or at least a migraine headache, is to continually rent to tenants who won't pay. There are enough qualified prospects to fill your vacant unit; all you have to do is advertise and then properly qualify them.

Advertising

The best way to prospect for tenants is to post vacancy signs and place classified advertisments in the local newspaper. Vacancy signs must be precise and to the point, qualifying the prospective tenant to a certain degree. For instance, your sign might say, "Vacancy, 1-Bedroom, Adults Only," or "Vacancy, 2-Bedroom, Kids OK." Stating certain facts about the available unit eliminates a lot of unqualified prospects who are looking for something you don't have. Your signs should be legible and large enough to be seen easily from a passing vehicle. Erect your vacancy signs on either side of the building, or post them on the lawn near the busiest street for maximum exposure.

Classified advertisments should also be precise and qualifying, in order to eliminate unnecessary calls from unqualified people. Good advertising achieves attention, interest, desire, and action (remember these as AIDA). To get attention, your headline should attract specific prospects. To stimulate interest, you should expand the headline and offer a benefit to the prospects that makes them read the rest of the ad. Arouse desire with good descriptive copy that makes the prospect want what you have to offer. Ask for action by making it easy for the prospect to respond to your offer. Here are some specific ideas for each objective:

- *Attention.* The purpose of the attention heading is to get the reader to distinguish your ad from all the others in the same column. For example, "Newly Decorated," "Large 3-Bedroom," or "Free Rent for 1 Month." (This last type of ad might be used in a rental market already oversupplied with available units. Free rent would definitely get more attention than the other ads in the same column.)

- *Interest.*   To develop interest, offer a benefit, such as "2 fireplaces," "newly carpeted," or "great ocean view," to entice the reader to finish reading the balance of your ad.

- *Desire.*   This will precisely describe what you have to offer: "2-Bedroom, Kids OK, $675" or "1-Bedroom, Adults Only, Pool, $575."

- *Action.*   The action getter can be simply a phone number so the prospect can call and inquire.

Classified advertisments are printed under specific headings, so there's no need to duplicate information that's already available. In other words, you need not state that your apartment is unfurnished when your ad is running in the "Unfurnished Apartments" column.

Begin your ad with the location, then the type of unit. For example, you might say:

NEAR DOWNTOWN . . . 2-bedroom, 1-bath, patio and large fenced yard, kids and pets OK. $675. Call 555-1212.

By giving the location first, you qualify people from the start. People usually look for rentals in areas where they want to live. Anyone looking for a two-bedroom in the downtown area will respond to this ad; anyone looking for a three-bedroom in a different area will look elsewhere.

After a full description, including any particular features, close the ad with the amount of rent you're charging and a phone number. The amount of rent is important, because you again qualify the prospect. If you're charging more rent than prospects can afford to pay, they won't bother to call.

The following is a sample advertisement that proved very effective. It ran in a local newspaper under the heading "Unfurnished Condominiums for Rent":

RENT WITH BUY OPTION . . . Spring Mt. & Jones, 3-bedroom, 2-bath, neat & clean, beautifully landscaped and decorated, w/tennis cts, pool & jacuzzi. $795. Call 555-1212.

Showing the Vacant Unit

At this point, your advertisement is running in the local paper, and your vacancy signs are strategically located around the available unit. Now it's imperative that the unit be ready to be shown, which means it should be neat and clean throughout.

If by chance you're renting an occupied unit that will be vacated shortly, then inform the occupants of your intentions. Request that they keep the unit tidy so that you can show it to prospects.

While you're showing the unit, point out its features, such as storage, cabinets, view, and so on. Do not bring up anything that you might consider to be negative, because what may be a negative aspect to some may not be to others. Also, be sure you know the exact square footage of the unit in case someone inquires.

If the prospects are interested in the unit, they'll usually begin by asking questions concerning schools (Which school district is this?), transportation (Do you know the bus schedules?), shopping, and so on—questions you should be prepared to answer. If you don't know the school districts in the area, for example, find out what they are.

Renting the Unit

Your prospective tenants have seen the unit and have decided to rent it. What do you do now?

First, get as much of a deposit as you can, and do not accept a check. Your prospects could stop payment on the check as soon as they leave the premises, and you would be stuck with a worthless check. Accept only cash or a money order for the deposit, and make sure it's for at least $100. Anything less could entice your prospects to renege on their obligation should they find something else before moving in.

After receiving the deposit and giving your prospects a receipt, have them complete a rental application form. (See Appendix A.) Be sure they fill out the application completely, because you'll use this information later to determine whether you'll accept them as tenants. Once they have completed the application, check for omissions, and if there are none, tell them you'll phone when you've made a decision on their application.

Qualifying Prospective Tenants

Based on the rental application, you now have to decide whether to accept your new applicants as tenants. Essentially, you're looking for someone who will take reasonably good care of the premises, pay the rent on time, and not be a nuisance. Bear in mind that you're about to develop a long-term business relationship with these people, and you don't need the headaches associated with tenants who fail to pay their rent on time. When tenants who occupy a unit decide not to pay their rent, you can remove them, only by due process of law, which is very costly and time consuming.

The best way to avoid this catastrophic situation is to investigate your prospects' credit history. Telephone a local credit agency and find out what is required for a credit check. If the prospects have no credit, ask their past two landlords about their rent-paying habits. Occassionally, I'll will ask prospective tenants to show me their credit cards. If they have active Visa or MasterCard accounts, that's usually a sign of good credit. Just to be safe, though, I recommend that you check with the past two landlords. If you call them yourself, check with the previous landlord, instead of the current one, to protect yourself from a landlord who might bend the truth to be rid of a bad tenant. Landlord Services (www.gofic.com) does credit checks for $10 a head.

Your next concern is whether your prospects will properly care for your investment while they're living in it. About the only way you can determine this is by calling the previous landlord and inquiring into their living habits. Incidentally, in my 30 years as a landlord, I have made certain observations about the habits of humans that may prove useful to novices. It has been my experience that people who take good care of their vehicle will, in most cases, take good care of their home. Conversely, people who drive a dirty, ill-maintained car almost always keep a dirty and messy home, and won't take very good care of your property after they move in.

This observation also usually holds true for children. If the kids are reasonably well dressed in clean clothes, it's reasonable to assume that the parents will also care for things. So, when you meet prospective tenants, pay attention to the car and the children. Later, if you have any doubts about renting to them, let your observations assist in your decision.

Finally, you must qualify your prospects on their ability to pay the rent. The rent should not exceed 29 percent of the tenants' gross monthly income. However, if they have no consumer debt (i.e., car loans and credit card payments), they can afford up to 33 percent of their gross monthly income. Do not include overtime pay. For example, if your prospects gross $3,000 per month and have some consumer debt, they really cannot afford to pay more than $870 per month in rent ($3,000 × 0.29 = $870). If they have no consumer debt, then they can afford one-third of $3,000, or $1,000 per month.

Collecting Deposits

Generally speaking, the more risk you expose yourself to, the more you should require in deposits. You face more risk when the family you rent to has children or pets. If you're going to allow dogs and cats in your unit, a minimum $300 non-refundable deposit per pet is recommended. The security deposit on an unfurnished home is usually 75 to 100 percent of the first month's rent. This amount can be adjusted upward for each child in the family. Except for the pet deposit, security deposits are refundable within 30 days of moving out if there's been no damage to the premises.

Another necessary deposit is the nonrefundable cleaning deposit. The cleaning deposit normally ranges from $75 to $150, depending on the size and value of the rental. Before your tenants move in, be sure to inform them that 30 days notice must be given before moving out, and that neither the security nor the cleaning deposit can be applied to the last month's rent when they vacate the premises.

Separate refundable deposits should be required for certain keys, such as access cards for parking or for tennis courts. Usually $10 is adequate for keys and $25 for each key card.

Moving Tenants In

Before your tenants occupy your rental unit, it's imperative that they pay all monies owed to you in advance, in cash or by money order. This includes the first month's rent (or first and last if it's a long-term lease) and all deposits, including security, cleaning, and key deposits. Be sure that the rental agreement is signed and that one copy is available for the tenants. Also be sure that the tenants have one set of keys, plus information on who to call to have all the utilities turned on. Finally, inform them that you expect the rent to be paid on time, and that there's a three-day grace period, after which a 5 percent late fee will be charged.

Rent Collecting

Your investment in real estate is purely a money-making enterprise, not a charitable mission. Investors who yield to delinquent or nonpaying deadbeats are courting financial disaster. Therefore, be firm with your collection policies, and inform your new tenants at the time of moving in what you expect of them. However, you can be flexible with certain things. All rents do not have to be paid on the first day of the month. Under certain circumstances, some tenants might receive their paychecks on the tenth or the fifteenth of the month. If this is the case, adjust their rent due dates to coincide with their paydays.

After the tenants have paid all move-in fees in cash, you should make a policy of accepting only checks or money orders for the rent payments. If you receive a bad check, your policy from then on should be to accept only money orders from that tenant. Check bouncers are a habitual bunch. If you continue to accept checks after one has bounced, you can be assured that it won't be the last.

Rent checks should be mailed directly to an address of your choice, or remitted directly to your resident manager. Once a tenant has established a good payment history, you can make allowances when unforeseen circumstances occur, such as the loss of a employment, illness, or death in the family. Whatever the case, tenants must make definite commitments as to when the debt will be paid, and you must immediately follow up if it's not.

Rent Collection Policy

If you have a resident manager for your multiunit building, you'll need to establish a rent collection policy. Rent should always be collected by check or money order. Absolutely no cash should be accepted. (An exception can be made in an emergency or when someone's payment is extremely late.) A policy of accepting only checks or money orders eliminates the resident manager's temptation to borrow small amounts of cash, and if there's no cash on hand, there's less risk that the rent monies will be stolen.

You can have the resident manager deposit each month's rent receipts. Order a rubber stamp that says "For Deposit Only . . ." from the printer, then have the manager stamp the back of each rent check. The manager can then deposit each month's checks into your bank account.

Occasionally a tenant will request a rent receipt. Furnish the manager with a receipt pad in triplicate. One copy is for the tenant, one is for the manager, and one is for your records.

Evicting Tenants

States and cities usually specify the legal procedures property owners must follow to terminate a lease or evict a tenant. The typical procedure pertains to (1) lawful grounds, (2) written notice, (3) time to cure or remedy, (4) time elapsing

 BEWARE

Here are two important reasons why you should never accept rent payment of cash:

1. If you never inspect vacant units, the manager could collect cash rent on a unit while telling you that the unit is vacant.

2. A no-cash policy reduces the risk that your manager will be robbed of the rent receipts.

Enforcing a policy of always inspecting vacant units and never accepting cash can curtail these attempts to rob you.

before a hearing, (5) allowable tenant defenses, and (6) time to vacate after an adverse ruling.

Learn this legal procedure as it applies in your city. Then follow it to a tee. Failure to be precise can get your case thrown out, which means you must go back and start all over again. (See the Landlord Tale that follows.) Never resort to changing the door locks; turning off the tenant's water, heat, or electricity; or confiscating the tenant's property. Also, never resort to taking the law in your own hands by threatening or assaulting a tenant. Trying to avoid lawful procedure can expose you to numerous types of criminal charges and personal injury lawsuits.

Eviction Procedure for Nonpayment of Rent

The following procedure for the lawful eviction of a tenant for nonpayment of rent is common in many states:

1. The tenant in default is served with a three-day notice to pay rent or quit the premises.
2. An unlawful detainer is filed with the municipal court clerk, and a summons is issued.
3. The tenant is served with a summons and a complaint.
4. The tenant has the legal right to file against the complaint, pleading his or her case. In that event, a trial is held.
5. The default of the tenant is taken and given to the owner.
6. The court issues a writ of possession.
7. The marshal receives the writ of possession.
8. The marshal evicts the tenant.

Managing Multiunit Buildings

Whether you own a fourplex or a 20-unit apartment building, somone has to be responsible on site. Someone living on the property should be responsible for showing vacant units, collecting rents, and generally overseeing the property. In a 20-unit building, the person responsible is the resident manager. But even in a smaller four-unit building, you should have a manager responsible for certain duties, such as showing units and maintaining the grounds. That way it won't be necessary for the owner to be constantly on site, because some responsibility is delegated to the resident manager. Unless you like getting angry calls at 3 A.M.

LANDLORD TALE

In 1976, when I managed foreclosure property for a 40-branch savings and loan, there was notable incident during the process of evicting a tenant from one of our properties. We had foreclosed on a house in Long Beach, California, and I was directed to be at the property at 10 A.M., when I would legally take possession of the property. Reportedly, there was a tenant residing in the premises, an elderly woman, and the marshal had been ordered to the house in case she remained on the property and had to be evicted.

The day before, my supervisor had instructed me about the situation, and said to me, "When you meet the marshal at the property tomorrow morning, under no circumstances allow the tenant back in the house once the marshal evicts her."

I acknowledged him, but apparently I hadn't really paid attention to his warning. Because this "sweet" woman duped me into making a horrible mistake.

The morning started out well—I arrived at the property on time, and the marshal was there waiting for me. We exchanged some pleasantries, then the marshal knocked on the door and the tenant, along with an old black cat, came to the door. When the door opened, the marshal handed the tenant, a small, pleasant, gray-haired woman, a writ of possession. He then said, "Ma'am you're going to have to leave the premises immediately."

She replied with a mystified look on her face, "But sir, what am I to do with all my furniture, and my cat?"

"Sorry Ma'am, but it is my responsibility to make sure that you're out of the premises so I can turn possession over to this man. You can work out the disposition of your possessions later with him. He now represents the new owners of this property."

She said, "Well let me get my purse, and then I'll leave."

While the marshal escorted her back into the house, I waited outside by the door with a new lockset, deadbolt and screwdriver. Moments later, the tenant and the marshal exited the house. The marshal looked at me and said, "The house is all yours," then walked to his car, got in, and drove off.

I started changing the locks out on the front door when the tenant (or now ex-tenant) walked over to me and with tears in her eyes said, "Excuse, me sir, but my poor cat I've had for over fifteen years is still in the house. I can't leave him in there—he'll starve to death!"

Now I was really perplexed, because I'm such an animal lover, especially old tomcats. I thought about the situation for a moment (obviously not long enough), then opened the door and said, "Ma'am, I'll get your cat for you." And I walked in the house and started looking for the cat. Within a few seconds, guess who walked in right behind me? She sat right down on the couch in the living room.

(continued)

LANDLORD TALE

When I saw her sitting there, I was flabbergasted. Then I thought to myself, oh God, what have I done? She just looked up at me and said, "Sir, I'm not leaving until I have all my possessions, including my cat!"

At this point, I pleaded with her to leave, but she wouldn't have anything to do with it. I surmised that there was nothing left to do but get my equipment and head back to the office. (I also wondered how many others she had duped out of possession in her lifetime, because she seemed to be such a professional scam artist.)

The end result was that we had to restart the eviction process all over again, and it took the court another 30 days to issue another writ. However, this time when we showed up at the property with the marshal and the writ, she and all of her household belongings were gone. Later I discovered she had moved out the day before, knowing that it wouldn't be so easy to scam me a second time.

from tenants who have locked themselves out, always have a manager on site. Cost: 5 to 8 percent of gross income.

Choosing the Resident Management Team

The ideal resident management team is a husband and wife, who should divide the responsibilities and maintenance according to their abilities and availability. Ideally, one spouse will have the stability and income of a full-time job elsewhere, while the other stays home to manage the building. The following are qualities you should look for in a management team, listed in order of importance:

1. Honesty
2. Eagerness to do the job properly
3. Ability to accept responsibility
4. Ability to make minor repairs (at least one spouse)
5. Pleasant personality
6. Willingness of one spouse to stay at home and assist in the overall operation of the property

Duties of the Resident Managers

The managers' responsibilities are primarily to collect the rent, show vacant units to prospective tenants, and keep the common area clean. But if one member of the team is capable of handling minor repairs and mowing the lawn, then you can eliminate the need to call a professional for those services.

It's very important that the spouse who agrees to stay home be on the job to show vacancies and keep order around the building. Someone who is active outside the home and has numerous social commitments is not a good prospect; a parent who prefers to stay at home with the children typically makes a better on-site manager.

What you pay the husband-and-wife team depends on the size of the building. The payment for managing a 20-unit building typically would be free rent. For a smaller building, such as a fourplex or a sixplex, a 25 percent reduction in rent would be typical. Buildings larger than 20 units usually involve free rent plus a cash salary. For competitive salaries, look in your newspaper's classified section under "Couples Wanted."

Supervising the Resident Managers

The duties of the resident managers must be fully explained at the beginning of the owner-employee relationship. Be sure they know exactly what is expected of them. Remember, the more responsibility you can delegate to the managers, the more time you'll have for other matters.

Monthly reports must be submitted to the owner for efficient accounting and ready reference. These reports include a summary of rents (income) collected and bank deposits made (if the manager rather than the owner makes the deposits).

Each entry on the summary of rents collected should include the apartment number, the date rent was paid and the due date, the amount paid, and the type of income (rent, cleaning fee, key deposit, or security deposit). One copy of the rent receipt is also kept on file by the manager, and the tenant receives the third copy, if requested.

Major expenditures, such as replacing carpet or a hot-water heater, should be billed directly to the owner. In fact, it will be helpful if the owner can establish charge accounts with various suppliers. This will reduce the managers' temptation to pad expense bills or take kickbacks from salespeople.

Once you have a qualified and responsible management team operating your building, you'll find that a monthly supervisory visit is sufficient. On such visits, you can make major decisions, such as whether to undertake expensive repairs or recarpet a particular unit. In addition, you can pick up the collected rent and inspect the premises. A responsible manager can enrich the joys of landlording, as you avoid the headaches and hassles many amateur owners experience due to slip-shod management practices.

Tenant Profiling and Discrimination Laws

As a landlord, you cannot legally refuse to rent to people because of their race, creed, color, national origin, sex, or marital status. This doesn't mean, however, that you are obligated to rent to anyone who has a fistful of money. In particular, for a multiunit building, you should have certain standards to promote harmony in your building. For instance, single adults prefer to live in a building with other singles. Likewise, families with children usually prefer to live in buildings that cater to families, and older adults prefer to live where they're not annoyed by barking dogs and children at play. Therefore, set certain standards if you own a multiunit building, and don't try to mix the elderly with the young, or singles with families.

Renting Furnished versus Unfurnished Units

Generally speaking, if you're renting out single-family homes, it will be to your advantage to keep your units unfurnished. If you do supply furniture, of course, you can charge more rent; however it's then your responsibility to maintain the furniture and insure it for theft and fire damage.

The major disadvantage of supplying furniture to your tenants is that it creates more turnover. It's very easy to get up and move away from a rented home that's completely furnished. It takes tenants much more effort to move when they supply their own furnishings. Once tenants have taken the time, effort, and expense to move all their belongings into a home, they're likely to stay awhile.

However, certain types of rental units must be furnished in order to attract tenants. If you live in a college town and rent the home as a boarding house to college students, or if you happen to own single or studio-type apartments that cater to more transient clientele, then supplying furniture would be appropriate.

Obtaining and Maintaining Appliances

Items such as refrigerators, washers, and clothes dryers are expensive to purchase and maintain, but when they're offered as an amenity, they do add salability to your rental unit. If you have the opportunity to pick up these appliances at bargain prices as part of the purchase when you invest in property, then by all means do so. The responsibility for maintaining and repairing such appliances can mostly be turned over to your tenants through a "no-hassle $100-deductible repair clause" inserted into your rental agreement. This particular clause states, "The first $100 in repair of the rented property, including appliances, is the tenant's responsibility." (The no-hassle clause is covered in more detail later in this chapter.)

If you own a multiunit apartment building with nine or more rental units, you have to consider whether to supply a laundry facility with coin-operated washers and dryers, and whether you should buy or lease the equipment. In smaller buildings—those with eight units or less—furnishing washers and dryers is not economically feasible, because the usage isn't enough to pay for the utilities to run the machines.

If you buy coin-operated equipment, the machines should pay for themselves within two years. That's the good part. However, you have to maintain the equipment and be responsible for acts of vandalism and the theft of coins from your machines.

Conversely, you could lease your laundry equipment from a reputable appliance leasing company. The company would be responsible for supplying and maintaining the equipment and for collecting coins from the machines. Generally, the leasing company retains 60 percent of the gross receipts and remits the remaining 40 percent to the building owner. You can take precautionary measures so that a responsible person oversees the removal of coins from the leased equipment, in order to help eliminate the temptation of skimming from the coin boxes.

Paying for Utilities and Trash Removal

Tenants who rent single-family homes or condominiums should be responsible for paying for all the utilities and trash removal. Also, most apartment buildings, especially more modern ones, have separate meters for gas and electricity consumption, and the respective companies bill the individual tenants. But the owner of the building is usually responsible for paying the water bill. When separate meters are not available for gas and electricity, the owner must add the cost of these utilities to the rent. Furthermore, trash removal service for multiunit buildings is best paid for by the owner, so as to maintain a cleaner common area around the building and avoid friction with the tenants as to whose responsibility it is.

Budgeting

The successful operation of a rental building ultimately depends on carefully planning a budget, then sticking to it without exception. The budget is basically a financial plan for the upcoming years. Income and expenses are projected to provide an overall view of the building's financial well-being. If you don't properly plan income and expenses, financial suicide is inevitable. Money must be allocated for certain replacement items over the years. When owners do not plan properly, they end up deferring maintenance. That, in turn, causes vacancies, which, in turn, causes loss of income and further deferred maintenance and eventual loss in value.

Good budgeting encompasses not only the planning of income and expenses, but also the future replacement of capital items, such as carpeting, roofs, pool equipment, and furniture. These items are very costly, but with a properly planned budget, they can easily be replaced when necessary. A contingeny fund should be set aside and held in reserve for this purpose. For example, carpeting has to be replaced every seven years, on average. New carpeting in today's market for a one-bedroom apartment will cost about $840. Therefore, about $120 per year per apartment ($120 × 7 years = $840) should be reserved in a contingency fund to replace carpeting. Likewise, replacement reserves must be set up for items such as draperies, roofing, furniture, and appliances.

The best way to budget these items is to estimate total outlay for all future capital expenditures, maintaining a fund for each item in one savings account. For example, you determine that the cost of a new roof is $4,800 and that it will last for 20 years. Divide the total cost by the total number of months, and the result is the amount that should be budgeted each month ($4,800 ÷ 240 months = $20 per month).

Expense items, such as property taxes and hazard insurance, also have to be budgeted. Taxes and insurance premiums frequently are paid out of an impound account, which is already part of your mortgage payment. If this is the case, you won't have to pay them separately. If the holder of the first mortgage is not paying the taxes and insurance premiums, you'll have to arrange to pay these items from the monthly budget. Property taxes are projected at one-twelfth of the annual tax bill per month. Be sure to allow for future increases by the county tax assessor. Hazard insurance is likewise one-twelfth of the annual insurance premium.

As a rule, 5 percent of gross collected rent is usually adequate to budget for overall replacement reserves. However, you'll have to increase this amount if your building has additional equipment, such as an elevator, a heated pool, or a whirlpool.

Keeping Records

Proper record-keeping procedures are necessary so the information will be accessible when needed, especially when income tax time arrives, or when the IRS decides to make an unexpected audit. Keeping records is simple when your investments are single-family homes. All you need is a separate 8.5- × 11-inch manila envelope for each home, properly labeled, to keep all records and expense items. All income collected can be noted on the outside of the envelope, along with the addresses of note holders, the balance owed on the notes, and the initial cost of the property. At the end of each year, you can start a new envelope for the upcoming year.

Multiunit buildings require somewhat more elaborate record-keeping systems, with a separate set of records for each building. Make up file folders and label them "General Records," "Tenant Records," and "Receipts and Expenses." In the general records folder, retain such information as escrow papers, insurance policies, taxes, notes, and deeds. In the tenant record folder, maintain all rental applications, rental agreements, and any other data pertaining to your tenants. All tenant information should be kept for credit-rating purposes and landlord inquiries for at least one year after the tenants move out. In the receipt folder, retain all paid receipts for all expenses related to the building and copies of all rent receipts. Later you can arrange the expense items chronologically for tax purposes. At the end of the tax year, this envelope should be stored separately for at least five years, in case the IRS decides to audit.

Tenant Records (Cardex)

Set up a filing system for each multiunit building. Set up a record for each tenant on a 5.5 × 8-inch Cardex (see Appendix A). Whenever a tenant makes a payment, you or the resident managers record it on the Cardex.

Journal of Income and Expenses

For each multiunit building, keep a separate journal in which you post all relevant income and expense data monthly. This journal should include sections on income, expenses, loans, and depreciation. This gives you easy access to all current data relating to income and expenses. As shown in Figure 20.1, the first section denotes rental income for each property for the entire year. The second section is for posting expenses (see Figure 20.2). All those receipts you've been keeping in a file folder are recorded here monthly. Anything you don't have receipts for can be recorded from your checking account record.

Once you've completed an entire page of the expense and payment record, total each column and bring the balance forward to the next sheet. Then start posting your later entries. After you have posted your last expenditure for the year, total the last sheet, and you'll have your income and expenses for each category of the building.

FIGURE 20.1   Journal of income.

Monthly Income Record   Page # _____

Address _____

Year _____

Unit	Jan.	Feb.	Mar.	Apr.	May	June	July	Aug.	Sept.	Oct.	Nov.	Dec.
1	400	400	400	400	400							
2	390	390	390	390	390							
3	425	425	425	425	425							
4	275	275	275	275	275							
5	415	415	415	415	415							
6	460	460	460	460	460							
7												
8												
Total	2,365	2,365	2,365	2,365	2,365							

Be careful not to post such capital items as carpeting or a new roof in your expense record. These are depreciable items, not expenses.

Depreciation Records

Depreciable items are property or equipment having an extended useful life that are considered to be improvements to the property. Some examples are carpeting, elevators, linoleum, roof replacement, and swimming pools. Each of these items must be depreciated on a separate depreciation record form, as shown in Figure 20.3.

Annual Statement of Income

The annual statement of income brings together all relative income and expenses for the year and reveals the net profit or loss. Figure 20.4 shows an example. Note that depreciation, not an out-of-pocket expense, is deducted last for tax purposes. The bottom line is the net profit or loss shared with the IRS.

FIGURE 20.2   Journal of expenses.

Expense and Payment Record

Address _____ Year # _____ Page # _____

Date	Paid to	Paid for	Total Paid	Mortgage Principal	Mortgage Interest	Tax	Ins.	Mgmt.	Repairs & Maint.
1. 1/1	Bank	1st mort.	760	122.80	427.20	120	90		
2. 1/1	Smith	2nd	125	92.40	32.60				

Handling Repairs

One principle the no-hassle management theory is to avoid some of the common nuisances of managing residential rentals. Landlords can solve the problem of who is responsible for certain repairs by making the tenants pay the repair costs, up to a certain limit. This way, the landlord doesn't have to get involved with minor repairs.

In the sample rental agreement (see Appendix A) you'll find a clause under "Repairs and Maintenance" that I refer to as the "no-hassle repair clause." It

FIGURE 20.3   Sample depreciation record.

Location   3850 Raymond, Los Angeles, CA
Description   19-unit apartment building

Date acquired	January 1987
New or used	Used
Cost or value	$220,000
Land value	$40,000
Salvage value	-0-
Depreciable basis	$180,000
Method of depreciation	Straight line
Useful Life	27.5 years

	Year	Prior Depreciation	Depreciation Balance	Percentage of Year Held	Depreciation This Year
1.	1987	0	$180,000	100	$6,545
2.	1988	0	$173,455	100	$6,545
3.	1989	0	$166,910	100	$6,545

FIGURE 20.4   **Sample annual statement of income.**

Location   3850 Raymond, Los Angeles, CA
Year   1988

Income
   Rent $28,471
   Other (laundry)   629

Total income		$29,100
Expenses		
Interest	$ 8,410	
Taxes	4,800	
Utilities	1,812	
Service, repairs	120	
Pest control	321	
Insurance	850	
Management	1,800	
Total Expenses		$18,113
Net income (before depreciation)		10,987
Less depreciation		−6,545
Net income (or loss) for tax purposes		$ 4,442

states that the tenant is responsible for the first $100 in repairs on the rented property. In other words, if a window breaks, the plumbing gets stopped up, or the washer breaks down, the tenant pays the repair bill, up to $100. This frees the landlord from troublesome phone calls requesting minor repairs.

One more point about the no-hassle repair clause: Be sure to inform your tenants of the repair policy when they move in. It's also advisable to give them the phone number of a competent repair person.

Points to Remember

Rental management can be a real headache, if you allow it to be. It can also be a hassle-free experience, but you have to be diligent. Make sure you have the right tenants, and let the others live somewhere else.

This chapter offers a concise, yet thorough, guide to total property management. Foremost among these guidelines are to properly screen your prospective tenants and to include the "no-hassle" clause in your rental agreements. These simple procedures will help to make investment property management a truly efficient, successful, and profitable experience.

LANDLORD TALE

This experience highlights why it's never a good idea to move out of town and leave the management of your real estate to someone else.

In 1989, I decided to relocate from Las Vegas, Nevada, where I owned three houses and a condominium. The three houses were already rented out, and after I got a tenant for the condo, I turned all manangement responsibility over to a so-called professional property manager, and moved to Naples, Florida. For a while, everything seemed to go well. Then peculiar things began to happen. According to the property mananger, the tenants in the house on Pleasant Road decided to move out without paying the last month's rent, and to make matters worse, they left a lot of trash behind.

While the house was vacant, I decided to have it cleaned up and listed for sale. Within a month, the manager called from Las Vegas and told me that the foundation was cracked in several places. He told me that I would be lucky to get $50,000 for it, rather than $150,000. Oh, and by the way, he added, we do have a buyer if you want to sell at $50,000.

Well, I smelled a rat, and I booked a flight to Las Vegas. When I got there, I hired a structural engineer to take a look at the foundation. There were no cracks anywhere. Apparently, the property manager was conspiring with the buyer to cheat me out of $100,000. And they figured to get away with it because I was 2,200 miles away.

I ended up selling this particular property for $145,000 with a different real estate broker.

LESSON: Never be an absentee landlord, unless you want people to take advantage of you.

When you own multiunit income property, be sure to protect yourself. Hold property in a limited liability company, if the roof falls in, tenants can't go after your house.

And if you're wondering whether it's a good idea to be an absentee landlord, the preceding Landlord Tale should assist you at making that decision.

For a sampling of useful management forms, see Appendix A.

CHAPTER 21

Selling Your Property

Sooner or later, regardless of your investment strategy, you'll want to sell one or more of your properties. When that time comes, you have to decide whether to use the services of a real estate broker or try to sell the property yourself. You have to consider not only the cost of the broker's commission, but also the helpful services that a broker can provide.

Broker Services

Successful selling a property requires a good deal of effort, time, expense, and expertise. Property owners who are reluctant to commit to these requirements are unlikely to find a qualified buyer.

Most property owners prefer to hire a professional. Realty brokerage companies can provide the following important services:

- A vast supply of prospects acquired from such sources as referrals by past customers, Internet and e-mail inquiries, hotel and motel managers, institutional lenders, educational institutions, insurance agents, lawyers, human resource departments, builders, newspaper advertisments, and "For Sale" signs.

- A full-time effort to locate qualified buyers. Realtors are not just available part-time in the evenings or on weekends.

- An accurate appraisal of fair market value, based on recent sales of similar homes in the area.

- Helpful advice on how the property should be prepared to stimulate a quick sale.

- Showings of the property that emphasize the features that appeal to each potential buyer. Realtors know what their clients want, so they show potential buyers only those properties that are likely to interest them.

- A determination of how much the seller will net from the sale after all closing costs have been paid, including payoff of the mortgage balance, other liens, and property taxes.

- Assistance in negotiating the sale, including advice regarding the pros and cons of each offer.

- Assistance to the buyer in overcoming obstacles to the purchase, such as selling an existing property, acquiring financing, or arranging an exchange.

- Follow-up on potential buyers who have seen the property.

- Prequalification of prospective buyers.

- Details of the prospect's true objections to the property, so the seller can try to overcome them. Prospective buyers are usually more revealing with a Realtor than with a property owner.

Most prospective buyers depend on realtors to assist them in finding properties. Property owners who attempt to sell their property themselves thus make themselves less visible to a sizable number of prospects.

Timing the Sale

Traditionally, there are good times of the year to sell residential property, as well as good times to buy. The spring and fall are good times to sell, primarily because that's when most buyers are looking for property, especially if they have shool-age children. The worst time to sell real estate is usually the winter holiday season, from Thanksgiving to early February. Potential buyers are usually too preoccupied to concern themselves with the purchase of a home during the holidays. However, the deficiency of buyers makes it a good time to purchase residential real estate.

Price It Right

You should have a realistic idea of what your property is worth from what you learned about appraisal in Chapter 10. Bear in mind, though, that you're going to be competing with hundreds of other sellers, and it's very unlikely that you'll find a naive buyer who's willing to pay more for your property than it's actually worth.

To establish the right price, first decide on the minimum offer you'll accept for the property. Then you can adjust your price upward from this point, allowing a little room for negotiation. Most buyers like to negotiate, so allow yourself a little flexibility. Price the property at a reasonable point above your minimum in order to stimulate bona fide offers.

Necessary Documents and Information

After you have decided on a selling price, you can start gathering the documents and information you'll need to consumate the sale.

You'll need the the following information from the loan documents:

- Is there a prepayment penalty on the first mortgage? If so, will the lender waive it if the buyer obtains a mortgage from them?
- What is the current principal balance owed on the mortgage?
- Is there a tax and insurance impound account? If so, what is the balance?

Note that the prepayment penalty is a cost to you, levied by the lender according to the original loan agreement, charging you a penalty (six months' interest on the unpaid balance is common) for repaying the loan before its maturity. This penalty charge covers the lender's cost in reclaiming and then reloaning the money that is paid back prematurely, and it may be waived, as mentioned earlier.

You'll also need the following documents:

- A copy of the tax receipts for the previous year.
- A copy of the property survey.
- Evidence of title.

Home-Selling Tips

Regardless of whether you use the services of a Realtor, you still need to prepare the property for sale. This section is a guide to preparing your property in order to get a quick and bona fide offer.

Realtors often use such phrases as "This property has good curb appeal" (meaning it looks good from the curb) or "This house shows well," when showing homes to prospective buyers. Their descriptive jargon is relevant, because in order to get the best price for your home, it's wise to prepare it to look its best.

Unless you want to sell a fixer-upper, or a house that looks like a fixer-upper, you have to put the house and the surrounding grounds in order so as to get the best price. Some of this is simply tidying up around the exterior of the house. But unless you're an extremely tidy housekeeper, you'll have to do some minor repairs and touch-ups to meet good-condition standards. Remember, anything in obvious disrepair will eventually be discounted from the offer price.

First impressions are most favorable. If the house isn't appealing from the curb, the prospective buyer might not get out of the car to look further. The following suggestions will help to sell your home quickly by getting the prospect out of the car and into your house for a complete inspection.

Exterior

- Tidy up all around the exterior grounds by removing any debris, old cars, and so on. Cut the grass and trim the hedges and shrubs. Arrange and organize items, such as outdoor furniture and firewood.

- Store away, or have removed from the property, such items as broken-down dishwashers, water heaters, or air conditioners. (Avoid the look of a junkyard.)

- Give the lawn a thorough raking, and sweep up the sidewalk and driveway.

- Tour the perimeter of your property. Repair any broken fencing and paint or stain areas that need attention.

- Carefully inspect your front door. It's one of the first items your home-hunting prospects will examine. If it shows signs of wear, give it a fresh coat of paint or stain. While you're at it, spruce up the house numbers with a touch-up paint job, or replace them with new shiny brass ones.

- Repainting the entire exterior of the house may not be necessary. Quite often you can substantially improve the appearance of the house simply by repainting the trim.

- Repair any broken windows or screens, then wash them for a brighter appearance.

Interior

- When you're finished with the exterior, start on the interior of your home. The objective here is to make your home look organized and spacious, bright, warm, and comfortable. Cleanliness cannot be overemphasized. Remember, a clean house will sell much faster than a dirty one.

- Brighten dull rooms with a fresh coat of white, beige, or antique white paint. Lighter colors make rooms look bigger and brighter, and neutral colors will go better with the new buyer's furnishings. Instead of taking the time and effort to pull down and replace wallpaper, try sprucing up the trim instead.

- Cluttered rooms with too much furniture show very poorly. Prospective buyers want lots of room. Rearrange your furniture to make rooms appear more spacious. Put excess furniture in storage. Unclutter your home, then rearrange and organize what's left. You'll be surprised how many unwanted things can accumulate over the years.
- Have a giant garage sale to clear out all your unwanted belongings. You can earn extra money, and you won't have to pay the movers to relocate all those unwanted items.
- Clean all windows and mirrors.
- If the carpet is dirty, have it professionally cleaned. If the carpet appears to be overly worn, consider having it replaced. It's unlikely that you'll recover the cost of a new carpet in the sale, but it will probably help the house to sell faster.
- Unclutter those kitchen counters to make your kitchen look more organized and spacious.
- Clean and polish all appliances in the kitchen. Finish in the kitchen by making the sink shiny and sparkling.
- Clean and shine the tubs, toilets, and sinks in all the bathrooms.
- Break out the tool box and start fixing all those little things you've been putting up with all these months—leaky faucets, loose doorknobs, and cracked electrical outlets and switch covers. Secure those loose moldings and towel racks and anything that wobbles.

These are all little items of disrepair that can detract from the beauty and function of your home. When prospective buyers examine your home, they mentally keep track of any shortcomings. Too many little things in disrepair will bring a lower offer—if any at all—than if the house were in excellent condition.

When it's finally time to show your home to prospective buyers, all the preparations will definitely be worth the effort, as your home will receive more and better offers than if you were ill-prepared. But there are a few additional things you should do just before you show the home that will add that little extra touch of comfort and style.

Just before your prospective buyers arrive, clear out the kids and secure the pets where they won't cause any distraction. Turn off the television and put on some soft music. Turn on all the lights in the house to make it as bright as possible, even during the daytime. If you have a fireplace, fire it up, too. Spice up your home with the aroma of freshly baked cinnamon rolls right out of the oven. Finish up with clean towels on the racks, and put out some fresh flowers to treat yourself for making your home such a tidy showplace.

When the prospects arrive, make yourself scarce (when using a Realtor). Your absence will put potential buyers more at ease. Your presence will only distract from the job at hand, that of showing your entire home and answering any questions, which is the agent's responsibility. If you must be there, try to avoid any conversation with the prospects, because the agent needs their full attention to stimulate interest in the features of your home.

Do not complicate the sale of your home by discussing the separate sale of certain appliances, or the fact that you wish to keep certain personal items. Personal property, such as furniture and unattached appliances, can be negotiated later, at a more appropriate time.

Always maintain your home in showplace condition, as you never know when just the right prospect might show up. Your agent will usually make appointments with you for showings, and if casual browsers drop in for an unexpected visit, it's best not to show your home. Ask for their name and phone number and refer the information to your agent.

Keep in mind that it takes time to sell a home. Be patient. Keep your home on the market for as long as it takes. Your home must be exposed to enough prospective buyers to generate a proper sale.

In closing, you might consider offering a one-year home warranty plan, which would provide a little more added value and overcome questions about the condition of major home systems. These policies are available through most national real estate brokerage companies, and will protect your buyers for one year against the cost of most major repairs.

Property Information Sheet

The property information sheet is necessary only if you intend to sell the property yourself. It's a list of all the vital measurements and other information about your home, which you will distribute to prospective buyers. Use a 50-foot or longer tape measure to measure each room, and do this as accurately as you can. Enter this and all other stipulated information on the form shown in Figure 21.1, and make copies for distribution.

Open House and the "For Sale" Sign

Traditionally, Realtors hold open houses on their listed properties over the weekend, when the majority of potential home buyers have time off from work and can easily go house hunting.

FIGURE 21.1 Property information sheet.

PROPERTY INFORMATION

Address _____ Selling price $ _____

_____

Existing first mortgage balance _____ at _____%

Existing second mortgage balance _____ at _____%

Monthly payments on first $ _____ plus taxes and insurance $ _____

Monthly payments on second $ _____

Architectural style _____	Const _____	Basemt _____
LR _____	Age _____	Heat _____
DR _____	Lot size _____	A/C _____
Kit _____	Garage _____	220 wiring _____
Dinette _____	Curbs & gutters _____	Hot water _____
Fam. rm _____	Paved street _____	Soft water _____
Other rm _____	Sidewalk _____	
Bath _____	Water _____	
Bath _____	Sewer _____	
Bath _____	Septic _____	
BR _____		
BR _____	Schools: High _____	Grade _____
BR _____	Middle _____	
BR _____		

Draperies and curtains _____

Carpeting _____

Items included

Oven _____	Range _____	Refrigerator _____
TV antenna _____	Disposal _____	Dishwasher _____

Items not included _____

_____

Owner _____ Phone _____

If you plan to sell your home yourself, the weekend is also the best time to hold your open house. If by chance other owners are holding open houses at the same time, you'll actually benefit from it. Many open houses in the same neighborhood mean that more prospective buyers will have the opportunity to see your property.

Unless your property is located on a well-traveled thoroughfare, you'll need several "Open House" signs to direct prospects to your property. Count the number of turns a prospect has to make from a major thoroughfare in order to get to your property. That will be the number of signs you'll need. Then, get permission from the property owners where you want to place your signs, and order as many as you need.

Your signs should be 24 inches square with red letters on a white background. Each sign should read "Open House" with the approprtiate address below, and a red arrow pointing in the correct direction.

The sign in your front yard should read "For Sale by Owner" in red with your phone number below. In addition to the "For Sale" sign, consider placing small pennants or flags near the street, which are excellent for attracting attention to your open house.

Advertising

The purpose of advertising is to get prospects interested enough in your property to come by and look for themselves. Place your ad in the classified section of your Sunday newspaper, because Sundays are when Realtors place their ads. Prospective buyers are accustomed to looking for home sales in the Sunday paper.

Most newspapers have a separate "Open House" section in the classifieds. (See "Advertising" in Chapter 20 for more about writing ads.)

The Sales Agreement

Your property is tidy and in complete repair, both inside and out. Your advertisments are running, and the phone is ringing off the hook with inquiries about your property. Prospective buyers have been walking through your home day after day. Finally, somebody says they're interested in purchasing your home, or that they want to sit down and discuss the terms of the sale at your earliest convenience. What you have now is not a sale, but a serious and interested prospect. It's time to negotiate and reduce the details of your negotiations to writing.

Once you and the buyer agree on all the details of price and terms, complete the purchase agreement checklist, shown in Figure 21.2.

FIGURE 21.2 Purchase agreement checklist.

PURCHASE AGREEMENT CHECKLIST

Note: This is not a legally binding agreement. It is simply a checklist to accommodate the drafting of a formal sales agreement between buyer and seller.

Name of prospective buyer(s) _____

_____

Currently residing at _____

_____ Phone _____

Are considering purchasing the property located at _____

_____

  for a purchase price of $ _____

Earnest money deposit of $ _____ to be held in escrow by _____

Buyer to assume existing loans of $ _____

Or, buyer to originate new financing of $ _____

Real estate taxes last year were _____

Contingencies to be included in purchase agreement _____

_____

_____

Items not included in selling price _____

_____

_____

Items that are included in selling price _____

_____

_____

Sellers will vacate the premises on _____

Date of closing escrow _____

Sellers to pay rent of $ _____ per day if sellers occupy premises after the close of escrow

Legal description of property _____

_____

This checklist is used as a guideline in the preparation of the sales documents. Your escrow officer or attorney can use this information to save time asking questions.

Qualifying the Buyer

Just because you have a prospect who has announced a readiness to purchase your home, does not mean that you have a bona fide sale. Many a hopeful buyer lacks adequate income or creditworthiness to attain financing, in which case it's futile to enter into a sales agreement.

If the buyer has already arranged for new financing or he has been prequalified by a lender for a purchase in your price range, it's not necessary to qualify the buyer beyond getting proof of this. In all other cases, you'll have to obtain certain information and qualify the buyer yourself. (See Chapter 4.)

Summary

Now you can compare the total cost of selling the property yourself with the cost of using a real estate broker who receives a 6 percent commission. Assuming a $120,000 selling price, the broker's commission would be $7,200. Deducting your own costs of sale from this amount yields your savings.

The following are approximate costs you incur selling the property yourself, not including normal closing costs, which have to be paid regardless of whether you use a broker:

"For Sale" signs	$120
Advertising	100
Copies of information sheet	10
Total cost	$230

Therefore, you'll save $6,970 ($7,200 – $230), or earn that much, if you look at it that way, by selling the house yourself.

CHAPTER 22

Pay Less Tax

Home-Owner Tax Savings

One of the greatest benefits of home ownership is that the IRS and most state governments allow you to deduct a certain amount of mortgage interest and property taxes when you file your income tax return. Furthermore, you have the added benefit of excluding up to $500,000 in capital gain when you sell your principal residence. As of this writing, mortgage interest, limited to $1 million, and all the property taxes on your home are itemized deductions. The IRS also allows you to deduct the interest cost on a home equity loan (second mortgage) up to a maximum of $100,000 borrowed.

Tax Rules on the Sale of a Home

The IRS allows an individual taxpayer who owns a home and lives in it for two out of last five years prior to the sale to completely avoid taxes on up to $250,000 in capital gains. Married taxpayers filing jointly can exclude up to $500,000 in gains.

The IRS also allows the home-sale exclusion when the gain includes the sale of vacant land that has been used as part of the residence, provided that the land sale occurs within two years of the sale of the residence.

Home owners who do not meet the two-year requirement might be eligible for a partial exclusion if the home owner had to sell the house because of health reasons, a change in the place of employment, or to the extent provided by IRS regulations, "unforeseen circumstances." Such events include divorce, legal separation, death, new eligibility for unemployment compensation, a change in employment that leaves the taxpayer unable to pay the mortgage, and multiple births resulting from the same pregnancy. Such unforeseen events must involve the taxpayer, a spouse, a coowner, or a member of the taxpayer's household.

Other unforeseen events include damage to the residence as the result of an act of war or terrorism, a disaster caused by either nature or humans, or the condemnation, seizure, or other involuntary loss of the property. For example, taxpayers who sell their homes because their place of employment has changed will automatically qualify for a reduced exclusion if a "qualified person's" new place of work is at least 50 miles further away from the old home than the previous workplace was. A qualified person can be the taxpayer, the taxpayer's spouse, a member of the taxpayer's household, or a coowner of the house.

The reduced exclusion is predicated on the length of time the taxpayer owned and lived in the home before selling it. For example, an individual taxpayer who would be entitled to a $250,000 tax exclusion if he or she sold the house after two years will be entitled to a $125,000 exclusion if he or she sells the house after one year, and meets the requirements for the partial exclusion.

Determining Principal Residence

For taxpayers with more than one home, relevant factors for determining which is the principal residence include the amount of time a home is used; the residence of other family members; the taxpayer's place of employment; the address the taxpayer uses for driver's license, car registration, tax returns, and voter registration; and the location of the taxpayer's bank, religious organizations, and recreational clubs.

Rules on Business Use of the Home

When the taxpayer uses a portion of the home exclusively for business purposes and takes a tax deduction for that use, the cost basis of that portion of the house is reduced by the amount of the depreciation deduction allowed. If a gain is realized, the taxpayer will be subject to tax on any depreciation deductions taken on the business portion of the home; however, the taxpayer will be entitled to exclude any amount above that up to the maximum allowable exclusion.

TIP

To find the percentage of your home operating expenses that is allowed as a deduction, you must determine how much of the dwelling is used exclusively for business purposes. Example: You own a 2,000-square-foot home and use a 400-square-foot room exclusively for business, so you're allowed to use 20 percent (400 ÷ 2,000) of your total home operating expenses as a deduction.

Mortgage Interest Deductions

Current tax laws allow you to deduct home mortgage interest (to a maximum of $1 million), but only up to the original purchase price of the home and the cost of home improvements. The limit for deductions on interest paid on home-improvement loans is $100,000.

If you later refinance and pay off your old mortgage and have excess money to spend, you cannot deduct the interest on the excess money, unless it is used for property improvements or for medical and educational expenses.

Rules for Vacation Homes

According to the IRS, a vacation home can be a condominium, an apartment, a single-family dwelling, a house trailer, a motor home, or a houseboat. Unlike your personal residence, the gains from the sale of a vacation home will be taxed as capital gains. However, if any rental income was earned from the vacation property, you're allowed to deduct some of the expenses incurred, according to the following rules:

- If the vacation home is rented for less than 15 days, you cannot deduct expenses allocated to the rental (except for interest and property taxes).
- If the vacation home is rented for 15 days or more, you have to determine whether your personal use of the home exceeds a 14-day or 10 percent time test (10 percent of the number of days the home is rented). If it does, then you're considered to have used the home as a residence during the year, and rental expenses are deductible only to the extent of gross rental income. Therefore, if gross rental income exceeds expenses, the operating gain is fully taxable.
- If you rent the vacation home for 15 days or more, but your rental usage is less than the 14-day/10 percent test, then you're not considered to have made personal use of the residence during the year. In this case, expenses in excess of gross rental income may be deductible. Previous tax court cases have allowed loss deductions when the owner made little personal use of the vacation home, and proved to have bought the house to earn a profit through resale.

Passive Loss Rules

The passive loss rules apply to investors who report taxable income in excess of $100,000 annually, and to those investors who take no role in the operational or managerial decisions that affect their properties. Essentially, the passive loss rules were enacted to keep high-income earners from sheltering their incomes through depreciation deductions—a popular practice of the wealthy prior to the Tax Reform Act of 1986.

Exemption from Passive Loss Rules

The IRS has created another tax category, "taxpayers in the real property business." This category includes owners of income property, converters, real estate agents, contractors, and property managers. If you fit this category, you have a big advantage in being exempt from the passive loss rules. Your income property tax losses can also offset the taxable income received from other sources, including salary, commissions, interest, dividends, and royalties.

However, there is a stipulation: You're required to work in a real estate-related business or trade a minimum of 750 hours per year, the equivalent of slightly over 14 hours per week. Furthermore, the majority of the personal services work performed each year must be within the definition of a real property business or trade. You couldn't, for example, just go out and earn a license to sell real estate and automatically qualify for this preferred tax status.

Reporting Rental Income and Deductions

Rental income and expenses are reported on Schedule E of your tax return. You report the gross amount received, then deduct such expenses as mortgage interest, property taxes, maintenance costs, and depreciation. The net profit is added to your other taxable income. If you realize a loss, you can reduce the amount of your other taxable income within certain limitations. (See preceding section.)

On the cash basis, you report rental income for the year in which you receive payment.

On the accrual basis, you report rental income for the year in which you are entitled to receive payment. You do not report accrued income if the financial condition of your tenant makes collection doubtful. If you sue for payment, you do not report income until you win a collectible judgment.

Insurance proceeds for loss of rental income because of fire or casualty loss are reported as ordinary income.

Payment by a tenant for cancelling a lease or modifying its terms is reported as ordinary income when received. You may deduct expenses realized from the cancellation and any unamortized balance for expenses paid in negotiating the lease.

Security deposits are treated as trust funds and are not reported as income. However, if your tenant breaches the lease agreement, you are then entitled to use the security deposit as rent, at which time you report it as income.

Capital Gains

Real estate investors benefit from lower tax rates for capital gains. Under present law, gains realized in the sale of real estate are taxed at a maximum rate of 20 percent (18 percent if the property has been held for at least five years).

The example in Figure 22.1 illustrates the essentials of the capital gains tax.

Present tax law requires that you recapture accrued depreciation at a tax rate of 25 percent, and the remaining capital gain is taxed at a rate of 20 percent. However, if you're in the 15 percent ordinary income tax bracket, your capital gains are taxed at 10 percent instead of 20 percent. The tax rate on depreciation recapture remains at 25 percent.

Note that to qualify for capital gains treatment, you must own a property for at least one year.

Selling on Installment

If you decide to finance the sale of real estate (carry back financing), it won't be necessary to pay all your capital gains taxes at that time. Instead, you pay them on a pro rata basis when the money is received.

For example, say that you sold a house on installment with a 20 percent down payment, and you carried back financing on the balance for 15 years. In this example, your total taxable gain from the sale was $100,000, which accounts for 50 percent of the selling price. You would immediately incur a tax liability on $10,000 ($0.20 \times 0.50 \times \$100,000$). From then on you would owe taxes on the pro rata amount of gain you'd receive in each of the following years.

FIGURE 22.1　Essentials of the capital gains tax.

Sales price	$400,000
Tax calculation	
Original cost	200,000
Less accrued depreciation	−50,000
Adjusted basis	150,000
Total gain	250,000
Depreciation recapture ($50,000 @ 25%)	12,500
Capital gain ($200,000 @ 20%)	40,000
Total taxes	$ 52,500

Depreciation Expense

Income property owners deduct a noncash expense referred to as *depreciation*. The IRS presumes that buildings, their contents (such as carpeting and air conditioners), and certain improvements (fencing, outbuildings) wear out over time. Therefore, the IRS depreciation schedules permits you to reduce your taxable income to compensate for this wear and tear.

Depreciation is not an out-of-pocket expense. That's why investors call it a *tax benefit*—you don't have to write a check to pay for it. Depreciation is added to expenses that are already deductible, such as repairs and maintenace.

What Can Be Depreciated?

Many different kinds of property can be depreciated, such as machinery, buildings, vehicles, patents, copyrights, furniture, and equipment. Property is depreciable if it meets all three of these tests:

1. It must be used in business or held for the production of income (e.g., to earn rent or royalty income).
2. It must have a useful life that can be determined, and its useful life must be longer than one year. The useful life of a piece of property is an estimate of how long you can expect to use it in your business or to earn rent or royalty income.
3. It must be something that wears out, decays, gets used up, becomes obsolete, or loses value from natural causes.

Land cannot be depreciated. Whenever you buy an income property, you must first deduct the land value before calculating your basis for depreciation. For instance, say you buy an income property for $240,000 and its land value equals $60,000. Your original depreciable basis is then $180,000. Tax law permits a maximum depreciable life of 27.5 years. Thus, divide $180,000 by 27.5, and the result is $6,545. This is the amount of annual depreciation expense that you can deduct against pretax rental income after the out-of-pocket expenses are deducted.

Depreciation as a Tax Shelter

Say, for example, that you invest in an income property valued at $240,000, and it produces a net operating income (rent less operating expenses) of $15,000 per year. The mortgage payments total $12,000 a year, of which $11,000 represents deductible interest ($1,000 equals equity payoff). Since you must deduct the land

FIGURE 22.2   How depreciation becomes a tax shelter.

Net operating income (NOI)	$ 15,000
Less mortgage interest	−11,000
Income before depreciation	4,000
Less depreciation	−6,545
Tax loss	$ (2,545)

value of $60,000 to arrive at a depreciable basis of $180,000, you then have an annual depreciation allowance of $6,545 ($180,000 ÷ by 27.5 = $6,545).

Figure 22.2 illustrations how depreciation becomes a tax shelter.

In this example, you actually earned $4,000 in NOI, yet because of depreci-
ation, you can deduct a $2,545 tax loss against your income from salary or other
sources. Thus, the tax-shelter benefit of depreciation.

Deductions from Rental Income

- *Real estate taxes.*   Property taxes are deductible, but special assessments for
  roadwork, sewers, or other improvements are not. They are added to the cost
  of the land.

- *Depreciation.*   Be sure to deduct depreciation on all income-producing real
  estate; it's the tax-shelter benefit of owning improved real estate.

- *Maintenance expenses.*   These include such things as repairs, pool service,
  heating, lighting, water, gas, electricity, telephone, and other service costs.

- *Management expenses.*   Include the cost of the resident manager, stationery,
  and postage stamps, or the total cost of a management service.

- *Traveling expenses.*   These include the cost of traveling to and from properties for the purpose of making repairs or showing vacancies.

- *Legal expenses.*   These include the costs incurred while evicting a tenant.
  Expenses incurred while negotiating long-term leases are considered capital expenditures and are deductible over the term of the lease.

- *Interest expenses.*   These include interest on mortgages and other indebted-
  ness related to the property.

- *Advertising expenses.*   These include the cost of vacancy signs and newspaper
  advertising.

- *Insurance expenses.*   These include the cost of premiums for fire and casualty coverage.

Improvements versus Maintenance

Only incidental repair costs and maintenance costs are deductible from rental income. Improvement and replacement costs are treated differently. Improvements or repairs that add value or prolong the life of the property are considered capital improvements. Their cost may not be deducted, but it may be added to the cost basis of the property, and then depreciated. For example, the cost to repair the roof of a rental property is considered an expense and is deducted from rental income. However, the cost to replace the entire roof is considered an improvement, and is therefore added to the cost basis, then depreciated.

It is wise to keep track of all receipts related to the upkeep and improvement of your home or rental real estate. When you sell your home, the IRS allows you to exclude from taxation that portion of your profit that is due to capital improvements.

For tax purposes, the IRS allows home owners to add the cost of improvements (but not of maintenance) to the original purchase price. The difference between improvements and maintenance is as follows:

- *Capital improvements* are things that you do to your home that permanently increase its value and lengthen its life. These may include such things as adding a deck, building a patio, landscaping, acquiring new appliances (as long as you leave them when you sell), installing a new water heater or roof, adding on or remodeling a room, and so on.

- *Maintenance and repairs* are the kinds of fix-up things that are to be expected from time to time throughout your home. These include such things as painting, repairing a toilet or a leaky pipe, repairing a leaky roof, paying someone to mow the lawn, and the like.

 TIP

You can deduct only the actual business portion of your travel costs, and there are limitations and special rules for deducting entertainment expenses. Furthermore, it's important to segregate business mileage from other driving you might do at the time you actually use the car. Keep a logbook in your glovebox and get in the habit of jotting down mileage at the beginning and end of each business-related trip.

Answers about Income Taxes and Real Estate

Question: I see that the Internal Revenue Service allows an exemption up to $250,000 on the capital gains tax of a principal residence when it's sold, if the owner lived in the property for at least two years. But what if I live in the home for one year before selling? Can I get a reduced tax exemption for a $60,000 sale profit?

Answer: It depends on whether you meet the requirements of the reduced exclusion. If the reason you sold the principal residence in less than two years is a medical condition or a job relocation that qualifies for the moving expense deduction, then you qualify for a partial exemption based on the number of qualifying months.

The IRS also lists seven other qualifying conditions for a partial home-sale exemption after less than two years of ownership and occupancy:

1. Death of the home owner, coowner, spouse, or family member.
2. Job loss qualifying for unemployment compensation.
3. Legal separation or divorce of an owner.
4. Damage to the home by disaster, war, or terrorism.
5. Multiple births from the same pregnancy.
6. Condemnation of the home by a government agency.
7. Change of employment with insufficient income to pay for ordinary living expenses or the mortgage.

If you qualify based on the preceding conditions, then $30,000 (half your gain based on 12 of 24 months you lived in the home), would be exempt from capital gains tax.

For details, see your tax advisor.

Question: Can I deduct interest on a loan for land that I plan to build a house on?

Answer: Interest on unimproved land is considered personal interest and is not deductible. Once you begin construction, 100 percent of the mortgage interest will then be tax deductible.

Question: Are points deductible?

Answer: Yes they are. Points on a loan to buy your home can be 100 percent deductible in the year the loan is issued. However, the points cannot be borrowed as part of the loan amount and have to be paid separately. If the points are added to the loan proceeds, they must be amortized over the life of the loan.

Points on a second mortgage or refinancing loan must be amortized over the term of the loan. When the house is sold, the remaining points are deductible. There is an exception: Points on VA and FHA loans are not deductible.

Question: I'm considering buying a recreational vehicle. Can I claim the motor-home as a second home and deduct 100 percent of the interest from my taxes?

Answer: Yes, you can if you don't own another vacation home and the vehicle has a kitchen, bathroom, and bedroom. The deduction is also good for house-boats or anything the IRS considers a second vacation home.

Question: My mother earns $32,000 annually and wants to purchase a fourplex. If she lives in one unit and manages the others as rentals, what tax benefits would she receive?

Answer: Since your mother plans to reside in one of the units, she can deduct one-quarter of the mortgage interest and real estate taxes. On the remaining three-fourths she can take a business deduction for interest and taxes. She can also depreciate the rental portion over 27.5 years and deduct the costs of maintenance and utilities. Because she plans to manage the building actively, she can deduct up to $25,000 in losses on the building from her regular salary income if the losses exceed any gains from other passive investments.

CHAPTER 23

Advanced Investment Strategies: Your Second Property, and Beyond

This final chapter introduces an array of investment strategies that you can choose as appropriate for your particular needs, capabilities, and locale. However, in order for these strategies to be effective, certain conditions have to apply. For instance, the method of "rent one and build another," requires an abundance of rural residential property surrounding a growing metropolis. This strategy would not be appropriate in a mature metropolitan area, such as New York City, because large residential sites are either not available or too costly to be profitable.

Advanced Investment Strategies for Higher Yields

Besides the traditional techniques of renting or fixing up and then selling the property, you can employ a variety of other strategies to hike your real estate returns and build profits faster. Consider the following investment techniques:

- Land banking
- Renting out part of the home

- Subdividing and building another home
- Rolling over a short-term purchase
- Converting property to another use

Land Banking

This is a great long-term holding strategy. You buy a detached single-family home in good location with a sizable plot of land. The objective is to keep it rented for now, with the long-term intention of converting the home to a more profitable rental use. (Commercial rent is usually twice that of residential rent.) You could, for example, buy a house on a large corner lot adjacent to commercial zoning. Presuming that the area is growing outward from its center as most cities do, you can eventually convert the building to office space, or perhaps build a corner minimart or small strip mall with lots of tenants paying commercial rental rates.

This technique has a great advantage over investing in similarly located unimproved land, because the house generates rental income until growth makes conversion profitable. If you just owned vacant land, you would have to pay the mortgage and taxes without the benefit of income. More important, without any improvements on the land you would have no tax relief, because there would be no building to depreciate.

NOTEWORTHY

When I managed property for a developer in Lansing, Michigan, the owner accomplished the ultimate in land banking. During the 1960s, he converted five locations into thriving McDonald's restaurants, each one paying 5 percent of gross monthly sales in land rent. (One of them was the third MacDonalds ever built in the United States.) In fact, the leases were set up so that McDonald's would pay a minimum of $440 per month for the land, including payment for the cost of property taxes, hazard insurance, and maintenance, or 5 percent of gross monthly sales, whichever was higher. McDonald's never did pay the minimum; the average rent at each location was an average of $1,500 per month. That's $18,000 per year in rental income just for use of the land, on lots the owner purchased for less than $10,000 each.

LANDLORD TALE

Fred and Annie found the perfect country home, situated just 90 miles east of New Orleans and 3 miles north of Mississippi's picturesque Gulf Coast. It was a beautiful two-story custom home featuring 4 bedrooms and 2¾ baths, with 2,000 square feet of living area downstairs and 1,200 upstairs, on a lovely 2.5-acre site with a white picket fence overlooking a tree-lined lake. Unfortunately, this great house was only perfect in Fred and Annie's dreams—not only was it too pricey for their housing budget, it was much too big for what they actually needed.

Knowing that they just had to have this house, they got creative. If the upstairs, which already had adequate living space, had an independent entrance and a kitchen, they could then rent out the entire upstairs. And the rent they earned would solve the affordability problem.

In the end, they bought the house for $220,000, spent an additional $8,000 to build a stairway entrance, and added a small kitchen to the upstairs. They put down $40,000 and took out a 30-year mortgage at 6 percent on the $180,000 balance. The monthly payment on the principal and interest was $1,079, but after renovations were completed, they rented out the upstairs for $850 per month, which meant Fred and Annie's monthly P&I cost was only $229. Adding $210 a month for taxes and insurance, their total monthly housing expense turned out to be only $439 per month. Not bad for 2.5-acre country home that first, seemed unattainable.

Renting Out Part of the Home

With this strategy the objective is to purchase a larger house than you actually need, rent out an independent portion of it. For instance, convert the upstairs into a private living unit, such as a studio apartment. Keep in mind, though, that it should have a separate entrance, with a kitchen, bathroom, and bedroom. This way the tenant has less of an opportunity to be a nusiance (using your entrance and kitchen). Now, under of current tax law you can depreciate part of your residence (the rental area), and deduct it against rental income, and you also have the benefit of having someone to look after your property when you're away and perhaps feed the dog and gather your mail.

Renting to College Students

If you live in a college town, consider buying a big house with lots of bedrooms, converting it into a boarding house, and renting out the bedrooms to several

NOTEWORTHY

When I was a sophmore at Michigan State University, I rented a room in one of the campus boarding houses owned by a local attorney, Jim Vanderbunte. In fact, Vanderbunte owned 19 rental houses around the campus area. He also practiced criminal law, but the student rental business became so profitable and engaged so much of his time that he eventually gave up the law practice. That year he told me that in the previous year, his rental real estate earned him 10 times as much as his law practice.

college students. Of course, you would have to furnish the house, and require substantial deposits to cover cleaning and potential damage. If you had large bedrooms, two students could actually share one room, while other tenants would pay more for their private rooms.

Location is important, too. If the property is reasonably close to the campus, students willing to walk or ride a bike to class are likely prospective tenants. However, students who own a car and prefer a more quiet, peaceful environment would likely be more attracted to a location outside the city, situated within 5 or 10 miles from campus.

Subdividing and Building Another Home

Buy a home out in the country on a large parcel of land. Later on, you can subdivide the land, build another home for your own residence, and rent out the old house. Be sure zoning laws allow you to build another home before you sign on the dotted line, though.

How It Works

Robb and Rubi spent months trying to find the ideal home in a great country location. Finally they found the perfect house, but Robb didn't like the location. Then Robb found the perfect parcel of land, a picturesque eight acres, but Rubi didn't like the house that was on it. The solution: Even though Rubi didn't care for the home, they purchased the perfect parcel of land anyway, because Robb promised Rubi that he would build their dream home on it. They would only live in the existing house temporarily, and when the dream house was finished they would move into it and rent out the other house.

This concept has several benefits. In most cases, you can build on preowned land for a lot less than it costs to buy a new house; thus, you have built-in equity when the new house is completed. You can ususally get 100 percent financing on the construction loan, too.

Check with a lawyer before you actually attempt this. Your lender will want to hold the only mortgage on the property. In other words, you will usually need to take out a construction loan to build the house, then get a new mortgage to pay off both the construction loan and the original mortgage.

Advantages of Buying a Large Site

Besides the benefits of great leverage with 100 percent financing and built-in value, this investment technique offers certain other advantages:

- Better financing, because the property will qualify as an owner-occupied dwelling. (The lender will require a lower down payment and charge a lower rate of interest, because the property won't be considered an investment purchase.)
- Because the rental will be virtually next door, it will be convenient to show to prospective tenants, and it will be easy to maintain and look after.
- Built-in profit, because the new house, when finished, will likely be worth substantially more than the cost to build it.
- Should you go away for an extended period, your tenant can look after your house.

Rolling Over a Short-Term Purchase

Although this book primarily recommends long-term investment strategies, you might find this short-term method more in line with your objectives. This technique could be called a "fix-up and flip" strategy, because it involves paying cash for property, quickly renovating it, then reselling at a profit to recoup the entire investment. It's ideal for the investor with access to $50,000 to $100,000 in ready cash. The investment capital can be generated from your own funds, a partnership, or a private institutional lender. The principle behind this technique is the fact that a cash purchase commands a bargain price, especially when the seller is motivated to sell.

For instance, say that you've located a particular property that can be purchased for $67,000 cash and, if renovated, could be sold within six months for $100,000. Assume that you have a lender that will lend you $75,000 for six months.

Typically, a short-term loan from a financial institution would cost about 10 percent plus 2 points. Loan proceeds consist of $72,000, of which $67,000 represents the acquisition cost, while $5,000 is the cost of renovation. Interest on $72,000 for six months is $3,600, plus 2 points at a cost of $1,440, for a total cost of $5,040. Although the cost to finance may seem excessive at first glance, this investment technique supports a high finance cost because of a great net profit, especially considering that this technique is so highly leveraged, using no funds of your own.

Granted, were you fortunate enough to possess the ready cash to acquire, quickly renovate, and sell the property without borrowing the required capital, you'd obviously be that much further ahead, because you'd save $5,040 in finance charges.

Figure 23.1 shows how the numbers work out.

The sales commission is another variable cost that is included in the analysis. Due to the short period of time involved in this technique, I usually pay a commission to effect a quick sale. However, if you can make a sale without the services of an agent, you would earn yourself an additional $6,000.

Ingredients of the Short-Term Rollover

The key to this investment technique, assuming you borrow the working capital, is to have made tentative arrangements with a lender. Then, as soon as you find a suitable property, you make an offer contingent on acquiring sufficient financing. If your offer is accepted, it is then analyzed by your lender. Should the lender agree, you're in business; if not, your offer is void.

FIGURE 23.1   Example of a short-term rollover.

Acquisition cost		$ 67,000
Cost to acquire and renovate:		
Closing costs	$ 500	
Cost to renovate	5,000	
Cost to finance	5,040	
Tax and insurance (6 months)	300	
Utilities (6 months)	200	
Total expenses	11,040	
Total acquisition cost and expenses		78,040
Property selling price		100,000
Less the following selling expenses		
Sales commission (6 percent)	6,000	
Closing costs	500	
Total acquisition cost and expenses	78,040	
Total overall cost	84,540	84,540
Net profit before taxes		$ 15,460

To profit from this technique, you can use this rule of thumb: If you can buy a property for no more than two-thirds of its selling price after it's fixed up, you have likely found a good deal. In the preceding example, the purchase price was $67,000, which is two-thirds of the selling price of $100,000. If you purchased a home for $80,000, the selling price would have to be at least $120,000 to incorporate the two-thirds ratio.

Properties that best qualify are those that have a substantial amount of equity and a seller unwilling to carry back a note; they require renovation, yet are sound in structure and overall construction. A large amount of equity means that the seller has, in most cases, owned the property for an extended period. Since the seller bought the property for substantially less many years ago, and is unwilling to carry a note or renovate the property, the seller will be inclined to sell at a bargain price to quickly cash out of the property.

Converting Property to Another Use

Gas stations now functioning as minimarts . . . Old homes converted to office space . . . Apartments now serving as condominiums . . . What was once a 40-acre farm on the outskirts of town is now a sprawling enclosed shopping mall. These are prime examples of conversions in which both land and buildings were adapted to a more profitable usage as the region has grown and changed.

Converting a Home to Office Space

Based on the premise that office space rents for twice the rate of residential space, converting a home to a dentistry center or law office offers much opportunity for profit. Of course, not just any home is ripe for conversion. The prime candidate should be located on a busy street with enough square footage and land to accommodate a thriving business.

For instance, on the west side of Las Vegas along Jones Boulevard, there are a number of luxurious ranch homes on half-acre lots. In 1989, what was once a quiet two-lane country road, expanded to a busy six-lane boulevard. The increase in traffic caused home owners to become disenchanted with their location (no more quiet enjoyment). Many residential properties along Jones soon began going up for sale.

It wasn't long before someone decided to buy one of these lovely ranch homes and convert it to a family dentistry office. The situation was ideal for a conversion: unhappy home owners situated in the midst of busy outward growth motivated to sell, and a large home ideal for conversion, with adequate parking on a large site in a good business location.

As this example shows, you have to keep your eyes open for certain changes occurring in your area. Expanding roads, new interchanges and such, all present opportunities for the shrewd investor who has the ability to make profitable conversions.

Bear in mind that if you consider a similar home-to-office conversion, you will likely need a change in zoning from residential to commercial usage.

Converting Apartments to Condos

Why would you want to convert, say, 15 apartment units into individual condominium units? Because you can often transform certain types of apartments into a higher, more profitable usage. What do you need to accomplish a profitable conversion? An apartment complex that can be purchased at the right price to produce a reasonable profit margin, with sufficient land for adequate owner parking. To arrive at the right price, you employ a two-to-one rule. This means that the sales price of each of the converted condo units should be at least twice that of the per-unit purchase price of the apartment building. For example, if the purchase price of the apartment building is $50,000 per unit, then the sales price of each condo unit must be at least $100,000.

To illustrate how you might calculate the bottom line in this situation, Figure 23.2 presents an example for a 15-unit building.

In this example, you can see why the two-to-one method is a good rule of thumb to quickly gauge whether a potential conversion project is feasible. Although the per-unit acquisition cost is only $50,000, after you add all the costs of conversion, the total per-unit cost increases to $70,000. In this instance, the two-to-one rule would yield the investor $30,000 per unit.

Keep in mind that the figures in this example simply demonstrate the conversion strategy. You may come across an entirely different conversion opportunity, in which every item from acquisition to incidentals is subject to big variances in cost. Much depends on local market conditions regarding condo prices, the amount of

FIGURE 23.2   Example of an apartment-to-condo conversion.

Acquisition price at $50,000 per unit	$ 750,000
Renovation cost at $8,000 per unit	120,000
Attorney fees (condo documents, government permits, sales contracts)	40,000
Selling costs (sales commissions, advertising)	45,000
Mortgage interest (1-year renovation and sellout)	60,000
Incidentals (landscaping, design costs, building permits)	35,000
Total costs	$1,050,000
Cost per unit	$ 70,000

required renovation, the degree of complexity of condo conversion laws, and the market strategy. To determine whether a project is feasible in your area, research condo prices, rental properties, and conversion laws and procedures. Do some quick two-to-one calculations on a note pad to determine whether any subject properties deserve further attention. If the preliminary figures appear profitable, talk with people who are knowledgeable and experienced in conversion procedures. Helpful people could be building contractors, attorneys, or Realtors experienced in condo conversions. With the advice gained from these talks, along with a closer examination of market conditions, you can make a final decision as to whether this conversion strategy will generate enough profit to compensate for the inherent risks in such projects including slow sales, permitting delays, and cost overruns.

Converting Apartments to Office Space

Office space usually rents for twice the rate of comparable apartment space. Just from this observation it would appear highly profitable to convert apartments to office space. But before you go ahead with such a conversion, you need to consider some important questions:

- *Is the property you wish to convert within a commercial zone?*   If not, can it easily be changed to the proper zoning?

- *What is the current vacancy rate for office space in the area of the subject property?*   If too much space is already available, it would be unwise to convert.

- *Do you have adequate parking for office space?*   Typically, the city will require one parking space for every 250 to 500 square feet of rentable office space.

- *How much will it cost to convert?*   Could you borrow the money to finance such a conversion? Finally, will the cost, legal procedures, time, and effort be worth the eventual profit you will realize?

Examine the situation carefully. Thoroughly analyze the finances of the projected conversion. Keep in tune with the requirements given, and if you can convert and finance at a reasonable cost and still earn a substantial profit, then go ahead with your plans.

Pyramiding Your Investments

To *pyramid your investments* is to build a portfolio of income-generating properties, using your initial holdings as the foundation.

Besides the benefits of appreciation, growing income, and tax sheltering, you also have a tremendous refinancing benefit. Every few years you can refinance certain properties, pulling cash out to reinvest in more properties.

For instance, after several years of appreciation and paying down the mortgage, you have likely accumulated a sizable amount of equity in the first property you purchased. You can use that equity to invest in another property, either by taking out a second loan or by refinancing the existing mortgage. That's the principle of pyramiding—using the acquired equity in the first property to invest in another property. You can then rent out the house you're presently living in and move in to the second property, so that you can utilize the benefits of owner-occupied financing (lower interest rates and smaller down payment).

Later on, when you've accumulated more appreciation and built-up equity in the second property, you can use that equity to purchase a third property and do same thing over again.

How to Retire on the House

Consider several investment scenarios. Buy just one house for $100,000 with a $10,000 down payment and a $90,000 mortgage at 8 percent with a 30-year term. Assume an annual appreciation rate of 4 percent.

At the end of 30 years, the mortgage is paid off and you own the home free and clear of any debt. Most notable, though, is that your small investment of $10,000 has grown to a value of $324,190, which equals the value of the house after 30 years of 4 percent annual appreciation.

Buy three or four houses in the next 10 years, and at retirement (if you're not retired already) your net worth could easily be in the range of $300,000 to $1 million. Presuming only modest increases in rents—at 4 percent annual appreciation, $1,000 rent today would equal $2,000 in 18 years—the income from those rental houses could reach $10,000 per month. And that kind of income is generated from owning only three or four rentals. Imagine how great it could be with even more rentals!

Ways to Tap the Equity in Your Home

Home equity can be tapped in several ways. Some home owners choose to *trade down*—to sell their present home and purchase a less costlier one to live in. For instance, home owners in the San Francisco area, where the average home is selling for $740,000, are selling their homes, taking their huge profits, and buying comparable homes for less than a third of the price in nearby Sacramento. They can then live off the substantial price differential between the two homes, which is often in the neighborhood of $500,000 dollars. Moreover, instead of accepting all cash, consider taking back a purchase money mortgage, and just watching all the money roll in for the next 20 or 30 years.

Still another way to tap the equity in your home is to refinance your existing properties and pull out tax-free cash, as outlined often in this book. You can use the proceeds to do whatever you wish.

Conclusion

I hope that this book convinced you that being a renter pales in comparison to being a home owner, especially considering the array of wonderful benefits one gains from owning real estate. Many property owners who had the wisdom to hold on to their properties for the long term are now able to live off the net rental income. Income property purchased today with a small down payment is unlikely to net an immediate positive cash flow, but as time passes, the property steadily appreciates and rents are gradually increased, while mortgage payments remain constant, which produces a substantial net income for the owner over the long term. So, the lesson in a nutshell is: Buy all the real estate you can when you're young, then enjoy all the great tax-free income benefits during the autumn years of life.

I wish you a very happy, hassle-free, and profitable home-buying experience, and hope that the advice offered will be useful.

Useful Forms

The forms in this appendix are for your use as you see fit, including duplication of each page on any type of photocopying equipment.

Application to Rent

You can overcome most of the problems encountered by novice landlords by properly qualifying your prospective tenants. Good paying tenants who will take care of your property as if it were their own are a valuable asset.

After your prospects have filled out the rental application (Figure A.1), review it carefully, making sure everything is legible and complete. Be certain the name is correct, because if Jim Jones later skips the premises, he will be easier to trace with his complete name of James Anthony Jones. If more than one person will occupy the premises, get names of all the adults, and make everyone responsible for rent payments.

Employment information is also very important. You definitely want to qualify the prospects on their ability to pay rent. As a rule, a maximum range of 29 to 33 percent of gross monthly income can safely be appropriated for rent—29 percent if there are some other debt obligations, and 33 percent if there are none. If your prospects qualify by their salary, you should verify their employment at a more appropriate time. A simple phone call to the employer is sufficient.

APPLICATION TO RENT

Name of first applicant _____

Home phone _____ Work phone _____

Name of second applicant _____

Home phone _____ Work phone _____

Unit to be occupied by _____ adults and _____ children and _____ pets

Present address _____

City _____ State _____ Zip _____

Current landlord/mgr's name _____ Phone _____

Why are you leaving? _____

Previous address _____

City _____ State _____ Zip _____

Landlord/mgr's name _____ Phone _____

First applicant's birth date _____ Soc. Sec. _____

Drivers license # _____ State issued _____

First applicant's employer _____

Address _____ Gross monthly pay _____

Position _____ How long? _____

Second applicant's employer _____

Address _____ Gross monthly pay _____

Position _____ How long? _____

Credit references: Bank _____ Account # _____

Other active reference _____ Account # _____

Reference for second applicant _____ Account # _____

In an emergency contact _____ Phone _____

Address _____

City _____ State _____ Zip _____

List all motor vehicles to be kept at the dwelling unit. Include make, model, year, and license plate number for each.

Vehicle 1 _____ License _____

Vehicle 2 _____ License _____

Vehicle 3 _____ License _____

I (we) declare that the above information is correct and I (we) give my (our) permission for any reporting agency to release my (our) credit file to undersigned landlord solely for the purposes of entering into a rental agreement. I (we) further authorize the landlord or his agent to verify the above information including but not limited to contacting creditors, both listed herin or not, and present or former landlords.

Dated _____ , 20 ____

Applicant 1 _____

Applicant 2 _____

Inventory of Furnishings

If you supply any kind of furnishings (appliances or furniture) you need an inventory to accompany the rental agreement for each individual unit (Figure A.2). It essentially identifies items such as the refrigerator, stove, and couch, and denotes the current condition of each. Later, if you should happen to have a lawsuit, it supports a claim of damage, excluding reasonable wear and tear, against the security deposit. The tenants may counter that the damage was caused before they moved in. Except in cases of gross and negligent damage, such a defense is difficult to overcome without proper documentation.

Have the tenants go through the unit room by room with you at the time they move in. Have them fill out the inventory, mark any comments, and return the form to you. If the space provided for comments is too small, have them make any additional comments on the reverse side of the form.

Tenant Record (Cardex)

For multiunit buildings, keep tenant records on 5.5- × 8-inch cards (Figure A.3). Each card is a ready reference of all monies paid by and due from a tenant, a description of the apartment type, including the floor plan (Fl. Pl.) and color of carpet (Clr.), plus other important tenant information.

Reminders to Pay Rent

You should not tolerate any rent-paying delinquency by your tenants. Good landlords react predictably and immediately to nonpayment of rent when it's due. Slow-paying tenants usually will react to this predictability and make paying

FIGURE A.2 **Inventory of furnishings form.**

INVENTORY OF FURNISHINGS

Rental unit address _____

Tenant(s) _____ Inventory date _____

Room	Item	Comments	Condition at Move-out

Tenant agrees that the above information is an accurate inventory and description and assumes responsibility for these items in the dwelling unit as of _____ , 20 _____

Move in   Move out

_____ Date _____   _____ Date _____

_____ Date _____   _____ Date _____

the rent a high priority. Normally there's a three-day grace period after the due date. If the rent is not received with three days of the due date, action has to be taken.

Collection experts agree that a first notice should be sent within five days of the due date, and a second notice after seven days. Use forms such as those in Figure A.4. If your slow-paying tenant has a history of continued delinquency, a three-day notice to pay or quit the premises could be used instead of the second notice.

FIGURE A.3 Tenant record (Cardex).

Address: _____

Key signature _____

Original move-in date _____
Lease dated _____ Expire _____
Tenant telephone number _____
Deposit _____
Rent _____

Date due	Date paid	Receipt number	Paid to noon	Amount paid	Security deposit	Clean fee	Key deposit	Basic rent	Refrigerator	Furniture	Parking	Month to month	Additional occupants	Other: Fireplace, Dishwasher	Air conditioner	Utilities	Total rent	Balance due

Bldg. _____ Apt. _____ Fl. Pl. _____ Clr. _____ Name _____ Date due _____

FIGURE A.4   Reminders to pay rent.

Three-Day Reminder to Pay Rent

To _____   Date _____

_____

Just a reminder that your rent was past due on _____ . According to the terms of your Rental Agreement, rent more than _____ days past due requires a late charge payment of $ _____ . We would appreciate your prompt payment.

Thank you,

_____

Landlord/Agent

Five-Day Reminder to Pay Rent

To _____   Date _____

_____

Your rent is now past due as of _____ . As of this date, the past-due rent and late charges total $ _____ .

You must settle this account, or our legal options will have to be considered. Therefore, please act to remedy this matter immediately.

Thank you,

_____

Landlord/Agent

Notice to Pay Rent or Quit the Premises

The notice to pay rent or quit the premises (see Figure A.5) gives the tenant three days from the date of notice to pay all monies in default or move out. You should issue this form to the tenant only after you have attempted to procure the amount owed through other means, such as the three- and five-day reminder notices.

Note: Exercise caution in using a pay-or-quit notice, because laws on this matter vary substantially throughout the country. This particular form may not conform to the laws in some states where new landlord/tenant statutes have been

FIGURE A.5   Notice to pay rent or quit the premises.

NOTICE TO PAY RENT OR QUIT THE PREMISES

To _____   Date _____

_____

Certified Mail ☐   Regular mail ☐   Hand delivered ☐

You are hereby notified that the rent for the period _____ 20, _____ to _____ , 20_____ , is now past due. As of this date, the total sum owing including late charges is $ _____ . Unless this sum is received within three days of this dated notice, you will be required to vacate and surrender the premises.

If it becomes necessary to proceed with legal action for the nonpayment of rent or to obtain possession of the premises, as per the terms of the Rental Agreement, you will be liable for recovery of all reasonable attorney fees and expenses. You will also be liable for any additional rent for the time you are in possession of the premises.

_____

Landlord/Agent

---

enacted. If this is the case, you should seek the appropriate form at a reputable legal stationery store, or consult with an attorney who specializes in such matters.

Rental Agreement

You may wish to use the sample residential lease in Figure A.6 or, buy a residential lease form at a local stationery store. The following items concern important points in the sample rental agreement:

- *Terms.*   Here your rental agreement can either be month-to-month or for a year. A term of one year or more should include some type of graduated rent increase after the first year, protecting the owner from loss due to inflation.

- *Rent.*   Here the amount of rent to be paid is spelled out. Be sure to include a late fee, which is commonly 5 percent of the monthly rent.

- *Repairs and maintenance.*   Here the clause "except for the first $100 in cost, which the tenant pays" is referred to as the "no-hassle clause." If you purchase a rental agreement from a stationery store, be sure to insert this clause into it. And be sure to inform your tenants that the first $100 in repairs is their responsibility.

RESIDENTIAL LEASE

1. This Lease made this _____ day of _____ , 20___ , by and between _____ , herinafter called Landlord, and _____ herinafter called Tenant.

2. *Description:* Witnesseth, the Landlord, in consideration of the rents to be paid and the covenants and agreements to be performed by the Tenant, does hereby lease unto the Tenant the following described premises located thereon situated in the City of _____ , county of _____ , State of _____ , commonly known as _____ .

3. *Terms:* For the term of _____ (months/years) commencing on _____ , 20___ , and ending on _____ , 20___ .

4. *Rent:* Tenant shall pay Landlord, as rent for said premises, the sum of _____ dollars ($ _____) per month payable in advance on the first day of each month, during the term hereof at landlord's address above, or said other place as Landlord may hereafter designate in writing. Tenant agrees to pay a $25 late fee if rent is not paid within five days of due date.

5. *Security Deposit:* Landlord herewith acknowledges the receipt of _____ dollars ($ _____), which he is to retain as security for the faithful performance of the provisions of this Lease. If tenant fails to pay rent, or defaults with respect to any provisions of this Lease, Landlord may use the security deposit to cure the default, or compensate Landlord for all damages sustained by Landlord. Tenant shall immediately on demand reimburse Landlord the sum equal to the portion of security deposit expended by Landlord, so as to maintain the security deposit in the sum initially deposited with Landlord. If tenant performs all obligations under this Lease, the security deposit, or that portion thereof that was not previously applied by Landlord, shall be returned to Tenant within 21 days after the expiration of this Lease, or after Tenant has vacated the premises.

6. *Possession:* It is understood that if the Tenant shall be unable to enter into and occupy the premises hereby leased at the time above provided, by reason of the said premises not being ready for occupancy, of by reason of holding over of any previous occupancy of said premises, the Landlord shall not be liable in damage to the Tenant therefore, but during the period the Tenant shall be unable to occupy said premises as herein before provided, the rental therefore shall be abated and the Landlord is to be the sole judge as to when the premises are ready for occupancy.

7. *Use:* Tenant agrees that said premises during the term of this Lease shall be used and occupied by _____ adults and _____ children, and _____ animals, and for no other purpose whatsoever other than a residence, without the written consent of the Landlord, and that Tenant will not use the premises for any purpose in violation of any law, municipal ordinance, or regulation, and at any breach of this agreement the Landlord may at his option terminate this Lease and reenter and repossess the leased premises.

8. *Utilities:* Tenant will pay for all charges for all water supplied to the premises and pay for all gas, heat, electricity, and other services supplied to the premises, except as herin provided: _____ .

9. *Repairs and Maintenance:* The Landlord shall at his expense, except for the first $100 in cost, which the Tenant pays, keep and maintain the exterior walls, roof, electrical wiring, heating and air-conditioning system, water heater, built-in appliances, and water lines in good condition and repair, except where damage has been caused by negligence or abuse of the Tenant, in which case Tenant shall repair same at his sole expense.

Tenant hereby agrees that the premises are now in good condition, and shall maintain the premises and appurtenances in the manner in which they were received, reasonable wear and tear excepted.

The _____ agrees to maintain landscaping and swimming pool (if any). Tenant agrees to adequately water landscaping.

10. *Alterations and Additions:* The Tenant shall not make any alterations, additions, or improvements to said premises without the Landlord's written consent. All alterations, additions, or improvements made by either of the parties hereto upon the premises, except movable furniture, shall be the property of the Landlord, and shall remain upon and be surrendered with the premises at the termination of this Lease.

11. *Assignment:* The Tenant will not assign or transfer this Lease or sublet said premises without the written consent of the Landlord.

12. *Default:* If the Tenant shall abandon or vacate said premises before the end of the term of this Lease, or if default shall be made by the Tenant in the payment of said rent or any part thereof, or if the Tenant shall fail to perform any of the Tenant's agreements in this Lease, then in each and every instance of such abandonment or default, the Tenant's right to enter said premises shall be suspended, and the Landlord may at his option enter said premises and remove and exclude the Tenant from said premises.

13. *Entry by landlord:* Tenant shall allow the Landlord or his agents to enter the premises at all reasonable times and upon reasonable notice for the purpose of inspecting or maintaining the premises or to show it to prospective tenants or purchasers.

14. *Attorney's Fees:* The Tenant agrees to pay all costs, expenses, and reasonable attorney's fees including obtaining advise of counsel incurred by Landlord in enforcing by legal action, or otherwise any of Landlord's rights under this Lease or under any laws of this state.

15. *Holding Over:* If tenant, with the Landlord's consent, remains in possession of the premises after expiration of the term of this Lease, such possession will be deemed a month-to-month tenancy at a rental equal to the last monthly rental, and upon all the provisions of this Leas applicable to such a month-to-month tenancy.

The parties hereto have executed this Lease on the date first above written.

Landlord   Tenant

By: _____   By: _____

                                                  By: _____

Web Sites

Here are several web sites that should prove useful in your home-buying experience, listed according to category.

City and Neighborhood Data

- The World Wide Web offers several tools that you can use to research the features of a particular community. Surf the Homestore.com family of web sites (www.homestore.com), and you'll find the following useful tools:

  —Theschoolreport.com provides information about every public school district in the United States. It includes data on class sizes, subjects offered, test scores, maps of school locations, and principals' phone numbers.
  —Homefair.com provides cost of living comparisons in different cities.

- The U.S. Department of Commerce's Bureau of Economic Analysis (www .bea.doc.gov) supplies state and local economic data. This site is ideal if you who want to review information about the economic health of a particular community.

Comparable Sales

- www.dataquick.com
- www.propertyview.com

Credit Information

- www.creditaccuracy.com
- www.creditinfocenter.com

Foreclosures and Repossessions
- www.brucebates.com
- www.all-foreclosure.com
- www.va.gov
- www.bankhomes.net

Home Improvement
- www.hometime.com
- www.askbuild.com

Home Inspection
- The American Society of Home Inspectors (www.ashi.com) offers a helpful site where you can find a certified home inspector and learn more about the home-inspection process.
- www.creia.com.

Insurance Information
- The Federal Emergency Management Agency site (www.fema.gov) shows where various disasters (such as tornadoes, earthquakes, and floods) are apt to strike. It also supplies helpful educational resources on such topics as flood insurance and disaster preparation and prevention.
- www.cpcu.com
- www.statefarm.com

Legal Information
- www.lectlaw.com
- www.lexis.com

Mortgage Lenders
- One highly recommended mortgage web site is E-loan (www.eloan.com). It offers a wide array of mortgage loans from a variety of lenders, and handy tools for comparing the cost of different loans.
- Mortgage Market Information Services (www.interest.com), supplies data to more than 300 newspapers. Its web site supplies rate quotes for a given loan type from a variety of lenders in your area, as well as informative articles on the home buying process.
- Another quality web site with lots of information on mortgage loans is HSH Associates (www.hsh.com).

- The Federal National Mortgage Association (FNMA, or Fannie Mae; www
.homepath.com), a big player in the secondary mortgage market, has a web
site that supplies useful consumer information.

Real Estate Listings

- A good comprehensive web site is www.realtor.com, sponsored by the National Association of Realtors (NAR).

- A national list of repossessed VA-owned properties can be found at www
.vahomeswash.com.

- The U.S. Department of Housing and Urban Development (HUD; www.hud
.gov) web site includes listings of homes for sale by HUD and other government agencies.

Do not accept any Web-based data as the last word. Verify all information.
Physically view comparable sales, visit schools, and check out neighborhoods.

BIBLIOGRAPHY

Brangham, Suzanne. *Housewise.* New York: HarperCollins, 1987.

Bruss, Robert. *The Smart Investor's Guide to Real Estate Investing.* New York: Crown Publishing, 1981.

The Complete Do-It-Yourself Manual. Reader's Digest, 1973.

Eldred, Gary. *The 106 Common Mistakes Homebuyers Make (& How to Avoid Them),* 3rd ed. New York: John Wiley & Sons, 2002.

Fogarty, Thomas A. "House Prices Picking up Steam Again," *USA Today,* February 19, 2003, p. 1D.

Graves, Sarah. *Unhinged.* New York: Bantam Books, 2003.

Irwin, Robert. *How to Find Hidden Real Estate Bargains.* New York: McGraw-Hill, 2002.

Max, Sarah. *The Real Estate Renaissance.* CNN/Money (Internet), January 23, 2003.

McLean, Andrew, and Gary Eldred. *Investing in Real Estate,* 4th ed. New York: John Wiley & Sons, 2003, p. 170.

Payment Tables for Monthly Mortgage Loans. New York: McGraw-Hill.

Tyson, Eric, and Ray Brown. *Homebuying for Dummies,* 2nd ed. New York: Hungry Minds, 2001.

Wedlick, Dennis. *The Good Home.* New York: Harper Design International, 2001.

Weiss, Mark B., and Ruth Rejnis. *The Everything Homebuying Book,* 2nd ed. Avon, MA: Adams Media, 2003.

Wilson, Craig. "Whodunit? Sarah Graves," *USA Today,* February 21, 2003, page 7D.

Andrew James McLean is a graduate of Michigan State University, with a diverse professional background in real estate. He has worked as a licensed Realtor, an appraiser, a loan officer, a manager of foreclosed property for a 40-branch savings and loan, a property manager for a commerical developer, and as a resident manager for a 363-unit luxury apartment building. He has also taught real estate investment (adult education) at the University of Nevada, Las Vegas. Most notably, he is the author of 14 books, including, with Gary Eldred, the best-selling *Investing in Real Estate*, now in its fourth edition. During the past 32 years he has personally owned and operated more than 20 individual properties (homes and rentals), including a 19-unit apartment building.